MW01045065

What people are saying about...

GRAVITY:

*Seven Essential Truths About
Influence, Leadership and Your Soul*

....

"Reading this book is like putting a jeweler's loupe up to your eye and discovering new facets of the leadership diamond that, somehow, you've been missing—truths that can put the sparkle of "gravitational attraction" and healthy influence back into the roles where you serve. If you care about lasting leadership that honors God and develops people, and if you love a good story that inspires vision and growth, read this book and be on the watch... brilliance ahead!"

Dr. Jodi Detrick, *Speaker, Coach, Mentor, former Seattle Times Columnist Author of The Jesus-Hearted Woman: 10 Leadership Qualities for Enduring & Endearing Influence*

"This is an excellent book. So many leaders misunderstand how to build great teams and motivate them to do great things. They pull on the wrong levers. They don't realize that the true energy in an organization is driven not by the leader's raw talent, but by the genuine love followers have for their leaders. And that requires that the leader needs to work on themselves, needs to become the kind of person that people want to follow. That means the virtues of the leader's own soul are paramount in becoming a great leader. It also requires a genuine, abiding relationship between the leader and Jesus. I was moved by this book to see how God has led me this far and to aspire to keep going further with him for the sake of my team, our mission and God's glory."

Steve Woodworth, *President of Masterworks*

"Packed with spiritual narrative and growth, this is a shining star of a book about the challenging and immensely rich road of life with Jesus. This is a great book for all leaders... pointing to the deeper "gravity" that we need in our lives. The narrative of Jason Cahill's life shows a journey to deeper connectedness with Christ, which has powerful impact on others. This is a great read."

David Fletcher, *Executive Pastor, First Evangelical Free Church - Fullerton, CA*
Founder/Director XPastor.org

"This book offers an inspiring call to sit down with the authors and enjoy new perspectives through a modern day parable. The authors are two wise sages who understand the pivotal truth that great leadership hinges on the conviction that until you know the true reality of your current condition healthy, significant, and sustained growth isn't possible. Like Picasso, whose artistry went through various "stages," so will your influence, leadership, and soul. Read this book and get ready to color your world with fresh new insights."

Dr. Vicki Farina, *Personal Leadership Coach and Mentor, Speaker*

"In this book, my friends Ron Kuest and Michael Forney move beyond superficial pragmatic answers to the real core of influence - How are you growing your soul?

Although hundreds of books discuss skills, practices and characteristics of leadership, very few dig into the more important foundational aspects. *GRAVITY* does just that. It looks at "why" people have or do not have influence. It reveals that leadership is more about who you are on the inside than about what you do. It leads you to think through how to develop your soul. This will result in real influence that lasts and empowers others.

I highly recommend *GRAVITY* to all who want to reach their full leadership potential. It will challenge and inspire you to grow deep."

Dr. Mel Ming, *Founding Partner of Leadership Development Resources*

"Leadership is more than an executive skill set... it is influence. But where does influence come from? In a compelling and thought provoking storyline, true to life characters will challenge you to change your perspective about Christian leadership by giving you new insight and biblical direction. You can expect this book to become your personal mentor as you discover, heal, and grow in areas of your life you never knew existed. Dare to step into the seven truths of spiritual renewal this book will take you on, and learn how the principle of gravitational attraction affects your influence and leadership. I've been changed from it. You will be too!"

Angela Craig, *Speaker, Coach, Author of Pivot Leadership*
Founder and President of Give Good Awards

"Growing up around the automobile business meant learning to lift the hood and hear the sounds of problems. *GRAVITY* allows mindful readers to listen closely and discern hidden sounds deep within the soul. I recommend reading this book as a part of your journey to soul driven success. It extends an invitation for an extraordinary exploration capturing a new vision for life and work."

Dr. Sam Farina, *Director of Assemblies of God Coaching*
Founder of The Farina Group

"The authors describe effective leadership as a two-way thoroughfare of attraction and influence, rooted in integrity. The integrity part is certainly not new. What is, however, is how they describe how leadership strength is born out of the condition, or mass, of the soul. What is more, this soul mass is both the expression and result of a life of love, rooted in God. This resonated with me greatly. The book unpacks its content within the context of a narrative of a leader named Jason, whose professional and personal life have hit a wall. There's a little bit of Jason in all of us. I found embedded in the story many nuggets of wisdom. As a narrative, *GRAVITY* could be a quick read. As a book about the leader's soul, however, it warranted my unhurried time and personal reflection."

Mark Van Valin, *Lead Pastor of Spring Arbor Free Methodist Church*

"Wherever you may be on your individual spiritual journey *GRAVITY* is an amazing resource for each of us. The authors have captured essential life and relationship lessons in the story of Jason and Lew that we will all use in shaping our lives."

Lloyd B. Robinson, *Executive Coach, Mediator*
Former President and CEO of ALPAC Corporation

"The church is often a confusing space to practice and develop leadership. All the normal 'shoulds' and 'outs' of leading in a corporate office are amplified inside a church office with terms like "God's will" and "eternal destiny". It's a twisty road to navigate and there are few leaders with the necessary combination of both corporate and church experience to guide the way. Enter the authors who have stepped into the fray and provided a resource that is not only immediately practical but a captivating read, as well. If Patrick Lencioni and JK Rowling wrote a book together, it still wouldn't have the storytelling power and priceless leadership insights that leap off of every page in *GRAVITY*. This is a game-changer for both leadership and books on leadership."

Jesse Rice, *author of The Church of Facebook*
Former Worship Arts Director for Menlo Church - Menlo Park, CA

"This book tells a story that any leader can relate to. The characters seem familiar and the wisdom imparted is timeless."

Jim Gray, *Host of the Shut Up & Listen Podcast on Frequency.fm*

"Reading *GRAVITY* is like eavesdropping on a dozen or so of the richest most revealing conversations. You will be stunned by the privilege of listening and watching God's grace unfold in the main character. And you will often pause and say 'me too! I long for this transformation too!'"

Jane Van Antwerp, *Pastor/Exec. Director of Beyond the Blue Ministries*

"Christian books on leadership abound, but rarely does one find a book that integrates leadership truths based on biblical principles in an entertaining and thought-provoking way. *GRAVITY* does just that. The book's narrative style will draw you in and give you a concrete way to understand the connection between influential leadership and your soul. *GRAVITY* is a must-read for leaders at all levels in business, the church, and non-profit organizations. I recommend it highly."

Skip Vaccarello, *Silicon Valley leader, Author of Finding God in Silicon Valley*

"In an era of post-modern philosophy, the effort has been to strip away layers of thinking, attempting to make the complex simplistic. Yet the lessons of life are not simple. They are multi-layered as is God (God is love, God is light, God is judge, God is Father, etc.). So too are the lessons of influence and leadership.

This is an appealing and sometimes mirror-like story as I saw myself in Jason and occasionally, Lew. Through the story they remind me of the many layers of influence I possess in my own leadership journey. Yet there is one layer above all others where *GRAVITY* separates from other lessons of leadership-the unexpected and essential layer of the soul.

Like life and God, this book needs to be experienced in layers. Enjoy it for the story, not unlike our own. Go back and read it again for the depth and richness of the principles of gravitational attraction and influence. Finally, drill down to discover the rich layer exploring the nature and essence of our soul-mass-the source of our gravitational attraction and radiating influence. This book has changed how I view and relate to those I lead and influence. I know it will do the same for you."

Dale Oquist, *Lead Pastor of Peoples Church - Fresno, CA*

GRAVITY:

Seven Essential Truths About Influence, Leadership and Your Soul

A Leadership Fable
by Ronald D. Kuest and Michael L. Forney

SOUL MASS PRESS
www.soulmasspress.com

© 2016 by Ronald D. Kuest and Michael L. Forney. All rights reserved.

Published by Soul Mass Press
1108 Wing Point Way NE, Bainbridge Island, WA 98110
www.soulmasspress.com

Scripture taken from the HOLY BIBLE, TODAY'S NEW INTERNATIONAL VERSION®. Copyright© 2001, 2005 by Biblica®. Used by permission of Biblica®. All rights reserved worldwide.

No part of this publication may be reproduced, stored in a retrieval system, or transmitted in any form or by any means, digital, mechanical, photocopying, recording, scanning, or otherwise, except as permitted under Section 107 or 108 of the 1976 United States Copyright Act, without the prior written permission of the publisher. The exception would be in the case of brief quotations embodied in the critical articles or reviews and pages where permission is specifically granted by the publisher.

While the publisher and authors have used their best efforts in preparing this book, they make no representations or warranties with respect to the accuracy or completeness of the contents of this book and specifically disclaim any implied warranty for a particular purpose. The advice and strategies contained herein may not be suitable for your specific situation. You should consult with a professional where appropriate. The publisher or authors shall not assume responsibility for any errors or omissions nor be liable for any loss of profit or any other commercial damages, including but not limited to special, incidental, consequential, or other damages.

The story used in this book is a work of fiction. Any similarity between the characters and situations within its pages and places or persons, living or dead, is unintentional and co-incidental.

Books may be purchased through most retailers or
directly from Soul Mass Press online: **www.soulmasspress.com**

Cover and Interior Design: 4th Avenue Media (www.4thavenuemedia.com)
Designer: Jana Raport
Production Manager: Lindsie Lauzen
Editor: Henry R. Schorr

ISBN: 978-1-944858-00-1
1. Spirituality 2. Leadership 3. Business

Printed in the United States of America
First Edition

This book is dedicated, first:

Ron: to my family–precious gifts beyond measure–my wife Pat, and our children and grandchildren; Jeff and Jodi (Casey and Emma); Kelly; and Kristy and George (Gracie and Nathan).

Michael: to my family; my wife Nancy, to my four incredibly beautiful and talented daughters: Loree, Ashley, Natalie and Rachel; and to my son in–law, Dustin. You all enrich my life and bless me in so many ways.

Second, we dedicate this book to all who read Gravity, and through it find they are more in love with Jesus, more intimate with their soul-mass.

Most importantly, this book is an offering of stewardship back to our Lord, Jesus Christ. Without him, there is no source to relational gravity.

ACKNOWLEDGMENTS

Ron

Thank you, Diane Johnson, who, out of the goodness of your heart gave me an editing review of the first beginnings when Gravity was still a non-fiction effort. Also, to Greg Ligon, who, in providing an editing review, simply suggested the first beginnings needed a little more "sinew and tissue" and sparked the creation of the principle and truths in a fiction-fable form that Gravity now appears. To Jim Ladd, my pastor, who has been an encourager and challenger and has prayed with and through the creative process. Most particularly, my wife, Pat, who has spent many hours helping to refine and clarify the narrative. And, of course, to Michael, who's idea of gravitational leadership as a metaphor sparked a marvelous collaborative effort of character creation and story refinement.

Michael

Thank you, Don Ross and Craig Mathison, who, connected Ron and I initially and sparked what has become a treasured friendship and collaboration. Also, to Lucas Mack, who, early in the project encouraged Ron and I to move forward and has been such an amazing help moving this book from a dream into publishable form. To Trey Schorr, who, spent much of his summer and fall reading, rereading, cutting, and leading Ron and I through the developmental editing process. To Jana and Lindsie for their excellent work on taking our vision for the book and make it so much better. To Annie and Josh for their contribution to the process and partnership turning the idea of gravitational leadership into reality. And, of course, to Ron, who took on the lion's share of the labor in converting our hours of discussion into a readable and referenceable form and for being willing to wrestle through many hours of debate, refining conversation to bring the work into its present form.

And, finally thank you to a host of friends and family, praying and cheering us on through two years of writing and refining.

FOREWORD

*L*eadership fascinates me. There is so much written on the topic, and yet, the mastery of the craft of leadership is elusive. As Vice President of the Leadership Network, I have the privilege of knowing leaders from all walks—ministry, business, non-profit and government. I've often wondered what is it that forms the essential make up of leadership: is it personality, appearance, intelligence or spiritual maturity marking them out from the crowd? The answer is probably yes to all.

So many leaders find themselves working harder and harder in pursuit of achievement. Their development focused around ever-increasing their mastery of leadership skills, yet never stopping long enough to hear the cry of their soul as it is crushed under the weight of demands. What if we stopped for a moment or two and listened to the cry of our soul? What if the key to significant leadership influence is not simply what we do, but whom we become? In story form, Ron Kuest and Michael Forney have skillfully illustrated that influence goes even deeper than insight, intelligence or spiritual maturity. It goes straight to the soul.

Not everyone can have the opportunity to sit face to face with Ron, who has influenced me, or Michael who has helped so many church leaders to learn these important principles of leadership. But thanks to their commitment to write *GRAVITY: Seven Essential Truths About Influence, Leadership and Your Soul*, you can experience their message and heart. In the pages of this well written story you will see yourself in the life of Jason, a young man being led to discover his meta-narrative, to deepen his relationship with Jesus so that others can follow and the Kingdom of God can be expanded.

This highly engaging story is about a young man, Jason Cahill, a non-profit executive. Through his journey of discovery, we learn that the core of influence is found in the mysterious substance of our soul-mass—that place where our human spirit and soul reside. But who is self-aware enough to explore the depths of our soul mass?

Most of us, I suspect, are like Jason. He has experienced a career crisis brought on by his excessive and dysfunctional need to control his environment. An experience not unlike so many in leadership. We are uncertain as to our true value and feel immense pressure to perform in order to prove our worth. Yet every success only raises the bar for future performance and the pressure builds inside until confidence is replaced by a sinking feeling that we might not be the leader we hoped. The fear of failure and pressure to succeed drives us to try even harder. We work hard to control outcomes, we seek approval for our efforts and, in the end, can't escape the feeling, like Jason, we are an imposter.

The solution for Jason, though not his first choice, is to engage with Lew Merton, a soul-mentor. Lew's oil exploration background provides a great metaphor for Jason to drill down deep into his soul mass to discover, heal and grow his soul mass so that his Christian faith and his influence to those around him is relevant and authentic.

Reading *GRAVITY* I discovered how the story provides a unique opportunity to present the principle of gravitational attraction and influence. Flowing from that principle, seven truths center around the metaphor that the attraction people have for others is like the properties of gravity and radiation. Like gravity, we learn that the center of that gravitational attraction is dependent on the size and density—the health—of our soul-mass.

This book provides a powerful springboard for personal reflection and the opportunity to shift the way you approach leadership and personal development. *GRAVITY* is full of rich truths stimulating transformational growth. It has been my privilege to have mentors like Lew Merton in my life who have helped me see past my immediate battles to the longer term targets and have invested in my growth as a leader. Now working with hundreds of leaders, I continue to learn those lessons in new contexts and endeavors and through new relationships of influence. This book has reminded and reinforced in my awareness how badly we all need mentors. Life-long friends who are wise, thoughtful and believe in our potential.

Nearly every day, through The Leadership Network and my own consulting group, I'm privileged to meet and talk and work with significant leaders who are impacting the culture they've been placed into. Through *GRAVITY*, I now have not only another essential lens to view what makes leaders effective but I've also gained important tools to assist me as I encourage, equip and develop spiritual leaders.

Resist the temptation to read this book as if it is just another in a string of leadership stories. Reflect on the truths presented and allow time for the Holy Spirit to work in your heart. My prayer for you is, like me, that you will be encouraged, inspired, challenged and transformed as you read. That God will use this book to shape you and free you to find your voice, your story and your unique contribution to advancing the Kingdom of God.

Greg Ligon

Vice President and Publisher
The Leadership Network
Dallas, Texas

AN INVITATION
to the reader

"No one can come to me unless the
Father who sent me draws them, and I
will raise them up at the last day. And
I, when I am lifted up from the earth,
will draw all people to myself."

John 6:44; 12:32

Has there been a time in your life when it seemed everything you tried ended in frustration or failure? Ever have a circumstance where you were exasperated with others because you knew the best way to get to success and no one would listen? Ever wish you could establish a legacy of credibility where you are admired and respected for who you are, not just for what you do?

Join Jason Cahill as he encounters these same questions. By his early 40's, life was finally coming together like we all hope it will for us too. Good job, great responsibilities, meaningful work, wonderful family and then, ka-boom. Credibility, influence, trust and security quickly exit the room. As you will see, Jason's reputation and career are up for discussion and for nothing more than trying to do a good job. Ever been there?

Like it or not, we are all thrust into positions of influence and leadership. We say something and others listen. We become parents and have the awesome and fearful responsibility of shaping a life. We find Christ and people now watch to see if anything is different, hoping to see a genuine change. We are

TIP.

Use this space to write,
sketch, and make margin
notes as you read.

given formal roles of responsibility at work and others think we are now a leader and expect us to act like one.

What we all suspect and yet no one talks about is a significant underlying problem. It's simply this: "Leadership is one of the most observed and least understood phenomena on earth." This often-quoted statement of James McGregor Burns, a respected commentator on leadership in the 20th and 21st centuries, expresses a deep truth and speaks to the problem at the same time. How can anyone be an effective leader when we know so little about leading? Isn't this the challenge we all face? We know about leadership. We just don't know how to do it well. And you can't shake the question. "Am I up to this?" You feel like an impostor living in fear of being outed for not really knowing what you're doing.

There's an elephant in the room but it's not the impostor syndrome. And we suspect it may not be entirely in the competency of our work. Could it be that it is found in the capacity of our souls? While the soul is one of the more important elements of our spirituality, like leadership, it too is poorly understood. Put these two mysteries together—understanding leadership and understanding the role of our souls—and we have the essence of all collective human interaction. As Jason slowly comes to realize, contained in that paradox of the soul is the source of our effectiveness or our failure as a leader.

You may be wondering where gravity comes into our story and how it relates to your soul. As you will discover, how you lead and influence others is like the principle of gravity. The extent of your attraction and influence is directly proportional to the size and density of your soul. But what is our soul? We have soul food, soul music and soul mates, yet like leadership, we *know* about the soul, but do we really *know* the soul? Then the questions come. When do we think with our brains, and when is it interaction with our souls? Is there really a soul or is it just a way to explain the unknown?

Lew Merton, a soul-mentor, explores these questions with Jason as he takes him through the Principle of Gravitational Attraction and Influence and the Seven Truths. For most, we are like Jason. We've made our soul a mystery and then put it away in our intellectual attics like an antique kitchen tool, unsure of its intended use.

As you read our story, we hope you will engage the Holy Spirit letting him teach you about your soul formation. Take time to reflect at the end of each chapter. Ask God to speak to you as you see yourself in Jason and as you hear the wisdom of Lew.

Our prayer is that this book will yield new information to hone your leadership competency. And even more so, that you are changed by allowing God to increase the source of your attraction and influence, transforming you into a gravitational leader wherever you are.

Ron Kuest
Michael Forney

THE PRINCIPLE OF
Gravitational Attraction and Radiating Influence

Love, like gravity, influences through
attraction. It causes objects to fall.

To be an effective leader requires others to fall in love with you. To be an effective spiritual leader requires others to fall in love not only with you, but also to fall more in love with Jesus.

Becoming a spiritual leader is a refined form of discipleship, and discipling is a refined form of love.

The Seven Truths

LIFE
is first about the kingdom of God

CHANGE
enlarges the kingdom of God

LOVE
is the force of gravitational attraction and radiating influence

LEADERSHIP
is the craft of a leader

LEADERS
are defined by their gravitational attraction and radiating influence

SOUL–MASS
and the Spirit of God determine influence

TRAJECTORY
is a leader's legacy

CHAPTER 1

Ka-Boom!

*Why are you like a man taken by
surprise, like a warrior powerless to
save? You are among us, LORD, and
we bear your name; do not forsake us!*

Jeremiah 14:9

J ason walked into the conference room and immediately
sensed something was wrong. The five board members of
New Horizons were already seated. *Did I get the start time
wrong?* he thought. If there was one thing Jason prided himself
on, it was being on time—early if he could swing it. He knew it was
about being in control, and control was one of his primary tools of
leadership.

Jason felt himself going on defense. *This meeting isn't about
New Horizons and its financial problems. Dang! I think this meeting is
about me.*

Melissa Foster, Chair of New Horizons, nervously cleared
her throat. "Jason, have a seat, and thanks for coming in on
short notice. I can imagine you've been caught off guard, and I
apologize for that."

Caught off guard! Ha! This feels like I walked into a trap, thought
Jason.

"We've called you in for this special board meeting because
we have a crisis and problem. You know as well as we do, we are
facing a financial crisis threatening our continued existence as a

family-strengthening nonprofit."

Jason could feel his throat tighten. Every sense in his body was yelling, *This is an ambush, and I resent it! Who do you people think you are?*

"I—we've got reasons for that. We've talked about them before," interrupted Jason as he folded his arms and leaned back in his chair.

Melissa was the CFO at a regional credit union. Jason thought they had a good connection. She seemed confident but not arrogant, genuine yet direct in her questions. This morning she was no different, but Jason still felt betrayed by her.

Melissa continued, "We are concerned about whether we're going to be able to continue as an organization. I said we have a crisis and a problem. Here is the problem: we believe you have not displayed the leadership abilities we know you have. Your executive style is threatening the survival of New Horizons. To be clear, your actions and behaviors in the past year have made matters worse, not better."

"For example?" Jason was hoping for some specifics so he could defend his actions. For every problem, he had an explanation. Or perhaps it was a justification. *This is ridiculous! I'm on the front line giving my all, and you think I'm the problem?*

Melissa ignored Jason's baiting question and continued, "I know this meeting comes as a shock. We are as concerned about you, our Executive Director, as we are about New Horizons and its mission. You are bright and talented and have done some very impressive things in the time you've been with us. Jason, this discussion is not about your potential, which is phenomenal. It is about what you're doing with it."

Potential? Yeah, Melissa, what I'm doing with my potential is trying to rescue this organization. What do you think I'm trying to do? And this is the thanks I get. Potential! Oh, come on, thought Jason.

It was Hal Keller's turn to chime in. Hal was VP of operations at Neu-Soft and had been a New Horizons board member since its formation. "Jason, I know you're aware of the bind we're in because you've been in the discussions. However, in the past year, you've over-promised and under-delivered on almost every project we've taken on. Your staff is as exhausted as you are, with little to show for it. The two large donors you promised who were, in your words, 'as good as gold', didn't materialize, but you convinced us to initiate the building project anyway due to the timing of the fiscal and grant year. Now we need to borrow money, put the heavy touch on some generous supporters, cancel the program, or possibly even close the nonprofit we've all worked so hard to build. All four are lousy options."

Melissa leaned in and looked directly at Jason. "It's important you hear me clearly, Jason. This isn't the end of your career at New Horizons. Yet some things have to change, and we want to help you. If you trust us as colleagues, we can get through this."

Trust! How can I trust you when you ambush me? Fortunately, Jason was able to keep that thought silent, yet every muscle in his body wanted to leap from the chair and bolt from the room.

Keeping his swirling emotions somewhat in check, Jason said, "I understand we are facing some tough challenges, but I have just led us through several others. Doesn't it matter that I was able to engineer an incredibly complex merger with Family Matters to increase our donor base, talent pool, and overall revenue? Doesn't it matter that we've been able to hire some of the top people in nonprofit development? Doesn't it matter that we've increased our program reach by 28% this past year?"

Hal looked defensive, sympathetic, and uncomfortable, all at the same time. "Of course it matters, Jason. As we've said, we're not questioning your ability to head up an organization like New Horizons. We've all been impressed with many of the things you've done. However, it has come at a significant price in terms of fiscal and staff stability. We're asking you to make a concerted effort to bring your managing and leading style into alignment with our fiscal and staff realities."

Jason felt blindsided. He felt out of control, and that almost took him to panic. He could feel anger, fear, defensiveness and betrayal. *I'm being fired, and nobody even gave me a chance to correct!*

Jason looked directly at Melissa. "Okay, folks, I get the drift.

Yet it feels like you have a *but* in there. You can't do a setup like this without a *but* coming," he blurted out, a little more edgy than he wanted. Jason could guess what the *but* was: "You're fired."

"No buts, Jason," responded Melissa. "However, there is a however. We want you to know we are not asking for your resignation. However, things can't continue the way they are. We've got to get on stable ground financially, and you've got to make some changes in the way you work with your team and build coalitions and alliances. You've got to step up your game."

Jason had been in enough termination meetings to know this one was feeling different. But how this was different, he couldn't get a sense.

"Here is what we would like you to do," said Melissa as she looked around at the other board members, signaling this was a collective decision. "Instead of giving you a laundry list of issues and problems, we'd like you to spend time with a coach or mentor. You determine where the problems are in how you lead and the resulting impact on your team and New Horizons. Most importantly, we'd like you to come back and tell us how you've made things different. We want to hear from your staff as well."

We? thought Jason. *We as a board? Yeah, right. How much of this has been engineered by Melissa and Hal? I've sacrificed huge to keep New Horizons afloat, and this is the thanks I get?* Jason felt finding a coach or mentor was more like an order than a helpful suggestion. *Just what I need,* he thought. *Somebody else to tell me how I'm not doing my job. I don't need advice. I just need people to actually do what I ask them to do. My problem is staff who have problems. Not me.*

Melissa continued, "Jason, like I said, your job isn't on the line, but, then again, it is. Everybody's job on the line. It's simple. No money, no jobs. I don't need to remind you, you've got people's economic security in your hands, both in the office and in the field—the people we serve. We've got to pull this out, and we believe you can orchestrate that if you begin working as a team and lowering the drama."

"Come on, Melissa. You don't think I get that? Do you know how many nights I've laid in bed trying to come up with a plan?

Q.

Jason seems bright. What do you think may be his problem?

Don't you think I'm as aware of the situation as you? Maybe more?"

"Yes, I know you're concerned, and I know you care. It's just that care and concern aren't going to save New Horizons. You have to lead us out of this crisis. Right now you're pushing everyone to disaster."

Hal chimed in. "Jason, bottom line, things need to change. You are a bright and talented leader. That's not the issue. However, your execution has to change. We believe in your capacity to personally grow, and we're willing to do whatever is required to assure New Horizons profits from your exceptional abilities; but that profit can't come at the price of the dysfunction we're experiencing."

"Okay. Is that it?" Jason asked as he looked at the other board members. Stone faces. Silence. Jason could see they were extremely uncomfortable; he couldn't tell who were merely going along and who were in agreement with Melissa and Hal. "You want me to find a coach and get fixed. Is that what you're asking?"

Yes, New Horizons is in a bind, and yes, some of it I'm responsible for. But they are making me the fall guy for what should be an "us" issue. Thanks a lot TEAM! Where's my "dedicated" staff? Why would they do this to me when I have done nothing but support and lead them? Why do I always trust people when I know they're going to let me down? Even the people closest to me always seem to turn on me in the end. Here we go again. Why can't they see the growth I've brought to this organization?

Melissa's voice broke into his cascading thoughts. "Yes, as a first step, we're asking you to look into contracting with someone and getting some help as you work this through. I was impressed with Lew Merton last week at Trinity Christian Church's leadership breakfast. I noticed you were there too, so you already know something about Lew. You might want to check him out."

Jason looked straight into the faces of each board member. "Is that it? Okay. I'll get to work."

"I know you will, Jason. We need you. Know that," said Melissa with an assuring smile.

Jason got up. As he walked to the door, he searched for

something to say for closure. He could only find the obvious. "Do you want this door left open?"

"No, please close it on the way out. We have a few other things to discuss."

Like severance, Jason thought to himself.

Why, my soul, are you downcast? Why
so disturbed within me? Put your hope in
God, for I will yet praise him, my Savior
and my God.

Psalm 43:5

REFLECTION QUESTIONS

1. *Have you ever been blind-sided like Jason?*
2. *How did you feel?*
3. *What were the issues and reasons leading up to it?*
4. *What positive insights or behaviors did you learn from the experience?*
5. *What negative reactions and memories, if any, are still present?*

CHAPTER 2

A Fateful
Encounter

A friend loves at all times, and a
brother is born for a time of adversity.

Proverbs 17:17

T he nights were the hardest. Jason would lay awake, unable to fall asleep, consumed with fear and worry alternating with anger and self-pity. *How could the board have blind-sided me like that? Who do they think they are? Why does everything seem to fall apart just about the time it's coming together? How am I going to take care of my family if I'm fired?* After the sleepless nights came the morning mind games. They were taking a toll.

Evenings with Sylvia after the twins were in bed weren't much better. "Honey, I can see you are on an emotional roller coaster since your meeting with the board. One minute you're depressed, the next you're angry, and then you get a burst of energy trying to make it all right."

"Well, look at you: Sylvia, the therapist. Did you also notice my stomach is in a knot and my back and shoulders are coiled up like a bedspring?"

"Tony, Alex, I can hear you jumping on the bed. Get down, now!" She laughed. "Sorry, Jason, but that is funny. You talk about a bedspring, and the boys are acting it out. I'm not making light of your situation because it affects all of us. And I know you don't like to talk about your feelings, but do you realize you're taking it out on us as well?"

"Hey! How about a little grace! I'm sorry, Sylvia, but until that board meeting last Saturday, it seemed life was moving just about the way we had planned and hoped. Then, just when things were going good, wham! Life is getting to look more and more like dodgeball. You never know when you're going to be taken out. I'm sorry it's showing and you and the boys are getting the brunt of it, but the questions keep coming and I'm not getting answers. I'm beginning to wonder if the problem is me."

"I'm glad you're starting to ask questions, sweetheart. No questions, no answers."

"Well, aren't you the philosopher too!" Jason paused, seeing the hurt look on Sylvia's face. "I'm sorry, I don't mean to make you my verbal punching bag..."

"Yes, dear, I know. Any bag will do. I just wish I could help you somehow."

"Cute. And, you can help me. Find me another job. There's got to be one other position I'm qualified for in the world. Maybe in a third-world country so we can survive on less income. Then again, maybe I'm not cut out for this nonprofit stuff. I'm exhausted. I don't have any more rabbits in the hat. Maybe I peaked early, and the rest of my career is a bounce down the ladder of humiliation. Why do I always end up on the short end of the stick? What's wrong with me?"

"Oh, Jason. Stop being so dramatic and feeling sorry for yourself. You are talented and gifted. Maybe that Lew guy you talked about can help. Why don't you give him a call? What do you have to lose?"

On a cold gray Monday morning, nine days since Jason's meeting with his board and two weeks after hearing Lew Merton speak, Jason was up early. Lew had a morning slot open. Sylvia was sleeping soundly. Chasing after twin boys under five was intense, and he didn't want to wake her as he quietly slipped out of the house. Twenty minutes later, he drove up to a 1920's two-story American Foursquare house, converted and remodeled into office suites. Jason wasn't sure he really wanted to go in. Deep down he felt this Lew guy, a soul-mentor, would see through his façade and expose a part of him he wasn't ready for. He knew Lew wasn't a counselor or a therapist, but he wasn't quite sure what he was.

Arriving early, Jason sat in his car in an empty parking lot trying to get up the energy to go in. *What I don't need right now is someone taking me down memory lane. What I want is a coach to help me finesse the staff, come up with a few new creative ideas for funding and I'm—we're—back on track.*

Even though Jason wanted to focus on the immediate future, he found himself going to the past. *Maybe remembering the good days will motivate me forward,* he thought. *Three years to get my business degree. Dad would have been proud. Only thing that would have made him more proud would be to have known I became a pastor like him.* The thoughts started turning dark. *Yeah, that sure turned out well.* Jason remembered how his dad would say, "Jason, just do what's right, and you'll have a blessed life."

And then there was Emily. Jason's fingers tightened on the steering wheel, and his suddenly moist eyes squeezed shut. He didn't want to go there, but the memories started to flow. Jason recalled how they met in high school, never dated anyone else, and got married in the fall after graduation, and their daughter, Sydney, followed nine and half months later.

Jason thought how, right out of college, he quickly worked his way up in a prominent beverage company into senior management, the youngest by a decade on the executive floor. He was clearly being groomed for the CEO chair. A gnawing emptiness caused him to make a life-altering decision to do something more meaningful. He left his corner office and six-figure salary to follow in his dad's footsteps and become a pastor. Jason had been volunteering at his church as director of discipleship and because of his impressive business experience and ministry family background, the senior pastor at Living Streams Christian Community asked him to join the staff as executive pastor. Jason immediately enrolled in a Master's program in missional leadership at Northcoast College. Life was good. He settled in and felt like he was on top of the world.

Should have seen it coming, you idiot! Put that much time into work and ministry and seminary, and who wouldn't go looking for affection in all the wrong places? Jason's fist hit the steering wheel, as if that would erase the mixed feelings of guilt and violated trust. Emily's affair came out of nowhere—but not really. Jason vividly recalled one of their arguments.

"Jason, I supported your move from Nordstrom's to Continental Beverage—and even leaving the good life to be a pastor like your Dad—but this school commitment is too much. Something's going to break. Your daughter and I need some of your time. I'm feeling like I'm in third place behind church and school."

For about the millionth time he thought, *Why did this happen to us? To me? I was a good husband and a good father. I gave up an amazing career to do good in the world as a pastor. What did I do to deserve this? What did I do to Emily to deserve this?* The aftermath of Emily's affair was ugly. Jason wanted reconciliation, but in the end, he couldn't get past the broken trust.

Then came the next crushing blow. "I'm sorry, but you can't continue on staff," the senior pastor had said. "Our charter with our denomination does not allow for divorced pastors. If I had any room to work this out, I would."

The lost career, lost marriage, and lost direction led to five years of serial jobs in managerial sales and service. He was good at producing, but his heart wasn't in it.

After several years in this dark time, Jason began volunteering for New Horizons, a family-strengthening nonprofit. The first glimmer of light came when he was hired as the program director for their new training program, helping struggling employed clients build marketable skills to raise their income. And then came marriage to Sylvia and the birth of their twin boys. Life had been getting brighter for five years. Two years ago came the promotion to Executive Director.

And now this, he thought, shaking his head. *Am I just caught in this cycle of life where it just repeats every half decade or so? Maybe Lew's got something for me to make this different. Like Sylvia said, what do I have to lose?*

The alarm on Jason's smartphone startled him out of his trip down memory lane. Jason shook his head to clear the vivid emotions and memories. An all-too-familiar mild anxiety flush overtook him. What would this meeting be like? All he knew about Lew was what he'd heard at the leadership breakfast, and he'd had to leave early. *Two weeks ago, I heard a speaker talking about gravity and the soul. A week ago Saturday I got a bomb dropped on my future, and the two events merge today. Bizarre. Okay, God, what's up? Are you messing with my life again?*

As he walked up to the building, Jason thought, *The last thing I want is to pour out my life to someone I don't know. Hard enough with those I do know. My only problem is I'm missing some pieces to tie this mess together at New Horizons. As soon as I find some deep pockets and smooth things over with staff—and as soon as they stop trying to sabotage me—I can pull this together. I always have before. I don't need a leadership coach or a soul-mentor, whatever that is.*

But a voice in the back of his head spoke. *So, Jason, what do you need?*

Jason frowned. Where had that thought come from? Wherever it had, it was on the right track. He whispered into the silence, "I don't have a clue. If I did, I wouldn't be meeting with this guy."

Jason stood at the door and scanned the signs of the tenants. There it was on the sign: Merton and Associates: 2A and B. *Associates*, smirked Jason as he opened the front door. *Every laid-off professional seems to have a consulting business, and they always seem to put Associates on the end to imply they are bigger than they really are. Lew didn't sound like that type when I heard him speak two weeks ago. But then again...*

The old wooden stairs creaked at his weight, and Jason winced and looked around, as if afraid someone might see him coming to a counseling session. At the top, a hallway stretched ahead through the center of the building, with acid-etched-glass inset doors leading to two rooms on each side. *Merton & Associates* was printed in gold-leaf letters on the open door to his left.

"You must be Jason Cahill," said a sweet voice beyond the door to the right. The voice came from a perky-looking young woman who appeared to be no more than five years older than Sydney, his daughter from his first marriage.

"I am, and you have a phenomenal gift to anticipate Lew's next client," Jason said, more edgy than he intended. *That was unfair,* he thought. *She sounded like she's really pleased to see me.* Jason hoped his smile conveyed his remark as a joke.

The young woman smiled, seemingly unoffended. "I'm Chelsea, Lew's associate and minder and attendant. Lew will be here in a moment, but go ahead into his office." She motioned to the door connecting her office with the next room down the hall. "By the way, coffee is on the table if you'd like a cup. I'm not the serving type. Besides, the Keurig dispenser makes it completely DIY."

Well, that takes care of the "Associates" part of the business, he thought. Jason pushed open the cracked door and walked into Lew's office, feeling like he was intruding. Yet, like a detective, he was curious to see the evidence telling him more about who this Lew was and what his gravitational agenda was about.

Lew's office was about 14 feet by 20 feet. *Nice size for conversation. Must have been the master bedroom at one time,* Jason thought. The aroma of sweet pipe tobacco—not stale, yet distinctively tobacco—conjured thoughts of a bygone era. It had been a long time since he'd been anywhere where that aroma filled the room. On the long wall by the door was a large whiteboard. At one end of the room was a small fireplace with a four-inch-thick oak mantle. The exterior wall had three square windows set high in the wall. Below the windows a bookshelf ran the length of the wall. In the age of e-books, the shelves seemed another anachronistic reminder of a previous decade. *Lew actually touches paper,* he thought. *And that wood trim around the doors, windows and baseboards looks original.*

Opposite the fireplace was Lew's desk. It was a heavy, antique oak desk, the kind in a million offices before Steelcase replaced them with lifeless metal boxes, only to be replaced, in turn, by particle board cubicle furniture. Behind his desk was a tall oak computer desk cabinet, the only clue Lew lived in this century. In the center of the room was a small, dark brown leather couch, a coffee table and two facing hunter green tufted leather chairs. Capping the room, in the corner by the fireplace, was an antique globe on a stand.

Talk about atmosphere! Unsmoked tobacco and leather. Classic bookshelves. Antique woodwork. This is the perfect man-cave. Someday, this is the office I want. The only thing missing is a smoking jacket and an Irish setter, he chuckled to himself.

"Ah, I see you made yourself at home. Good to meet you, Jason," Lew said in a somewhat out-of-breath greeting, as he rushed into the room. Lew looked like a college professor. He was about five feet, eight inches. It was hard to tell his age: sixty, maybe sixty-five. His hair was still brown, although slightly receding, and his face showed many hours in the sun. His blue wool jacket and a green-striped business shirt, no tie, wool slacks, penny loafers and round tortoise-shell glasses completed the picture. Lew took off his tweed, Irish Donegal cap and tossed it on the couch along with his jacket, and then he went to the coat rack and put on a dark brown cable knit cardigan.

Reaching out his hand to shake, Lew said, "Jason Cahill. I've heard a lot about you."

Yeah, I bet, thought Jason.

"Don't worry, all good. Sit down, sit down," Lew said, still a little out of breath and motioning to the leather chairs. "So how'd you get to me?"

"You were speaking at Trinity a couple of weeks ago at a leadership breakfast. I popped in late and had to leave early, so I missed the fine points of your presentation."

"Well, Jason, that tells me where you met me, but it doesn't say anything about your excursion to get here today. Let me ask again, how'd you get to me? And, by the way, I don't need the therapist's story."

Don't worry you aren't going to get it, thought Jason. "I'm here, Dr. Merton, because my job is on the line. I've had almost a 20-year run of building my skillset as an organizational entrepreneur, which was doing fine, I thought. Only problem, my board chairman told me I needed to get fixed."

"Really? Your chairman said that?" Lew pressed raised his eyebrows and peered over his glasses.

"No, that's my one-floor elevator speech for where I'm at. If you want the 43-floor one, it will take a little longer."

"I may be mistaken, Jason, but I think that's why we're meeting." Lew pulled a pipe out of his cardigan and looked to see if it needed to be repacked. "Jason, I'll tell you more about how I want to approach our time in a minute, but first, what do you want to happen out of our time together?"

Jason felt vulnerable and guarded at the same time. He crossed his arms and gave a safe response. "I think that the point of our meeting is to make sure the board and staff are happy. I'm not sure what I want out of our time is really that relevant. But if you really want to know, what I want is for the board to get off my back so I can get back on mission. Since New Horizons is paying your bill, I'm sure the board will be happy with that result."

Lew leaned in to Jason's personal space. "To set the record straight, Mr. Cahill, I'm working for your soul. New Horizons may write the check, but I answer to your soul."

Reflexively, Jason leaned back in his chair. "That's a little unnerving, but whatever makes your business work is fine with me. I just have to get over a significant speed bump on my career path. If I sound a little edgy, it's because I am. I've been in positions of responsibility since before graduating from college, and now the board and probably my staff are pulling the rug out. I've done my homework to be successful. I've read all the classic books on leadership and management, and I've brought New Horizons to a level of service they've never had before. We've taken some big risks and grown substantially, and with that comes some stretch

Q.

Jason is entering into a mentoring relationship with Lew. Have you ever had a mentoring experience?

marks. I just need the board's support to help me ride out some challenges we're facing as we go forward. I guess that's why I'm here. So, Dr. Merton, do your thing."

"By the way, Jason, it's neither Doctor nor Mister. If we are going to spend time together, it's Lew. What do you think your board would say they want you to get out of our time?"

"Good question, ah, Lew. Did you ask them?"

"No. Our time together is our time. I'm not a consultant for New Horizons. But I sense you may have tried to dodge that question. What do you think they want?"

"I'm not really sure," Jason shrugged. "I guess they want New Horizons to get back on sound fiscal ground. The problem is, I feel like I'm caught between contradicting expectations. You've been in corporate business, right?"

"I have," Lew nodded.

"So you know big gains require big risks. Problem is, I feel the board wants the big gains but isn't willing to support the big risks. That's a zero-sum game in my book. And they probably want me to back off on some of my intensity with staff."

"How will backing off solve your problem with the board? And are you clear on what problem we're both talking about? Is it with the board, your staff, your clients or with you? Seems to me you'd better know your location before you undertake a major reconstruction project. So, permit me to ask the question again. How will that solve your problem?"

"For me, the problem is solved if the gains we've made are stabilized, I still have a job and everybody's happy, I guess." Jason shrugged as if it were fairly obvious. "I've heard them use the old cliché more than once: 'Bring us solutions, not problems.' But they can't decide on good solutions if they don't understand the problems. I feel like I'm in a box. If I tell them the problems, they think I'm not doing my job. If I don't tell them our problems, they think I'm being secretive and hiding things. See my dilemma?"

"Perhaps there is no dilemma. Ever consider the possibility your board wants you to crawl out of the self-justification box and be the best you can be? Might they think that will be the best for New Horizons?"

"Never thought of it that way."

"Perhaps you should. You said you had to duck out early from my talk. Did you get the overview of gravitational influence?"

"I was just hearing your run-up and had to leave. But it would be helpful for me to know how you are going to get this train of mine back on the track."

"Like I said, Jason, I'm not a consultant to help New Horizons get their collective act together. And you need to understand if we are to continue, I'm not your executive coach to help you get to your next-level career stop on your allegorical train ride. And, be sure of this, I'm certainly not going to be your counselor or your therapist."

"Okay, you've taken care of what you're not. So what are you going to do for me?"

"If we move forward, I'm going to be your soul-mentor. That means we're going to become long-term friends, and in the process I'm going to help you discover, heal and grow your soul-mass. Let me stop for a minute. I want to make sure you got those three points. Discover, heal and grow. I'm going to do that by using the metaphor of gravity I've found very helpful in my own journey. You know, I'm beginning to get tired of that word, *journey*. Overused to meaninglessness."

Jason could feel a tension rising up. *Oh no. No one gets inside me besides me,* he thought. "Listen, Lew. I've been to seminary, and I was a pastor. I'm not sure you should be the one to take me on a spiritual ... process."

Lew held up his cold pipe. "Excuse me a moment. Not many places left to indulge in my habit." Lew, the wiser one, was letting Jason's resistance take some time to subside as he tended his pipe. Lew opened his humidor, opened a sealed pouch and took a pinch of tobacco. His tamping touch from experienced fingers got the tobacco to the right compaction in the bowl to sustain a burn without burning out or burning too fast. "With tobacco this fragrant, I'll never forget where I put the humidor," Lew said with a smile. Pointing the pipe at Jason, Lew asked, "You mind? Not many places or people I can do this with anymore. Second-hand smoke and all."

"Not at all, Lew. My grandfather smoked a pipe, and it will bring back memories."

Lew grabbed a two-inch match from a cut-glass container originally made for toothpicks. He lit the match with his thumbnail, touched the yellow flame to the strands, pulled a draw on the pipe and slowly exhaled while shaking the match out. The smoke lingered around his head before blowing around the room, propelled by the overhead fan.

"Anyway, where were we?" asked Lew.

"I think you were trying to get into my spiritual business while telling me how you got into your business."

"Here's the long story, hopefully made bearable. I spent 32 years of my career as an oil exploration engineer, yet my assignment was drilling into the hearts and minds of people who worked for Banner Oil. I was a pioneer in developing the concept of human systems engineering. You heard of it?"

"No, can't say that I have," replied Jason.

"Of course not. It was my invention. I had this great idea: if you designed optimal systems and carefully screened for optimal team players, you could have phenomenal work teams. Looking back, that was scary thinking because, as we know, people pegs don't conveniently slip into predetermined holes. Here's the key I discovered. What pulls teams together, makes them cohesive and then accomplishes great things is influence. It's intangible, squishy and sometimes scary.

"Paralleling this investigative curiosity at Banner Oil was the beginning of my spiritual journey. My growing spiritual hunger and curiosity drove me to questions such as the nature of God. That search took me to the nature of our souls and our human spirits. As I drilled down, I began to see that this mysterious property of influence is a gravitational attraction, and the source of that gravitational attraction is the mass and density of our souls. I sensed my exploration of work teams and my search for the substance of our spirituality—our souls and human spirits—were beginning to overlap and merge. I knew I was on to something but I wasn't yet sure what it all meant."

Lew paused for another draw at the pipe. "I finally reached core. In finding that core, the answers began to come as I explored the depth of this mystery—our souls and our human spirits. Like you, I bet I hear the term *soul* a dozen times a day. Soul food, soul music and soul mates. As a trained scientific explorer, I was hooked. I was drawn to find the core inside of me—inside what I've come to call my soul-mass—that combination of human spirit and eternal soul. And for me, it centered around trust. How do I really trust God, trust others and become a trustworthy person? The answer, I've come to believe, is found in the health of our soul-mass. That, my friend, is what I want to help you to discover. Let me ask you some questions."

"Shoot."

"Tell me your understanding of the principle of gravity."

"It's a force of attraction pulling smaller objects towards a larger mass. If I remember my high school physics class, it's an irresistible property of attraction possessed by everything of substance in the universe."

"Good."

"Okay, let me see if I get your drift. You're saying that gravity is a metaphor for the attraction and influence one person has for another." Jason had moved back to the edge of his chair, looking as if any interruption would give him an excuse to quickly exit.

"That's extraordinary, Jason. I think you've got one more piece to this. And that is...?"

"And that is that love is the power of relational gravity and is directly proportional to the size and density of the soul. Am I right?"

Lew drew air through the pipe but without inhaling. He slowly blew the smoke out through his pursed lips. "I'm impressed.

But keep in mind, getting it and living it are two different things. You in?"

"In what? In trouble, in deep, in over my head? Yup. I also think I'm in for whatever you might have for me. Because if I'm not in I'm probably out. Out of a job, out of chances and out of luck."

"You have a great way with words and a sharp wit, Jason."

"Thanks, Lew. But words and wit don't seem to translate into job security at this moment."

"Maybe they do. It's interesting. I've been around unorganized people who have been able to get incredible things done. I've been around neophytes who needed a map to get to the restroom, and yet they were able to put teams together who worked their hearts out and did impressive things. What was going on there, I wondered. I've also seen brilliant people who could teach at Harvard Business School or the Colorado School of Mines who couldn't organize a group to decide where to have lunch. What was going on there?" Lew shrugged his shoulders. "You tell me."

"I guess we call it having a great personality, right?" said Jason.

"But?"

"I've been around those people, the ones with flashy personalities. There's something attractive about them. Problem is, while they're making you feel good, they're picking your emotional pocket. Okay, that's a little dark. But you really think there's something wrong with their souls? Or are you trying to make something out of nothing?"

"Great question. You tell me when we're finished."

"So I presume this is what we're going to be talking about? You're going to fix my broken, wounded and wretched soul?"

"Broken? Probably. Wounded? Definitely. Wretched? Not a chance. And fix? Hah! I don't fix anything. That's your job, and it can only happen through the Spirit of Christ within you. He is in you, right?"

"He's there. He's got his space. I've got mine. We don't talk a lot, but we're still friends."

"Hum? Interesting. Let me wrap this up so you can think

about what we talked about. What evolved from my research was a principle, along with seven truths to explain it. As they formed, it became clear I was ascending into the spiritual realm of conversation, and I was having a hard time keeping my professional work separate from my spiritual awakening. About that time, Energon bought out Banner Oil in a hostile takeover, and human systems engineering wasn't on their strategic dashboard. I got a golden parachute with a very generous early retirement package.

"Great timing, huh?"

"It was. I was able to pull my cash, and two years later Energon was no more."

"Yeah," Jason laughed, "other than the former execs pleading for reduced sentences on their walk of shame."

"Permit me to ask you an important question, Jason. You think you're in the middle of good timing?"

"Ha! I didn't realize humorist came with your title too."

"No jokes. Let's not waste our time and New Horizons' money. Are you serious about moving forward? Because if you are, we'll start on a road through seven truths proving this principle of gravitational attraction and influence. In the process, I fully expect you to become intimately acquainted with your soul. I expect you will find it, as you've suggested, battered, wounded and depleted due to a lack of care."

Jason sat back in the chair and raised his hands. "Look, Lew. I don't mean to make this difficult. It's just that I've found the best way to survive in life is to not let people let you down. It's happened too many times for me. I get what you're trying to do, and I get what the board wants. It's just that if this turns out bad, I'm not sure what options I've got left."

"Sounds to me like you're trying to control outcomes, and unintended consequences keep coming out."

"Nice play on words, but you're right. I do try to control outcomes. I am intrigued by what you've said. I just can't handle getting screwed over again. You understand?"

"Completely. I'm not going to ask you to trust me in the beginning. That will take time. All I ask is that when you find me reliable, you have confidence in what I have to say. Fair?"

"Fair. Let's get to work."

"Great. So, here we are and here's the principle." Lew pointed to a framed statement done in fine calligraphy, hanging on the wall next to the whiteboard.

Love, like gravity, influences through attraction. It causes objects to fall.

To be an effective leader requires others to fall in love with you. To be an effective spiritual leader requires others to fall in love not only with you, but also to fall more in love with Jesus.

Becoming a spiritual leader is a refined form of discipleship, and discipling is a refined form of love.

"No offense, but from our conversation, you're certainly not a therapist, and you're definitely not a theologian. So what are you?"

"No offense taken. By the way, you seem a little more than touchy about this therapist thing. Are you afraid I may find something in your heart or in your soul in need of repair?"

"I just don't like people messing with my head."

"Don't worry, no messing allowed," said Lew as he smiled and slowly drew and blew a stream of pipe smoke. "Besides, you're not alone. My soul-mass was in the same state as yours when I started this ... process. I'm going to help you find ways to restore your soul to health and reestablish a wholesome relationship with the Holy Spirit in you. You up for it?"

"I was until you laid the 'falling in love' thing on me in the principle."

"How so?"

"You're saying that in order for me to lead, people have to fall in love with me?"

"You're a good listener, Jason. That's exactly what I said. What's your point?"

"That makes me feel uncomfortable. I love my dog, I love my sports teams, I love my wife and kids, and I love God. But

Q.

*Why is Jason having
push-back on the love
topic?*

to think others have to love me in order to follow me makes me uncomfortable."

"Well, first of all, I hope your love list isn't in the order you gave it to me," laughed Lew. "What makes you uncomfortable?"

"I'm not sure. It just doesn't feel right. It feels sexual and if not sexual, at least intimate. I'm not sure I want people I lead to fall in love with me."

"You mean, to get that close to you? What do you want them to do?"

"Well, follow, respect and trust, mostly. Even liking me would be okay."

"All good, Jason, but consider that what you want are all derivatives of love. I try to make things as simple as possible. Tell me what's wrong with this logic. God is love, right?"

"Of course."

"Did Jesus not say, love one another as I have loved you?"
"Yes."

"Did the Apostle Paul not say to walk in love?"
"He did."

"Then your problem is, what?"

"Jesus was perfect. He didn't hurt people or use them or make them feel stupid. He didn't let people down."

"That's true, although he did make the Pharisees feel stupid. What's your point? Is it possible you don't want the pressure or burden of love?"

"You really know how to make a guy squirm, don't you? You're good."

"Obviously, I'm not going to let you off the hook. I'm also not going to change my principle for you, and I know you're not asking me to. But if we go forward—and that's an if on your part—know we'll be exploring influence and love. Take your time to think it over. I don't want to waste your time or mine."

For the first time ever, this guy is getting into my head. No, no, this guy knows how to get to my soul ... wherever that is, thought Jason. *I'm intrigued, scared, curious and desperate, all at the same time. Is this guy safe? That's all I want to know. Can I trust him? Can I trust him? If he drops me on my head like so many others, I'm not sure I can come back without becoming the worst cynic in the world. Yet, what do I have to lose? Maybe my soul.*

"Lew, my opportunity to spend more time with you is a little more than intimidating. And yet, I'm intrigued. Of course I want to go forward. I'm out of tricks in my bag."

"Good. Looks like it's finally time to start getting real. By the way, I've got a few things for you to do before we meet again. First, I'm going to send you two assignments. One is an 'I Am' worksheet. I want you to list as quickly as they come to mind and finish the phrase, 'I am...' There are twenty responses. Second is a 'How I Add Value' worksheet. In this one, just respond to the questions. When you're done, email them to Chelsea. Last thing, I want you to connect with Alisha Bishop. She runs the Margaret Corbin Brigade, and you'll find her fascinating. I'll text you her address. Oh, and here's a scripture I want you to ponder. It's Genesis 2:7. 'Then the LORD God formed a man from the dust of the ground and breathed into his nostrils the breath of life, and the man became a living being.' Lastly, I want you to be thinking on the first truth, which is, life is about the kingdom of God.

"Oh, and one other thought about your love issue. Perhaps you push back because you feel unworthy of their love. Think about it. Check in after you've met with Alisha."

For what will it profit a man if he gains the whole world and forfeits his soul? Or what shall a man give in return for his soul?

Matthew 16:26 (ESV)

REFLECTION QUESTIONS

1. *Jason is entering into a mentoring relationship with Lew. Have you ever had a mentoring experience?*

2. *If so, what has or was it like? Rich and continuing? Short-term and transactional?*

3. *If you've never had a mentoring relationship how do you think one would be helpful in your spiritual growth?*

4. *Lew said to Jason that in order for people to have influence, the people you influence must begin to progressively fall in love with you as their leader? Why do you think Jason is having push-back on that statement?*

CHAPTER 3

Well, That's Life!

LIFE IS FIRST ABOUT
the kingdom of God

So it is written: "The first man Adam became a living being"; the last Adam, a life-giving spirit. The spiritual did not come first, but the natural, and after that the spiritual. The first man was of the dust of the earth; the second man is of heaven.

1 Corinthians 15:45–47

"Get out of the kill zone!" A dazed Alisha Bishop mustered the energy to give an order to her driver. A US Marine Corps Captain, she looked down through her shredded, blood-soaked flak jacket and saw her right arm loosely connected to her torso.

Blood, bone fragments and flesh splattered on the bulletproof windshield, and her now-bloodied fatigues were visual evidence her team did not dodge the bullet. She didn't know if it was an IED or a shoulder-fired TOW missile. Didn't matter at this point. There was a shrill ringing in her ears, yet behind it was an eerie silence. "Let's move!" she screamed. It was the last thing she remembered before losing consciousness.

Captain Bishop's team had been on their way to a town near Musa Qal'eh, Afghanistan. Alisha was a member of a Female Engagement Team. Their role was to gather and communicate information to local women without violating cultural standards.

Six days after the explosion, Alisha was a patient at Walter Reed Army Medical Center. Her role was to recover from devastating injuries, not least of which was an amputated stub that used to be her right arm. It had been necessary for surgeons to take the limb to stop a life-threatening infection. Her badly lacerated face would require facial reconstruction surgery when her body stabilized from the amputation and infection. Her pelvis, wired together like a '51 Chevrolet in Havana, Cuba, was a reminder she would always walk with pain and a cane even with her hip replacement. Walter Reed was to be her home for the next 13 months for surgeries and rehabilitation.

Driving down Century Park Boulevard, Jason looked for Alisha's address. He'd driven past Bio-Dynetics Systems' massive office and warehouse building three times, but saw no signage for the Margaret Corbin Brigade, yet his map app said that was where it was. *Lew must have dropped a number or written it down wrong, Jason thought.*

Frustrated, he decided against his instinctive wiring and stopped at Bio-Dynetics to ask directions. Walking through the lobby doors, he stepped up to the receptionist desk. A phone with a sign to dial 3146 had long ago replaced a live body.

"Welcome to Bio-Dynetics Systems. How can I help you?" said a friendly male voice through the speaker.

"Excuse me; I'm trying to find the Margaret Corbin Brigade. I've driven around and around and can't seem to find the location. Can you help me?"

"It's here," said the voice. "Mrs. Bishop shares offices with us. You're not the first one to have difficulty finding her. Is she expecting you?"

"Yes. Jason Cahill, New Horizons."

"New Horizons," said the receptionist. "My wife and I just attended one of your workshops. Great stuff! Thanks for putting it together. Hold on just a minute, and Mrs. Bishop will be right out."

In less than two minutes, Alisha walked through the door separating the lobby from first-floor workspaces. Alisha was six feet tall. She carried herself in a stately manner, exuding dignity in spite of her broken frame and obvious limp. Her mahogany complexion and jet black hair conveyed a beauty in spite of visible scars. A cane hung on a prosthetic right arm that had all the appearances of a bionic masterpiece. She extended her left hand to shake.

"Nice to meet you, Jason. Lew told me you were just starting the Gravity experience with him."

"Ah, yeah, that's kind of how he explained it." *Not all the plastic surgery in the world could erase the disfiguring lines of her trauma,* Jason thought.

Alisha saw Jason in the all-too-familiar uncomfortable place, trying not to look at the scars on her face, as if pretending they weren't there. Putting Jason at ease, Alisha gave an assuring smile. "I would have shaken hands with my right limb but that sometimes freaks people out if they aren't used to being around amputees and prosthetic limbs. Come on back to my office."

"I'm not familiar with Bio-Dynetics or your Margaret Corbin Brigade. What do they do?"

Reaching her office, Alisha offered Jason a chair. "Bio-Dynetics is the world's largest developer of prosthetic devices. They are creating limbs now that actually respond to brain waves. That's what I'm wearing, and I'm on retainer as a consultant for the company. I speak to groups on the topic of life after discovering you're an amputee. In exchange, Phil Spencer, the founder of this wonderful company, gives me an office and lets me run my nonprofit, the Margaret Corbin Brigade, out of his building."

"Is Margaret a friend of yours?"

Alisha laughed. "Hardly. Margaret's about 225 years older than you or I. During the War of Independence, she fought alongside her husband at Fort Washington in New York. When her husband was killed, she continued to load and fire the cannon. She was the first woman soldier in the United States to get a military pension."

Alisha slowly eased into her chair. "Our purpose at the Brigade is to provide support to women returning from deployment with everything from disabling injuries and PTSD to unplanned pregnancies. We are also gearing up to do the same for first responder women stateside."

"Hadn't thought of that as a need."

"I run into that perspective all the time, Jason. We say 'soldier,' and we automatically see a male in our mind's eye. The female combat soldier is strangely invisible. These women come back from deployment with all the baggage of their male comrades and then bring their own suitcases as well. They are often the overlooked casualties of war."

"Let's talk. At New Horizons we're always looking for alliances and networking," Jason offered. "Maybe there are some projects we can team up on."

"Perhaps there are some possibilities." Alisha had learned to be careful about who, how and when alliances were made. She had enough pain in her life to avoid unnecessarily bringing on more. "But enough about my world. Besides, I don't think networking is why you're here. I presume your world just got rocked by your own version of an IED."

"Yeah. I really didn't see it coming. But look, this is nothing like what you must have gone through."

Alisha's smile dropped from her face. "For you and your world, I'm sure it felt the same." Changing subjects, Alisha asked, "If Lew is on point, he probably gave you a scripture, right?"

"Yes, and quite frankly, I haven't a clue as to how it fits into this whole *Gravity* gig of his."

"You sound a little skeptical or even suspicious."

"Look. I'm sure I could have come to Lew on my own if I thought I needed his help. But I assumed I was doing okay. I thought I had brought New Horizons to a new level of visibility and service. And I was able to snag some real high-value talent to help expand our programs, then boom. I don't like the either/or way the board told me to get fixed."

"So you got an ultimatum?"

"Well, no. It just felt that way. I don't feel like I have any choice. I know there's some tension with staff. We all have our backs against the wall and futures on the line. I know we're on rocky financial ground, but I have confidence I can turn this around. I always have.

"I've heard a lot of I's in your statements," said Alisha. "You might want to think about that. Can we stop a minute? Can we talk about this defensive skepticism of yours?"

"I'd rather not, but yes. I know I'm here to talk with you about things other than—or in addition to—your war experiences and your current efforts. Obviously, Lew has a plan for us meeting. You just need to know talking about me is not one of my favorite topics. I'd much rather talk about how we can partner in service."

"So I noticed."

"But considering my current situation, I'll go to the fire pit and see how quickly I can run through the coals. Like I said, I don't like to talk about me, so let me give you the Cliff Notes version. I grew up in a pastor's home. When I was 13, my dad died of a heart attack. He'd given his life to ministry. I bet he said it a thousand times if he said it once that God would provide for us. Well, God didn't provide. Dad had no social security, no life insurance, and my mother had no skills outside our home. Can I just say it was rough?"

"I can imagine. I have friends with similar life stories."

Jason continued. "With academic and financial need scholarships, I put myself through school, majoring in business. I did it in three years with honors. I was on a mission to be one of the youngest execs in a Fortune 5000 company. I tasted the well of corporate success and at 29 still felt empty, so I made a career change. I guess I couldn't get too far from my Dad's influence and my roots. I went on staff with a church while getting a Master's in missional leadership. Well, that didn't turn out the way I hoped."

"Sounds like you've had a few people let you down."

Jason paused, wondering if he was venting too much to someone he just met, yet he felt he wanted to explain his situation to a person unconnected to the outcome. "Let's just say, except for my mother, over the years just about everyone in my life has let me down. Actually, one of my current life mottoes comes from an unlikely source. I'd like to tell you it's from the Bible. Only problem is there isn't much scripture speaking to me right now."

"So what's your motto?"

"It's from Nietzsche. You know, the 'that which doesn't kill me makes me stronger' guy." Jason swiped his phone several times. "The quote of his that makes most sense to me is this. 'The individual has always had to struggle to keep from being overwhelmed by the tribe. If you try it, you will be lonely often, and sometimes frightened. But no price is too high to pay for the privilege of owning yourself.'"

"It sounds like you view yourself as a self-made man." Alisha smiled.

"You're very perceptive," responded Jason, enjoying the safe banter. "Besides, the nice thing about being self-made is, God doesn't have to be embarrassed with the results."

"I can identify with where you are. I too at one point was very driven. I had a lot to prove. I grew up in the rural South, raised in a Christian home where women had their place. But that place wasn't for me. I adopted the faith of my parents but never really owned it. What I owned was determining my destiny. I guess you could say everything I did up to the explosion was to prove a point."

"Which was?"

"To prove to my dad and three brothers I had a God-given right to be whatever I wanted to be—including a Marine officer. Somewhat like you, I was out to prove I was a self-made woman." With a grin, Alisha said, "Now with these artificial body parts, I guess you could call me a man-made woman."

Jason snorted, trying to hold back a laugh. "Please excuse me. That was a great word play. I don't know what to say."

"How about, 'That's funny.' Let me get serious for a minute. I presume you are still a committed follower of Christ."

"Yes," Jason said, nodding his head. "It's just that..."

"Yes, yes, I know," Alisha interrupted. "You've got all the fine print provisos for your own micro-theology. Am I right?"

"Hey, don't get me wrong," said Jason, holding up his hands and leaning back a bit. "I am a committed Christian. That hasn't changed. It's just that all the clichés from my childhood and even seminary are pretty thin when it comes to my life experiences."

"Sounds like you're madder at the Church than at God. What do you see needing recalibration?" Alisha pressed.

After a moment of gathering thoughts, Jason answered, "It's just that I see way too much preaching around trusting God when what they're really meaning is blind faith. I know enough about the Bible and spirituality to know that kind of teaching can be deadly. It didn't serve my family. I'm not a 'God helps those who help themselves' kind of believer, but I do think that if anything is going to happen in life, it has to start with you. You have to open doors if you're going to see different scenery. Right?"

"Interesting. I thought in Luke 11 Jesus said, *'For everyone who asks, receives; and he who seeks, finds; and to him who knocks, it will be opened.'* You're the preacher, Jason, but I don't recall it saying knock and then open the door or knock it down. I'd like to come back to this before you go, but let's step back a minute. Would you like a cup of coffee? Anything in it?"

"Black is just fine."

"Yes, it is," winked Alisha.

Alisha returned with two mugs. "This is one thing I don't miss about the Marines."

"Coffee?"

"Ha. No, bad coffee. Watch out, it's really hot." When she had sat down, Alisha asked, "Have you been thinking about the scripture Lew gave you?"

"Yes, it's about God creating Adam, the true alpha male."

Alisha smiled. "Nice play on words, but I'm not going there. So what does it say, and what does it have to do with the first truth Lew gave you? You do know what the first one is, don't you?"

"Yes. It's, 'Life is first about the kingdom of God.'"

"And what's the scripture?" asked Alisha.

Jason reached for his smartphone and pulled up the verse. "It's Genesis 2:7. 'Then the Lord God formed a man from the dust of the ground and breathed into his nostrils the breath of life, and the man became a living being'."

"Fine. First point: this scripture talks about life and living. It would be helpful to make a distinction between the two."

"How so?"

"See if you can tell me."

Shrugging his shoulders, Jason replied, "I don't know. I think the meaning's fairly obvious. It's about Adam being formed from the dust of the earth."

"That's how most people read the verse. It's about the first man being created. A little ego-centric, isn't it? Take away the forming part. Now what do you have?"

"God breathing life into Adam."

"And?"

"And the man became a living being. Huh. Never saw that before. It's not just about the first man being created. It's about life and a living creature. That's powerful."

"So, Jason, what would you say you now see in that passage? What's the distinction?"

"I guess it's saying living is what I do day to day. Life is what God gave us all, starting with Adam."

"Well done. I can see your education wasn't a complete waste." There were times when the Marine in Alisha kept breaking out.

"You know, it's obvious Lew has made his point. Perhaps I need to focus on the life I've been given instead of the living I'm experiencing. Man, that is so basic and yet big. How did I forget this basic stuff, anyway? You're pretty good at pulling that out. You should be teaching in a seminary." Jason laughed as he became more comfortable with Alisha. "And I see you can take a woman out of the Marines but you can't completely take the Marine out of the woman."

"It shows no matter how hard I try."

"Stop trying. It becomes you. You know, as I've tried to analyze why I got shot out of my metaphorical vehicle at New Horizons, the conversation is always about why me, why now and what's next. Instead, maybe the conversation should be about what am I doing with my living—even though it feels like it sucks right now."

"Good thinking, Jason." Changing subjects, Alisha looked straight into Jason's eyes. He could feel an intensity that was comforting and intimidating at the same time. "Owning it and living it are two different things. I can certainly identify with where you are, Jason. I was in nearly constant pain at Walter Reed for 13 months, recovering from my injuries."

"What did you do with your time?"

"Being hospital- and bed-bound gave me months to think about my life. What I didn't realize was, just as you pointed out, I thought my life was over, when in fact, it was only my living that was severely disrupted."

"You must have had a rock-solid faith when you went in to endure all that."

"Not at all. When the explosion shattered my body, it took my fragile faith with it too." Alisha's stoic Marine persona began to soften. Her shoulders slightly dropped. "Until then, I thought God must be so proud of me. Look what I'm doing. All I ever wanted from the time I was a high school junior was to be a Marine and prove that a woman does not have a ceiling. So you might say I thought I was letting God open the doors while I was trying to blow open the ceiling. My career goal was to be the first female Marine Brigadier General. Then in an instant, a Taliban Afghani took away my dream. I felt used up, worthless and that God had let me down."

Alisha's voice remained as if she were in charge as she told her story, but her body continued to tell a different one. Jason noticed her gaze was off to a corner of the room, her functional arm was slightly quivering and her voice took on a monotone cadence. "While recovering from countless surgeries and in rehab, I couldn't help but believe my life was over. No arm. A disfigured face. A hip and a leg that will always need a cane."

As if Alisha snapped out of being in another place, her eyes burrowed into Jason's with an uncomfortable intensity. "Too broken to be a Marine. Depressed. Add to that all the sedation and narcotic medication, and I hit rock bottom. My life was over, and I felt if I died, so what? At least I wouldn't be in pain any longer.

"Jason, do you know what it feels like to be stripped of

everything you thought other people valued in you? It was Markus, my husband, who began to change my view of how we value others and ourselves. He was there for me through it all. Before the attack, he used to say, and I know he was joking, 'If you ever get ugly, I'll still be there for you.' Well, I did, he still is, and he still makes that joke. For him, my living isn't as pretty as it used to be. But here's the thing you need to know. After my injury my life has become richer and fuller, not lesser and empty."

Jason felt himself sliding his body back into the chair because of Alisha's intensity, yet leaning forward as he became completely engaged.

"You know what was the scariest part? It wasn't my fear of death. It was feeling useless. I was terrified of becoming a burden for others to care for. Yet, I had it all backwards. You see, for me, I defined life in terms of what I did. And when I thought I could no longer do, I thought my life was over. One day a Navy Chaplain stopped to visit me. We had a good talk, and when he was leaving, he handed me a scripture. It was John 10:10. *The thief comes only to steal and kill and destroy; I have come that they may have life, and have it to the full.*"

Alisha regained her composure, and the tension in her face, voice and body began to relax again. "Talk about a gift from God. As I grabbed hold of those words, something began to change. I could feel it. I went from depression and despair to anger. Not at God or even the unknown Afghani behind the explosion. I became angry at my circumstance."

Jason nodded, feeling a small identity with her anger.

"Let me tell you, Jason. Something strange happened when I looked at death, eyeball to eyeball, and death blinked. I was no longer afraid to die. I know, I know, this sounds hokey, but when I was no longer afraid to die, I was also no longer afraid to live in whatever condition I finally healed into. This was when I discovered my mission, my purpose in living. My life wasn't over. I was still alive, and I had to determine what to do with my living. My new living was going to be difficult and painful, but I now had a renewed purpose. You could say my story is a gift with a very expensive price tag. And I know this gift is to bless others. I would like to tell you this realization came in a flash. Didn't happen that way for me."

"How did it happen?"

"Somewhere between realizing God had a plan for my living and taking an inventory of my Marine experience came my purpose. Listen carefully, Jason. My purpose isn't grounded in what I do. That's my living. Purpose is grounded in who I am. That's my life. Get this distinction, Jason, or you are wasting your time with me and Lew."

This is one strong person, thought Jason. *I feel like I'm in the infantry and I should say, "Sir, yes, sir!" Now there is a person I would follow into a sure-death mission. She is a true leader.* Instead, he asked, "What happened to get you to that realization?"

"Sometimes the truth we need comes in hard ways. Before Walter Reed, I was a doer. When I landed in a bed there, completely helpless, that was a new experience. I couldn't do a thing for myself or for those helping me. I felt indebted and humiliated at the same time. I was more terrified lying in bed than deployed in Afghanistan. I was scared stiff of being useless. In my total helplessness, I began to experience, through Markus and others, what a free gift of love felt like. And then I saw that's how God wants us."

"Excuse me, Alisha, I don't mean to interrupt, but are you saying God wants us in a helpless state? I thought that was why he gave us a brain—so we wouldn't be helpless."

"Well, you can form your own theology. For me, I realized I had to become spiritually in the same state I was physically. To be an instrument of his love, I had to realize how helpless I am without his love, saving grace and power. I had to stop proving to God that I was qualified on my own works to receive his love. He created me in love, and I'm completely helpless without it. For me, it changed my outlook on life as well as living."

"So how did it all come together for you?"

"Fortunately, preparing for the Female Engagement Team required leadership training along with basic life skills. We got a crash course in medical care, critical incident training, conflict resolution, cross-cultural communication and you-name-it. I began to see all that training was valuable if I could just find a place for it. I had paid a huge price for the training. But I had it, and I intended to use it. "

"Sounds like a contradiction. You're helpless, yet your prior training got you strong?"

"You listen well, Jason. As you clearly saw from the scripture and gravitational truth, there is a significant distinction between having a life and experiencing a living. I believe God wants us to be strong and courageous in our living while experiencing complete dependence on him for our life."

"Wow. Deep." Uncomfortable with the clarity of the truth, Jason shifted gears. "How did you get here—to Bio-Dynetics?"

"I met Phil at Walter Reed. He had just received a contract from DOD DARPA for field-testing his state-of-the-art wonders built to look like prosthetic limbs. In the course of time, I became one of Bio-Dynetics' guinea pigs. Phil took me under his wing and connected me to Lew. Lew helped me reconnect with my soul, and the rest is history."

Jason wished he had a Phil Spencer in his life. *Where were all the advocates in my life when I needed them?*

Alisha looked at him intently. Strangely, the deep scars in her face seemed to fade. "So you think you're the best door-buster in the region, Jason? I get it. Everything in life validates door busting. Let me give you the main point; then you can kick it around a little."

"I could listen to you all day, Alisha. I think we come from a similar root: that hard work is the proof of worth. I think Lew sent me here not only to learn it but for another purpose as well."

"Right you are, Jason. My experiences taught me that when we forget the meaning of grace, our spiritual lives look like how we're living—doing—instead of our living looking like our life full of grace and the father-heart of God."

"That sounds circular."

"It is, and the key is where you start to draw the circle. It begins with life and then translates to our living. Not the other way around. I said we'd come back to our conversation about Luke 11 and doors opening. Think about it in relation to our conversation today."

Leaning forward, Alisha put her hands on her desk to rise. Jason was amazed, seeing her bionic arm in sync with her natural arm. "I have another appointment, so let me finish with this. I know you said you were a pastor at one time, so you already know the basic truth I had to almost die to learn. It's simply, all God wants from us is eternal fellowship with Him, and that comes through Jesus. That's it. Bottom line, relationship is the heart's cry of the Father. That is life, and this is the reason for our living day to day. It's the reason from Adam to now."

Jason thought, *When did I lose this basic truth?*

"You are going to hear this again, Jason. It will, no doubt, come from Lew. But let me set you up so when it comes by again it will really stick. Your value is not in your works. Your value is in the health of your soul. And your attraction—how much others love you—is not found in what you do or what you look like. It goes deeper than that. Your gravitational attraction is proportional to the core mass and density of your soul."

Alisha extended her right hand, the mechanical hand mounted on her artificial limb. Jason wondered what it would feel like. The machine-driven marvel encased in a soft leather glove gently squeezed his hand as Alisha said, "Jason, it was a pleasure to meet you. I know your Gravity journey is going to take you places you cannot imagine. I can't wait to see how it turns out for you."

Driving away, Jason couldn't get one phrase Alisha had said out of his mind. "When we forget the meaning of grace, our spiritual lives look like how we're living instead of our living looking like our life full of grace and the father-heart of God." Jason mused, *I'm starting to wonder if I've spent most of my life focused on my living. Seems a little short-sighted. Hopefully Lew can help me sort it out.*

Jason was a few minutes early for his appointment with Lew.

As he walked up the stairs, he saw Chelsea's door open. He poked his head in and saw Chelsea in her sweats, with her hair pulled back in a ponytail.

"What are we doing, casual Tuesdays now? How are you?"

Chelsea looked up from her laptop, smiled and said, "Marvelous, in spite of digs from clients. How was your time with Alisha?"

"How was it? That's probably going to be the question from Lew, but let's say interesting, fascinating and challenging."

"Is that multiple choice or all three?" asked Chelsea. "Pull up a chair if you want."

"Looks like you're deep into something," said Jason. "Don't want to interrupt."

"No interruption at all. You have me curious. What did you find interesting?" Chelsea asked, closing her laptop.

"I didn't realize how many women are experiencing war injuries. I guess the little bit of chauvinist in me makes me cringe even more than for male soldiers. Seeing her physical condition really bothered me."

"Times are a-changing, huh? What was fascinating about your time?"

"Her bionic limb. I had no idea robotics and neuro-programming had come so far. I was amazed at the dexterity Alisha had in her right limb. Guess you can't call it an arm."

"And, Mr. Cahill, for your last and final question before you get the grand prize of a dinner at Pogo's, the all-you-can-eat chicken diner down the road, what was challenging?"

"Well, obviously her story. Alisha is one impressive and inspiring woman."

"Not just an impressive and inspiring *person?*" Chelsea poked. "And what made her challenging?"

"I've got to be careful with you, Chelsea. You listen too carefully," he said, smiling. "Actually, the real challenging part was comparing my job crisis with her experience. Guess who came up the chump and who is the hero? Kind of put my career crisis in perspective."

"So what were your takeaways from your time with her?"

"Got a notebook?"

"No, but I hope you're keeping a journal," nudged Chelsea.

"Well, the obvious was she found her life while struggling with her living. I never thought about the connection and contrast between life and living. Very interesting."

"Progress, huh?" said Chelsea with a grin. "Anything else? Pardon my curiosity and poking. I hope you don't mind, but I'm fascinated by this process of Lew's. I'm doing an internship with him, and I'm working on my final project."

"Glad to be useful," said Jason. "Can I ask you a question? What are you finding in your research?"

"Just starting, but I'll let you read a draft of my dissertation when I finish. You may find your story in there if you give me permission."

"Well, let's wait and see if my part turns out a mystery or a dry autopsy report."

"Okay, now I have a question for you. It's the same one Lew will ask."

"Fire away."

"Who do you think you are?"

"What?"

"I said, who do you think you are?"

"Last time I heard that coming from a female it was my mother. What do you mean, who do I think I am?"

"Just what I said. Who do you think you are?"

"You caught me cold on that one. You sent me the 'I Am' worksheet. You already know what I wrote. I'm a man, a husband, a father."

"Interesting. You said in your 'I Am' worksheets that you were a *good* husband and a *good* father. Is that to be contrasted with bad? I also noticed you didn't say you were a *good* man."

"Where are you going with this, Chelsea? Is this part of your research?"

"Yes and no. I'm starting to gather that you are a very accomplished doer who's experiencing some difficulty with your being. Am I warm?"

"You tell me. You're the expert intern. I've seen my share of be-ers in the world. And you know what? The reason why we are experiencing the good life is because of doers, not be-ers."

"Sounds like you just told me. Please don't take this as impolite, but how's the doing working for you? When Lew accepted me as an intern, he said my job description was simply to be a detective. And then he said as he helps clients walk through this Gravity adventure, he wants me to look for clues. 'Keep your eyes peeled and your ears open.' That's all he said besides, 'Welcome aboard.'"

"And so what are you seeing and hearing, Detective Chelsea? Sounds like you've already gathered a lot of opinions as evidence."

Chelsea laughed. "Seriously, I'll give you my observations after you tell me what you observed in your time with Alisha."

"I saw a very strong *person* who's got a firm grip on who she is."

"Bingo. Her identity is rooted in who she is, not in what she does," said Chelsea.

Jason asked, "How about you?"

"Hey, hey, hey, clients don't get to ask questions! Besides, how about me, what? How about my opinion on Alisha? How about my opinion on identity?" Chelsea laughed. "Okay, since you're new, here's my two cents and the answer to your questions."

Chelsea leaned back in her chair and steepled her fingers. "First of all, Alisha is one well-put-together person. Just pray neither of us has to go through what she did to get what she has.

"Next, my opinion on identity. Let's make this one about you. I can tell you are angry and feeling like you're not in control. I only have a narrow-window view of what issues brought you to Lew, but my guess is you may be in for a hard ride before coming out the other side. Like I said, in your worksheets, your responses seem to be a lot about doing."

"You read me fairly well. I do believe in working hard and doing the best job I can. To me, that's how you serve others. Let me repeat myself, what about you?"

"Here's my cultural context, not that it has any relevance to your meeting with Lew. I grew up in a wonderful home in

Connecticut. My parents are now Christ-followers, but back then I would say they were God-knowers. Like so many New Englanders, simplistic religious clichés put them off. Have to say, like them, I'm still a skeptic on some of what the Church says and then actually does. Lew's been helping me walk through this, and it's been really helpful."

"I'm curious, what's been so helpful for you?" inquired Jason.

"I presume you already know this since you're the preacher-man."

"I think you know that's part of my history. Not sure it's part of my future, though," said Jason as he folded his arms and leaned back in the chair.

"Well, no matter where you are, your history is what makes your present."

"Little deep for an intern, isn't it?"

"Whatever. You asked me a question about how Lew's been helpful to me. He's helped me see my human spirit is selfish at the core, and without continuous transformation I allow it to form my identity."

"I get that. So how's that helpful?"

"I didn't realize my skepticism, which I inherited from my parents, was deeply rooted in my human spirit. Between my spiritual mind, heart and will, my worldview—my identity—was shaped by viewing my world through distorted lenses of control, gratification and preservation, all filtered through a humanistic mindset."

"That's deep. So is that where you are?"

"Thank goodness, no. Lew helped me see how the Holy Spirit changes everything. With a healing and renewing soul, I try to filter out the messages of the 'old woman' in me and concentrate on the voice of God speaking through his Holy Spirit and resonating in my soul."

"Is this when I take the offering?"

"Man, you are beyond a skeptic. You sound like a cynic. Are you really that bitter?"

"Obviously, sometimes," replied Jason. "I guess that came off a little darker than I intended."

"Here's something else I've learned from Lew. Take it for what it's worth. The relationship God desires we have with others is like the relationship God wants us to have with him."

"Really? You mean distant and at arm's length?"

"Well, aren't you truly the cynic? Listen, Jason, I just met you; fortunately you're not paying me for time, so here's some free counsel. Your skepticism or cynicism doesn't become you. It sounds like you've justified your life on the basis of what you do, and you've come up short. So now it's ,'Wah, wah, wah!' You know this. You just don't want to admit it."

If this young woman wasn't hitting me where it's true, I could get offended, thought Jason. "You really know how to get in someone's face. But come on, how much do you think really gets done without works? To me, the worst kind of Christianity is where someone is in need and I just tell them I'll pray for them."

Q.

Ever think about the difference between proof and evidence?

"Oh, come on, yourself. You're smarter than that. God doesn't need our works. Our works aren't *proof* we're worthy. Our works are *evidence* the worthy One is at work in us. God so desperately wants our companionship that he was willing to sacrifice his own son. I'm a late arriver to being a follower of Christ, so this is still relatively new to me. You probably had all this down before grade school."

"Yes, but knowing and owning it are two separate issues. Like I said, you really know how to get in someone's face. And if I didn't feel you were right, I should be offended."

"Thanks, Jason. I really did push into your life—and further than I had permission or the right to do. I apologize."

"Apology accepted."

"This is still new to me, so I get emotional discovering these profound truths. When in my walk of faith will I become ho-hum and yet angry like you?"

"Ouch. The correct answer is, 'Hopefully never,' as Alisha made so clear. Unfortunately, my living has normalized the precious gift of life. Shouldn't. But it has."

Chelsea looked at the clock. "Oh, by the way, Lew had something come up. He left just before you arrived. Didn't you get the text? He also asked if I would let you know he'll pick up the conversation when he returns. Hope this wasn't a waste of your time?"

Jason blinked, stunned. "I think I just got a bait-and-switch deal. Did Lew plan this all along?"

Ignoring Jason's question, Chelsea wrapped up the conversation. "In the meantime, he'd like you to be thinking about a couple things. First is the second truth about gravitational attraction and influence. You got the list, but just to refresh, it's, 'Change enlarges the kingdom of God.' Second, he has two scriptures for you. They are 1 Corinthians 15:52 and 2 Corinthians 5:17.

"I've got to run too," Chelsea said, grabbing her hoodie, "but Lew said to call him about when to meet here for your next session."

Jesus answered, "I am the way and the truth and the life. No one comes to the Father except through me.

John 14:6

REFLECTION QUESTIONS

1. *Jason's scripture is Genesis 2:7. It describes the moment when God created Adam. He breathed into him life and he became a living creature. Have you ever distinguished the difference between the life you've been given and the living you're experiencing?*

2. *Have you ever had an experience where you felt you had been stripped of everything you thought others valued in you? If so, how did you respond? Did you find God in the midst of the feelings of emptiness and isolation?*

3. *Like Alisha, have you ever been confronted with an event where you realized the possibility you may die? How did you respond? How has it changed your view of life?*

4. *Alisha told Jason, "My purpose isn't grounded in what I do. That's my living. My purpose is grounded in who I am. That's my life." What does that statement mean to you?*

5. *Chelsea asks Jason, "...how's the doing working for you?" So, how's the doing working for you? Is it in harmony or in collision with your being?*

6. *Chelsea tells Jason, "God doesn't need our works. Our works aren't proof we're worthy. Our works are evidence the worthy One is at work in us." What does that statement mean to you? How do you distinguish the difference between proof and evidence?*

CHAPTER 4

Change and Changes

CHANGE ENLARGES
the kingdom of God

For I, the Lord, do not change.

Malachi 3:6a

*I*t was a sunny day with the temperature hovering near freezing. Lew had a late-morning opening. Traffic and a last-minute "crisis" at work caused Jason to arrive late.

I don't get my staff, he thought. *We have procedures and protocols in place to deal with issues that come up, and yet they still want me to hold their hands. I guess it's nice to be needed, but why can't they just follow the outlined steps? It's not that complicated.*

Finding a parking space in front of the building, Jason hastily exited his Audi TT and walked briskly up the stairs. He hated being late. If he was stuck in traffic with his clock ticking past a meeting time, he could feel anxiety bubbling up. Something about not being in control of his space bothered him.

As Jason reached the top of the landing, he realized he was looking forward to conversation with Lew. He respected Lew's wisdom and his uncanny ability to know what was going to happen before it did. *Yeah, as if he hasn't been through this with others dozens of times.* The whole soul-mass thing was intriguing. *How could I have been as far into ministry as I was without getting this down?* he thought. Glancing at Chelsea's office, he could see she was out, but Lew's door was wide open. "You in there?"

"I am," Lew called out.

"Sorry I'm a little late. I hate it when that happens," Jason said, walking in.

Lew rose from the oak desk chair as Jason entered. "Good to see you, my friend. Sorry I had to ditch you at the last meeting. Did Chelsea get your questions asked?"

"You mean answered?" said Jason, a little confused.

"Chelsea's got a knack of going right to the meat. She's insightful that way. Got time for an early lunch?" Lew said, grabbing his Harris Tweed overcoat and donning his Irish Donegal cap.

Settling into the passenger seat, Lew asked, "You like your TT?"

"I do. It's my one indulgence."

"Fine car. I drove the Audi R8 Prologue Avant concept car at their proving grounds in Chandler, Arizona. Awesome experience in a 150K speed machine. It was equipped with their new autonomous driver system."

"Congratulations, Lew. You just caused me to sin with envy. Thanks!"

Lew laughed. "Let's go to C'est le Bon on Miller Street. There's someone there I want you to meet."

I knew it! thought Jason. *This guy has every step planned.*

Jason was familiar with C'est le Bon, a French boulangerie and café. "Great place for lunch. I like to hang out there. I remember doing a case study on C'est le Bon when I was getting my missional leadership degree. Oh my, that was almost fifteen years ago. As I recall, in a five year period, C'est le Bon went from a single bakery shop in upscale Westport, Connecticut, to a chain of over 200 company-owned cafés and 300 franchise outlets."

Lew nodded; he was familiar with the story.

"I believe," said Jason, "it was started by a husband and wife team, Bill and Marge Courtland."

"Good memory."

"I recall reading in the Wall Street Journal, the company went through some turbulent times, which was a part of the point of our case study."

"Let me change the subject, Jason. What's your soul saying about what you're going through?"

"Ha!" Jason huffed. "I've never been able to get to a one-on-one with my soul. The most I've gotten from my soul are cryptic, unsigned messages."

"Do you believe your soul has a voice?"

Jason shrugged his shoulders as he checked his side mirrors, focusing more on the traffic as the questions got more personal. "I don't really know. All I know is, the soul is a spiritual part of me, and it's eternal. That's about it. You'd think I'd have more to show for my time at seminary, but I don't think we ever spent more than one class session on the soul."

"Jason, if I put myself out there as a soul-mentor, how do you think I'm going to accomplish that? Any ideas?"

"Probably by asking difficult questions."

"Well, think about it. We'll have more conversations over time about the condition of your soul and your human spirit."

"Fine." *Can't wait. That will be a thrilling experience!*

"Right now, let's talk about the next gravitational truth. Have you got it down?"

"Yes. Change enlarges the kingdom of God, and excuse me while I make a lane change."

When they were safely in the new lane, Lew asked, "And? Are you experiencing change? Do you see the kingdom of God enlarging? How is your work life at New Horizons?"

"Your Honor, the prosecutor is badgering the witness." He sighed. "Seriously, Lew, my work life is uncomfortable."

"How so?"

"The staff knows of my conversation with the board. Not sure how, but information like that seems to leak. It usually does. No doubt, one of the board members said something about the Saturday meeting."

"You'd better slow down, Jason."

"Huh?" *Is he trying to tell me not to leap to conclusions?*

"Traffic light's changing; I don't think you'll make it. Tell me about what is happening."

"I'm not sure. I think my staff is afraid my job is on the line, and that's creating insecurity for them. I think they are hoping my next big project will solve the debt and operational issues. I've done it before. Everyone in my life—my family, my staff and the board—has high expectations for the changes *I* need to make."

"So are you just making changes, or is real change taking place?"

"Not sure what the difference is. Give me an example."

"How about you tell me what you've been doing."

"Well, I've had a lot more meetings."

"And?"

"And I let people have their say."

"And?"

"And we waste a lot of precious time getting to an answer. Doesn't anyone else understand we've got our back to the wall?"

"What do you think real change would look like?"

"People would come to meetings prepared. I wouldn't even mind them colluding before the meeting if it meant we could get to solution faster."

"We'll come back to this later. I want you to see that more meetings are *changes*. How people make decisions involves a *change* in the culture and process of how you direct and lead. Think about that."

Dodging in and out of traffic feels like my job. Merge, collision, pile up. Yeah, something's on the way; just hope one of Lew's skillsets is in collision investigation, thought Jason.

"While you're weaving in and out of traffic, permit me to weave in and out of topics of our conversation. They will all merge, I assure you. Tell me about your time with Alisha. I know her story, so tell me your response."

"Hearing Alisha's story got me thinking about some big issues."

"Such as?"

"Such as the same questions I asked in my freshman year of college. Why am I here on earth? Who am I? What's my purpose? You'd think I would have answered those questions long ago."

"Hum?" said Lew as he pushed his glasses back up on his

nose. "Most people don't go that deep. Finding anything coming up in your drill bit yet?"

"I'm realizing more and more that God placed me on earth for a purpose. Yeah, I know, I've heard that from the time I was in youth group. Finally, though, what's clearer is, my purpose is not a specific task or accomplishment. Haven't been able to shake that feeling I had when I left Continental Beverage to do something meaningful. Yet I can't shake the fear I'm going to end up like my mom and our family when Dad died: struggling to make ends meet."

"And?"

"And I feel like I am tied to two trucks moving in opposite directions.

"Where do you feel you're being pulled?"

"One truck is pulling me to serve people. The other is pulling me towards financial security and a feeling that I've got my life under control. The good news is, I'm beginning to put my issues with the board and New Horizons in a broader perspective. The bad news is, what I thought were changes to fix this mess I'm seeing are more like patches than fixes."

Lew smiled. "Perhaps you are beginning to see your life as a *change* agent instead of just a *changes* agent. I have clients who kick and flail a lot longer while their self-centeredness continues to fight for preeminence."

"Maybe, but I feel like the battle inside me isn't over and is far from being won. For my entire life, I've been validated for what I do. I've always been confident in every situation. I believe in what I can do. However, if my purpose isn't about what I do..."

Lew pursed his lips. "Correct me, but I think Alisha faced those same questions. I wonder, Jason, if the question you're facing isn't so much about belief in yourself and your faith in God as it is about trust."

"Interesting you raise that thought, Lew," said Jason as he changed lanes. "I do have a trust issue. I gained it the hard way. You know my story. Dad died when I was 13. My wife cheated on me when I was 30. My church fired me a year later when our divorce was final. I understand grace. I really do. But my life experiences tell me that relying on my works is more trustworthy than leaving myself wide open for sucker punches from who-knows-where."

"And?"

"To tell the truth, I feel stuck between what appears to be truth and what I know is reality. I'm struggling with the works versus grace thing. I'm just not sure how grace fits into my current living."

"So, Jason, let me see if I understand. You're saying you can only trust what you create through your works, yet what seems to be falling apart is what you created. Do you see any contradiction in your logic?"

"Doesn't sound good coming back that way, but you might be right."

"So how's that working for you now?"

"It isn't, but what's my alternative? I'm not sure how many more shots I can take from people I thought were trustworthy. Either I take control over the events in my life, or I become a punching bag. Seems like making the necessary changes in the way I deal with New Horizons and taking more control over the direction of my life makes more sense."

"More sense than what?"

"More sense than putting my trust in people I don't completely trust."

Q.

How hard is it to be at the mercy of others?

"Perhaps you're confusing trust with control. What I'm hearing you say is, you can't trust people you can't control."

Jason pulled into the C'est le Bon parking lot.

"We can pick this up later, Jason. After our conversation with Bill, some of the pieces may fit together better. Bill's a good friend from way back. He's in town on business, and I thought he'd be a great guy to talk with."

Walking into C'est le Bon was a treat to the nose and eyes. It smelled like Grandmother's house the day before Thanksgiving, with bread baking, cookies and pastries fresh out of the oven and a soup pot on for early arrivers. The décor was authentically French country, and it felt both homey and classy at the same time.

"Hello, Bill," Lew called to a tall, lanky man in his mid-fifties sitting in a booth near the back of the café. He looked dapper. Wool slacks, penny loafers, blue striped Polo dress shirt and graying sideburns. He looked like a typical CEO who'd just stepped out of a board meeting to greet an old friend. "Great to see you," he said as he warmly hugged Lew.

"Thanks for making time to see us. I am glad we could connect. I want you to meet my friend, Jason Cahill. Jason, this is Bill Courtland."

"Jason, it is a pleasure to meet you, and I'm delighted you have connected with Lew. Your journey with him will be truly life-changing."

"I'm a little speechless, Mr. Courtland," said Jason as he shook Bill's hand. "I've been following you since I did a case study about C'est le Bon in a leadership class at seminary. I followed the business as it grew in your first decade and how you fought to take the chain private after it nearly tanked. I had no idea we were coming to meet the founding partner."

"Bill, would you tell Jason a little of your story? We have just started talking about change and changes, and you being in town is a little more than fortuitous."

Bill motioned for them to join him at his booth. "I'll try. This will be a short fly-over, pointing out the highlights and lowlights of our journey with C'est le Bon. Please feel free to interrupt.

"Marge and I were fresh out of college and knew we wanted to do something on our own. We both came from a long line of great home cooks, so why not start a small café and bakery, we thought. With quality food and a simple menu, we soon became a place where people liked to hang out. As we hired more staff, we wanted them to catch the reason for our success. We called it the TCE—Total Customer Experience. We made sure every employee believed and lived out our basic business principle. So, from the beginning, we determined to sell an experience, and it just so happened we used food as the vehicle. An authentic French café look and feel completed the atmosphere. We actually recorded French radio stations to get the background conversation that goes with the music."

It was clear to Jason: Bill loved telling the story of their beginning. "If a total customer experience was our brand identity, we soon discovered two guiding principles for our success. First is generosity and quality in *everything*—ingredients, leadership, employees, facilities. You can't be generous with something less than your best. The second is this: whether as individuals or as businesses, we leave a footprint in our execution. It's our stewardship responsibility. For us, it had everything to do with developing and investing in our staff. It had to do with our generosity and what we believe to be our stewardship role in helping build healthy and sustainable communities."

Jason finally worked up enough courage to ask, "How did you scale your concept?"

"As you know, Jason, our growth was phenomenal. We joined with a venture capitalist who shared similar values. We began opening cafés as fast as we could develop properties and train and indoctrinate employees. Four short years later, we decided to take our company public to raise more capital for a nationwide launch of our brand. Half our locations were franchised for quick cash infusion and the other half, corporate-owned to enhance long-term value growth."

Bill stopped and stood. "Got to talking and forgot about our eating. Let me get you lunch. We have some new menu items, and I'd like your feedback on a particular sandwich."

Jason was a little dumbstruck to think the owner of a huge café chain was serving. *Isn't that what wait staff are for?* he thought.

Bill returned to the booth with coffee. "Lunch will be right up. Now, where was I?"

"Going public," said Lew, taking a mug of coffee from Bill.

"Yes. Thank you. In going public, we brought in a broader base of experience for our board of directors and some consultants to improve our efficiencies. We developed systems and procedures, created efficiencies in our supply chain and established necessary HR policies and procedures. Running a business out of my hip pocket had to change."

"I think I hear a *but* coming," said Jason, feeling more relaxed in the presence of a genuine and truly humble man.

"You are right. The problem was, somewhere in the process of our growth, C'est le Bon misplaced its soul. Now I know corporations don't really have souls. But vision and values come from our souls, as leaders. What happened was, Marge and I dropped the ball and lost our focus on the core values of our enterprise. Here's the lesson we learned from our experience; it's the same one you two, no doubt, have just begun talking about: we failed to distinguish changes from change. Actually, we flipped our understanding—focusing on changes instead of change—and in doing so, we almost lost the company."

Lew looked at Jason and knowingly nodded.

"How so?" asked Jason.

"As we transitioned from a family-run business to a corporate model, we let our changes drive our change. By concentrating only on the transactional side of business management, we lost the transformational focus on enterprise leadership." Bill slowly shook his head.

"As you would expect, we began to slide. We were still opening stores on schedule, but the customer-driven volume was decreasing. We had all kinds of excuses, including the economy, shifting demographics, etc. We were now getting pressure from board directors to keep our stock price steady. The name of the game became a spin game to our investors, stake- and stockholders. There was a barrage of changes in menu and décor, trying to find the lost combination. We really thought making these changes would help us bang a uey and go the right direction again."

"A bang a what?" asked Jason, frowning his brow.

"Obviously you're not from New England. A U-turn," Bill laughed.

"I never realized things got that serious."

"Now listen carefully, Jason. This is the core of what I want you to hear: in the midst of making necessary changes in how we

Q.

How much in your life is about change or merely changes?

did business, we failed to protect the company from unwanted change due to vision and values drift. I hope you understand what a serious problem it signifies that we even cut employee hours to avoid benefit costs. We stemmed the cash hemorrhage, but the patient was going soul-dead. Employee morale and commitment were tanking. There was talk of unionization of our supply chain employees. I have nothing against unions, but when there is union talk, it means the company has lost trust with its employees. We were in free-fall, almost entirely because we missed the distinction between change and changes. Interesting. Never realized until our crisis how much making a word plural diminishes its value. When we went from change to changes, everything changed."

"Bill, can I interrupt for a minute," Jason interjected with a puzzled look. "In fifteen years you amassed a fortune. Why not start another venture with your accumulated cash? Why not invest your time in charity or missions work? Why not do something like that?"

Bill leaned back and steepled his fingers, thinking for a moment. "This may sound trite, but it was an integrity issue. It truly was not about money or our loss of control and influence in the company's direction. It was about our word to long-term employees who hired on and stayed on because they believed in our vision and us. We knew their life stories and prayed with them and for them. They trusted us. We owed them a return for their trust.

"This was the time to show that values do trump the bottom line and values do strengthen a robust bottom line at the same time. We needed a complete realignment. It began with our employees. No, actually, the change started with us. We re-centered our vision and values for C'est le Bon."

"How did you get back on track?" asked Jason.

Bill hefted his mug of coffee. "This was the pivot point. I was visiting one of our franchise outlets. After meeting with several managers, I got myself a cup of coffee, sat down and looked at the Total Customer Experience, as if I were a new customer. The atmosphere was no different from a dozen other cafés in the area. The coffee wasn't exceptional, and the pastry was bland.

Remember our first principle, quality in everything? This was when I realized just how far we had gone wrong. I knew we no longer consistently donated our days-end bakery inventory. We'd cut hours to scrimp on benefits. Our starting pay had barely changed in years, and merit increases for longevity weren't keeping up either. We had become a money machine using humans as one of our ingredients, like flour, sugar and coffee. And, frankly, the restaurant looked like the way we treated our employees—shabby. I looked around to see the evidence of our collective soul, and it wasn't there."

"What happened next?" asked Jason.

"We went through a culture audit. This reawakened our eyes to a number of things. First, our company had to again be an extension of Marge and me. C'est le Bon had to be an extension of our collective souls. Second, we had to return to the fundamental premise: our company exists to bless others. In our race to hugeness, we lost the values of generosity and stewardship, quality and footprint execution."

"So you understood what was right and wrong. How did you recover?"

"We were able to leverage a buy-back of our shares. We took the company private, dismissed all but two board directors, and essentially started over. Except we now have over 700 cafés and 27,000 employees between our warehouses, franchisees and company cafés. We have come a long way from one bakery and 15 employees."

A waitperson bringing lunch interrupted their conversation. "Lew, Jason, this is Sadat, one of our influencers-in-training. Eventually he'll be a manager, but right now he has one of the more critical roles in our business—making sure you are well served." Sadat had a self-conscious smile on his face. It wasn't every day you were introduced to your customers by the founder of the company.

"Bill, this soup and sandwich combo is right on. Great combination. I like it." Jason still felt hesitant to call him by his first name, but he felt so comfortable sitting and talking with him. "Here's one customer who thinks you nailed it."

"Thanks, Jason, your input is important."

"Hey, Jason," prodded Lew. "You'd better pump Bill for all he's worth. He doesn't have all day!"

"Pardon me, Bill. I'm a little in a state of groupie awe. What did you and Marge learn from this experience?"

Bill laughed as he said, "It better have been something, and it better have been good! And it was. Someone once told me one of the great tragedies of life is to have an experience and miss the meaning of it. Permit me to become a teacher for a moment.

"Like I said already, what Marge and I realized was in the growth of our company, we neglected our souls, and because we did, our company began to lose its soul connection. That's why my business card now says Bill Courtland, CSO, Chief Soul Officer. That's my exclusive job now. It's a leader's responsibility to put soul and keep soul in an organization. As leaders, we reproduce what and who we are. Who we are reflects what we think, say and do."

Bill sat back in his chair, and his eyes went to a reflective gaze for a moment. "Jason, it doesn't take an insightful genius to see the lack of integrity in others. That's easy. What's hard is seeing your own integrity black holes. They show up in how you deal with others. These integrity black holes are turning points. These are deep change opportunities, and you don't want to miss them. It is very costly when you do."

"I know, Bill. That's why I have the great privilege of having lunch with you."

"What Marge and I hopefully will never forget is: the healthiest organizations are ones where leaders have a clear vision and intention for their life goals. And, as a result, they live them out with integrity through where they work, worship and experience community. We understood the vision and mission for us is bigger than C'est le Bon, and yet C'est le Bon's vision and mission is bigger than Marge and me. Does that make sense?"

Man, thought Jason. *This is profound. I hope I can remember it all.*

"Let me sum up my assessment of the need for deep change as Marge and I found in our life experiences. I intentionally said *deep change* instead of simply change for an important reason. For us the *deep* part means that kind of change coming from our souls. For example, I'm going into a meeting in a few minutes with our company's regional managers. I will address some *changes* issues affecting vendors, pricing and employee benefits. And I will speak of *deep change* issues coming from our souls. The deep change issues assure we have an enterprise on mission and fulfilling our purpose for existence. Through the years, I've come to realize one of my key responsibilities is assuring we don't vision drift. Even more importantly, we don't culture drift. See the difference?"

All Jason could do was nod.

"I need to be wrapping up, but let me leave you with three cautions when you experience the need for change. Our first reaction is to resist. We find comfort in predictability, and change by its very nature means more disruption. Yet the only change that moves organizations out of status quo is disruptive change. Anticipate resistance. Your soul desires wholeness that comes through deep change, yet your human spirit demands control. As a result, you will resist change as much as you long for it. Confusing, huh?

"Second, change involves unknown risks, so we tend to avoid the moment and the need in order not to face the reality of risk. On the surface we feel our soul is deeply wounded and we want the pain to go away, but strangely, we take the current state of pain over the risk of the unknown—even though it means the way out of our current pain. Of course, the easiest way to resist is simply to deny there is a problem.

"Finally, the reason we find change so difficult is because in resisting change we reward something in our current state for not changing, blinding us to the need for change in the first place. For example, someone may need to lose weight, but they love to eat whatever and whenever they want. Unfortunately, what usually results is a triple threat—resistance, denial and giving in to the immediate reward.

"As leaders gently holding the trust of others, we've got to be attentive to key trends triggering alerts on our strategic dashboard. If we're not careful, the possibility of change creates its own blinders, and we slip into the narcotic nod of status quo.

"To get to a process of commitment for deep change requires you, as Lew would say, to drill to the root. However, don't even think of going to deep change unless you are passionate about the desire and need to change—that your current reality is simply unacceptable. Deep change will disrupt the convenient mindsets you've formed about what's true, what's not true, who your enemies and friends are and what is crucially important to living your life. Deep change is not for the faint-hearted."

Bill glanced at his watch. "One last thing. You need to go into this deep change process knowing your soul-mass is more wounded, tender and in need of restoration than you thought. This is a spiritual process, not a procedural one. Only God can restore your soul, Jason. You assist by taming your will and disciplining your human spirit. You also assist by consuming the wholesome bread of God's word; and that nourishes the soul. But remember, you're not the physician. You are just an orderly who has the privilege of being in the operating room with the Great Physician."

Bill got up from his chair while extending his hand. "Jason, what a pleasure to meet you. I hate to run, but I have a group of regional managers who are waiting for me." Bill put his hands on Lew's shoulders. "Lew, my dear friend, what a pleasure seeing you again. Marge and I can never repay you for your help through some very difficult times."

Lew smiled, thoroughly enjoying the company of Bill and the opportunity for Jason. "Give Marge a hug for me. Take care."

Therefore, if anyone is in Christ, the new creation has come: The old has gone, the new is here!

2 Corinthians 5:17

REFLECTION QUESTIONS

1. *Jason was awed when he met Bill Courtland. What do you think is the "experience" people describe when they meet you? What do you think creates their response?*

2. *Bill said C'est le Bon has a corporate soul. Describe the "soul" of your church. Describe the collective soul of your family. Describe the collective soul of your immediate workplace. What evidences point to your conclusions?*

3. *Jason said, "I believe God's grace through Jesus is sufficient for my eternal life. I'm just not sure where grace fits into my living." Have you had similar questions? How are you resolving those questions?*

4. *Bill said he founded C'est le Bon on a foundation of (1) generosity and stewardship, (2) quality in everything, and (3) excellent customer experience. What are the pillars of your workplace? Your family? Your place of worship?*

5. *Describe how you see the terms quality and excellence being similar and different.*

6. *What kind of a "footprint" are you leaving?*

7. *Describe a time in your family, work or church, when you felt it lost its soul. Did you use that moment as deep change opportunity? What did you do or not do as a result?*

8. *In speaking about churches and places of employment, Bill Courtland said, "The vision and mission of its leaders is bigger than the organization and yet the organization's vision and mission is bigger than its leaders." What does this mean to you and the organization where you contribute influence?*

CHAPTER 5

Integration and Disintegration

CHANGE ENLARGES
the kingdom of God

"For I know the plans I have for you,"
declares the LORD, "plans to prosper
you and not to harm you, plans to give
you hope and a future."

Jeremiah 29:11

D riving back from C'est le Bon and their meeting with Bill
Courtland, Jason was unusually quiet.

"Deep in thought?" Lew asked.

"No kidding. That was a lot to take in."

"So what are you thinking?"

"Well, first of all, I realize you engineered our meeting for the specific purpose of emphasizing change and changes. I'm grateful. Right now, however, I'm having difficulty sorting out for my living what needs change and what changes I need to make. This is a new concept and distinction for me."

Jason pulled to a stop at a red light. "Look, you may know where I'm going with this since you've apparently worked over other clients the same way. I'm realizing I'm not the person I want to be at work or at home. I'm demanding because I believe I will save people time by telling them what they eventually are going to figure out for themselves. I pride myself on having the best ideas in the pack, but that's come with a price. I feel pressure to perform to expectations even though I grind on people when I achieve my expectations."

"Well, that's encouraging, Jason. At least you're in touch with reality," smiled Lew.

"Maybe, and reality is a little raw right now. There are times when I'm on the edge of panic attacks, wondering if there is one more trick in my bag or if this is it. I'm smart enough to know this performance track eventually reaches a cliff or a box canyon. Either way, I feel the sense of impending doom, but I can't or don't want to get off the track. And even with all my life experiences, I'm still confused where my soul fits into this."

"I think I'm hearing you say you want and don't want to get off the performance track. I can see how it is confusing. Let me ask, what are some possible reasons for you not wanting to change?"

Jason took a deep breath, hesitating. *Oh well*, he thought, *I'm in this, what do I have to lose?* "Just as Bill said, I think I'm resisting change because I don't trust the unknown. I know I'm not happy where I am, but it's certainly safer than the unknown. Frankly, the other reason I'm resisting is I believe what I'm doing now is beginning to work—current financial realities at New Horizons notwithstanding. I think I'm getting back on track."

"Really ?" asked Lew. "I think we began this topic on the way to C'est le Bon, when you acknowledged things weren't going so well. You know it's a deadly temptation to confuse the little control dot you're standing on with the greater security developed through trust. I'm going to venture a wild guess. May I suggest your root issue is trust, not control? And because you find it hard to trust, you compensate with control."

"I think I've heard you say that before, and I thought you said you weren't going to be my therapist."

"I know very few people who don't struggle with what you're going through. And those few are very heavily medicated!"

"Obviously, you don't think I'm heavily medicated—or do you?" Jason joked, raising his eyebrows signaling he was wanting a response.

Lew ignored the cue. "Ever heard the Rudyard Kipling story about how monkeys are caught in India?"

"No, but I have a suspicion I'm going to find out."

Q.

Like Jason, are the challenges you face more rooted to trust?

"They put a nut in a jar with a narrow opening—just large enough for a monkey's fingers and palm to go through. Smelling the nut, the monkey puts its hand into the jar, grasps the nut and attempts to remove it. It is impossible to do while its hand is in a fist, and the monkey will not release the nut. Catching a monkey is tough. Putting a five-pound jar on the end of its fist makes the odds even."

"You could say that."

"Sounds like you may be satisfied with the fist, my friend, but tired of dragging the jar. What are you trying to hang on to?"

"Control, I guess ... To be honest, there have been too many people in my life whom I've let hold my jar. I'm tired of getting my arm ripped off, if you want to use your Kipling story. Look, Lew, I've spent time in thought and prayer, and right now my head is speaking louder than any insight from God. But here it is. I don't think my soul is ready to rely on the quality of its condition, whatever that is, to be the influencing force in my life."

Lew nodded. "Soul-searching is always a good expedition."

"Since we've connected, I've thought about my soul more than I ever have before, but I still don't know much. This is what I know at this moment. I am more secure in taking charge over my doing than I am in my being, even though you think I've made a fist of it. Does that make sense?"

"You might want to go."

"What?"

"You might want to hit the gas. The light changed."

"Oh. Yeah." Jason laughed hitting the accelerator.

"As far as your question, yes, it makes sense. You are getting to the heart of your heart and soul. Look, Jason, every day we make choices about who we listen to. You know this. Too often we drop our filtering guard allowing Satan to do his number on us. He whispers lies about who we aren't and then backs up the lies with factual indictments of our pathetic behavior. And we take what he says lock, stock and barrel, and we turn it into a fist. By the way, where do you think your need for control resides? Here's a clue. It isn't the soul. You might look in your human spirit. Don't you think it is time to begin to let go, experience trust and release the nut?"

"Are you talking about me or your monkey story?" laughed Jason.

"Yes," said Lew as he looked out the window and smiled.

As Jason pulled into the parking lot, Lew said, "Jason, do you have time to extend our conversation? I'd like to finish discussing more than this car ride will allow."

"Sure, it would be good to sift and grind this conversation while it's still warm. Besides, I feel a serious case of deep change coming on."

"Oh, starting to get deep on me, huh? There's hope for you yet!" laughed Lew.

Settling into Lew's office was beginning to feel to Jason like putting on an old shoe—comfortable and familiar. *I wonder if he planned it to feel like this?* Jason thought.

Lew found his pipe in his cardigan, put in a load of sweet and spicy smelling tobacco, struck a match and lit the tobacco strands.

"Let's go back to the topic of our discussion for today: change, control and trust. Let's dig into change first. Do you feel something in your living has to change—your relationship with God, your marriage, your job—or are you just about where you'd like to be?"

"I said in the car that things are now moving in the right direction. Not really. I know the direction of my life has to be different. I thought I could make a few changes and normal would appear. Bill's conversation on change and changes cleared that up. What I *do* is a reflection of who I *am* at this moment. I get that. For me to go through deep change will require me to know my deep values so that what I do is an authentic response to who I am. The gravitational truth—Change enlarges the kingdom of God—is beginning to make sense. The problem is, knowing and living it are two different worlds."

"Wow, did you feel the earth shake? Seriously, how is this making sense?"

"It's really basic. It's clear the quality of my relationship with God affects the health of my soul, which in turn determines the quality of my relationships with others. It's so basic and obvious, but I've ignored that truth for a long time."

Lew smiled. "A quality relationship with God. That is precisely what I meant by increasing the density of your core—"

"Which increases the gravitational attraction and influence I have on people around me," Jason interrupted. "Yeah, I get it! I'm beginning to feel like some slightly unhinged genius, like John Nash in *A Beautiful Mind*, who sees connections to everything."

"Good. Sounds like some deep processing going on. Have you determined what is going to change? What's going to remain the same? And, most importantly, do you know what is deep change and what efforts are merely changes?"

"No, not really. I'm starting to admit what I've been doing isn't working. But this is a little overwhelming right now. Obviously, the deep change starts with my soul-mass. But there is still a part of me that just wants to fix the broken pieces in front of me and move on."

"Good processing, Jason. No point in making either change or changes if you don't know what you want the outcome to be. Like Jesus said, if someone starts to build a tower but doesn't count the cost and fails to finish, he is a fool as well as looking like a fool. Let me ask, what might be the costs for your change?"

"I really don't know, but I fear what the cost *will* be if I don't change. I am seeing the unnecessary stress I've put on Sylvia and our marriage by trying so hard to make it not like my marriage to Emily. It feels like one of those bad dreams I had as a kid. The faster I tried running from the monster, the closer it came."

"It's always good to know what you're running from, my friend. However, it is even better to know what you're running to. Keep your eyes on that." Lew paused for a deep draw on the pipe.

"Obviously, Jason, the board meeting was a significant event in your process of continuous change. You didn't wake up a week before the meeting and decide to screw up New Horizons and sabotage the working relationships with your team, did you? In fact, I suggest this has been a process occurring over the time you've been there because it simply reflects the man within."

Jason frowned. "So you're saying I was unqualified for the position, and this is the inevitable result of incompetence?"

"That's not at all what I meant. I'm sorry if it came across that way. What I'm suggesting is, the board meeting was the culmination of a series of preventable events, great ideas and performance notwithstanding. You are qualified for your position. Yet, from what I'm observing, I don't think you took advantage of your qualifications and potential. I think you may have run too much on talent and not enough on soul-mass."

Jason took a deep breath, studying the Persian rug on the hardwood floor. "Okay, you may be right. No, I'm sure you're right. But how do I change?"

Lew walked over to the Keurig and prepared a mug of coffee. "Want some?"

"Sure," responded Jason.

Waiting for the coffee to fill the mug, Lew took some short puffs on his pipe. Jason could hear the tobacco strands popping as fire in the bowl reddened. "Let's start with your soul. Every time you believe a lie about yourself, your soul gets punched by that fist, and it withdraws. Every time you believe an indictment about yourself that would be true without the covering of grace, your soul shrinks. After a time, you no longer believe in the goodness of your soul. Yet you believe in the evil that's infiltrated into your selfish human spirit. How you respond to change is a reflection of the health of your soul-mass. Now, hold on to that idea, and let's get back to change.

"Here you are," said Lew. With his hot mug in hand, Jason settled back into his chair, preparing to hear wise teaching.

"Change is the common experience of all living beings on this earth. Change is evidence we are alive and growing. Now here's what I've come to understand about change. First, change is disruptive, it's essential and it's resisted.

Q.

Do you agree?

"I get the disruptive part. But essential? I'm not sure."

"Help me out here, Jason. What do we call the state before there is a change?"

"Eden? Heaven?" guessed Jason.

"Good answers, and true in a cosmic sense. But in our living we erroneously call it *normal*. What we really mean is *constancy*."

Lew got up from his chair, went to his whiteboard and wrote,

CHANGE → DISRUPTIVE → NORMAL → CONSTANCY

"So," Jason thought aloud, "I guess you could say normal is the lukewarm place we all experience in those brief moments between crisis and peace."

"Good observation, and I think it's a dangerous illusion."

"Is this the place I should ask, 'Why?'" interjected Jason.

"Yes, I had the same question too," smiled Lew. "Here's how I understand it. Normal is a dangerous illusion because, first of all, normal is a label only for those who occupy or long for it. That makes it highly subjective. Secondly, if it exists at all, it stays about as long as a pendulum does in the place where the downswing ends and the upswing begins. When we search and strive for normal, we are looking for something that doesn't exist."

"So you mean *normal* is a false impression?"

"Exactly. We are spiritually wired for an expectation of *constancy*, not *normalcy*."

"Explain, please."

"Constancy is the opposite of change. That's a state where nothing ever changes. Normal is repeatable chaos. Therein rests the dynamic tension of life. We—our souls—long for constancy, but we live with the disruption of change. Yet we are persistently trying to create a false sense of normalcy because it's the closest we can get.

"Constancy is a desire of all heaven-bound souls. However, I believe we'll only experience constancy in eternity. What makes

Q.

Have you ever looked at change from this perspective before?

our current life challenging is we are in a process of continuous and discontinuous change."

"So let me get this straight, Lew. You're saying change is essential to jar us from our complacent state of searching for normalcy—our chaotic state of disobedience—in order to recognize our longing for constancy."

"If I said that, write it down. That's good and you've got it." Below Change Lew wrote **CONTINUOUS** and **DISCONTINUOUS** on the whiteboard.

"Wasn't always that way. Adam and Eve were the first to experience this paradox of change. In Eden, they had life. They didn't have a concern about living. Eden was perfect. Nothing needed to change. After the fall—the first discontinuous change, by the way—Adam and Eve still had life. But they also had the experience of living, the experience of continuous change—living, and the event of discontinuous change—death."

"Fascinating point, Lew. Never saw that in the Genesis story before, but you're right. Keep talking. Maybe if I become all ears, my fist will relax."

Lew looked straight at Jason and held a pose for a moment as if he were looking right through Jason.

"Question, my friend. How many meetings with your staff did you catch them off guard, just like the board caught you? How many times did you introduce an idea that you had a week to plan for and they got fifteen minutes to buy into? And you did it so you could overwhelm them with your data, thus paving the way to get your way. No one likes being blindsided. Just because you are the leader does not give you the right to introduce disruptive change because someone pushed your button or you got a hot-flash of an idea and didn't want to entertain opposition."

"I see your point. You been reading my emails?"

"No, but I know how control freaks behave. You see how control is beginning to elbow its way into this conversation? Just like you, I was a control freak. I too thought very little about how disruptive change affected others around me. However, blindsides happen to everyone. Too often, they come from the person you expected to protect you."

"Tell me about it," Jason said with a frown.

"I used the phrase 'process of continuous and discontinuous change.' Do you understand what I mean?"

"Somewhat, but layer on your understanding for me."

"I'll give a drilling example from my former life. Over about a half billion years, vegetation, algae and primitive shellfish decayed and became oil. That is a process of continuous change—living organisms becoming a carbon-based organic combustible mixture. Then, Banner Oil came along, rammed a tube into the oil deposits and pulled the gooey stuff out. That's discontinuous change. Notice also that Banner put that crude oil in a pipe, sent it to a refinery and then distributed it to users. That's an example of control. See the differences?"

"I think so. Continuous change has a pattern and a rhythm. Take financing New Horizons, for example. Continuous change means donors come and go. Employees need cost of living and merit raises. Infrastructure and equipment ages and needs replacing. Grants for funding come and go. Service needs arise and have high visibility for a time, then become routine or phased out. Finally, I put procedures and policies in place, attempting to make change controllable. Is that what you're talking about?"

"You've got the picture. Continuous change can be anticipated. I've found the best response to it is to be alert, prepared and most particularly, flexible. Best approach I've found for continuous change is to manage it—actually to control it as best we can. Let me get some of this on the whiteboard and while I'm doing that, I want to give a tip of my hat to Virginia Satir who pioneered a lot of this thinking."

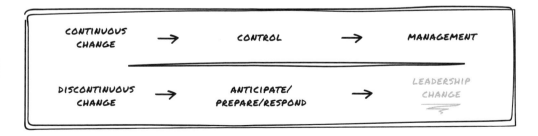

CONTINUOUS CHANGE → CONTROL → MANAGEMENT

DISCONTINUOUS CHANGE → ANTICIPATE/ PREPARE/RESPOND → LEADERSHIP CHANGE

"Now what are examples of discontinuous change?"

Jason was fully engaged, sitting on the edge of his chair. "Well, some events of life we don't see coming, like earthquakes, fires, physical attacks, illness, death, resignations, embezzlement, moral failures and interpersonal meltdowns ... along with Saturday board meetings. Right? But I guess good things could also fit: unexpected acts of kindness, miracles, gifts and opportunities."

"Good answers. Do you think it's possible to prepare for any of those?"

Jason thought for a moment. "Well, it seems like the tools to keep us alert and flexible are planning and administrative guidelines. They help us navigate through continuous change. So, if that's the case, then contingency planning and training are the tools that prepare us for discontinuous change. Am I right?"

"Great. And how do you think is the best way to approach discontinuous change?"

"Obviously, now I can see you lead it. It's during times of unexpected change, both challenging and blessing, we look to leaders, who have to be solid—have a healthy soul-mass. It's just like Bill was saying earlier: recovering from the discontinuous change of financial collapses had to begin with him and Marge. I can see now that getting lulled into managing continuous change almost put them out of business. And I'm beginning to see that I didn't do a good job of leading discontinuous change. I was doing okay at *managing* but completely missing the understanding of *leading*."

Lew nodded. "In every case, when it happens, you have two choices. You can embrace change and help others navigate through the process, or you can embrace individual and organizational chaotic decay. You pick."

"Thanks. Not that I feel any pressure right now."

"You should feel pressure. Influence carries with it great responsibility for how it affects others and how it changes you. Just remember, few do well with disruptive and discontinuous change without a leader helping them tolerate, embrace, navigate and arbitrate through the change. Just like with Bill and Marge, people are depending on you to get through this time of change in your life and to emerge wiser and more mature. If you aren't successful with change in your life, Jason, it will cause an avalanche of change and changes in other people's lives as well."

"I can see that now."

"That's the impact of gravitational influence. Your presence causes change in the people around you. As you'll hear over and over in our time together, the impact of change in the lives of others is directly proportional to the size and density of the core mass of your soul."

Lew went to the whiteboard and wrote **FOREIGN ELEMENT**.

"Now every change we experience needs something to get it started. It's a foreign element—that's the initiator. In the Genesis story, the Fall due to temptation and self-centeredness and initiated by the serpent, was a foreign element for the world's first couple. For us, sinful behaviors are foreign elements too. A foreign element causes the dominos to begin tipping over. Foreign elements are not always bad. They just disrupt the status quo."

"I don't need to belong to Mensa to know my Saturday board meeting was my foreign element."

"Yes, I think that's fairly obvious. Let me give an example again from my past. When I was with Banner Oil and we were doing environmental mapping, preparing for oil exploration in an area, we would often come across natural oyster beds. We would sample harvest and then baseline the oysters' mineral content and organic composition.

"Once in a while, opening the shell, we'd come across a natural pearl. As you know, an oyster requires an irritant to grow a pearl. The oyster resists the foreign element by trying to smooth over the aggravation with iridescent shell. Eventually the foreign element, the irritant, becomes a pearl of great value.

"So it often is with us. Irritants first disrupt the normal flow of life. No one wants an irritant. No one wants to be the irritant. Yet, eventually, we all want the pearl. We all want to be the pearl."

"Are you saying the more I disrupt other people's lives, that's a sign of success? I've sure done that!"

Lew laughed. "Exactly and not exactly. A foreign element can be any disruption to our normal life flow. Usually it comes in the form of discontinuous change. A birth, death, promotion or demotion. Even a new way of thinking or doing. A foreign element is anything altering the false impression that all is 'normal,' predictable and thus controllable. To be a perfect pearl means that in the irritation and disruption you add value."

"Yet part of me even now still doesn't want to change."

"Any ideas why?"

"Yeah. Even before we started meeting together, I was aware of my tendency for being a control freak. Of course, I'm going to try and resist anything I can't control."

Lew wrote **RESISTED** on the white board.

"How does it feel?"

"What, the resistance? Terrible, of course. Why do you think we resist change so much? And please, no open-ended volley back to me."

"In my own experience, it's because I either don't want to admit I was wrong or someone else was right, or it's just plain laziness. I don't want to go through the effort of learning something new. At a deeper level, resistance is that longing for constancy as much as it is the fear of the unknown. Change involves risk, so oftentimes our first response to a foreign element can be resistance."

"And I suppose you're going to tell me my Saturday board meeting was just the thing I needed."

"I think you just told yourself. It was what was needed for you to do something different. Consider where New Horizons would be today if your normal chaos wasn't disrupted by the board meeting. The way I see it, if you don't kill the illusions of normal, you'll never be motivated to find truth."

"Whoa! I've never seen it that way before. I am a walking contradiction. My first response to change is resistance because I want consistency and predictability—okay, control. Yet I desire the truth that only comes from change. Maybe this is why we resist the gospel. Deep down everyone who hears the good news knows his or her life will significantly change. Resistance is often the first reaction."

Lew walked back over to his Keurig coffeemaker to freshen

his mug. "Jason, as you ponder this heavy subject of change and changes, think about this. Making *changes* is a control issue. It's not necessarily wrong. Managing processes and systems comes out of making changes. But when a person isn't healthy in their soul-mass, changes often come out of insecurity and uncertainty. On the other hand, deep change is a trust issue. You want some more?"

"Huh? Do I want more deep change? Uh, yes and no, of course."

"That's funny. No, I meant, do you want to refresh your coffee?"

"Sure. Thanks." As Lew punched buttons on the machine, Jason added, "I really do want deep change. Just not sure what it will cost."

Lew smiled and lifted his coffee mug as if in a toast. "It sounds like the heart is catching up." He brought a mug over to Jason. "You may have found your transforming idea."

"What do you mean?"

To the right of Foreign Element, Lew wrote, **TRANSFORMING IDEA**. "There is always a nexus point in a leadership challenge—you're currently experiencing one—when a transforming idea is required to move forward. This is what makes change a potentially positive experience. Jason, what do you think is your transforming idea?"

"I have a suspicion it will be found as I experience the principle of gravitational attraction and influence. That's why we're meeting isn't it?"

"I certainly hope so. Now let me add one more element to this progression of change. Based on that transforming idea, these are the times when we, as leaders, take the people we influence down a path leading to integration or disintegration."

Lew wrote **INTEGRATION** and **DISINTEGRATION** coming off of **TRANSFORMING IDEA**. As the leader, that transforming idea will either move you forward due to a unified vision or make things start to fall apart due to individual agendas. This is the moment when the need for a leader, not a manager, becomes paramount. Do you know what I mean?"

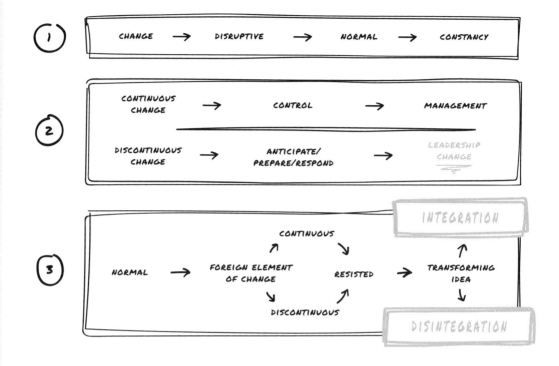

① CHANGE → DISRUPTIVE → NORMAL → CONSTANCY

② CONTINUOUS CHANGE → CONTROL → MANAGEMENT

DISCONTINUOUS CHANGE → ANTICIPATE/PREPARE/RESPOND → LEADERSHIP CHANGE

③ NORMAL → FOREIGN ELEMENT OF CHANGE — CONTINUOUS — RESISTED → TRANSFORMING IDEA — DISCONTINUOUS — INTEGRATION — DISINTEGRATION

"Okay. I'm seeing connections you haven't made yet, Lew. Since we were talking about constancy and the soul's desire for it, I have a thought. Christ is the transforming idea as well as the reality of eternity. Without the grace that he offers to negate our sin, we would be doomed to disintegration. It's only through him and his work on the cross that I have the opportunity for integration."

Lew, finished with his diagram, walked over to his green leather chair. "Powerful connection. You see, the Holy Spirit is not your distant roommate, as you thought. There's work going on in there."

"So we're coming back to the gravitational influence topic, huh?"

"Why do you say that?" Lew asked with a smile.

"I think I can sum up our conversation this way. Perhaps we—

okay, I—understand the paradox of change in the realization that I only want change I can control. What an illusion! The more I try to control change—in other words, to resist inevitable change—the more change occurs. My flesh wants and resists change, yet my soul desires constancy."

"Glad to see the ownership of your change experience showing." A pleased smile lit up Lew's face. "As visionary leaders, we are agents of controlled chaos. Effective leaders find balance in the dynamic tension between order and chaos, much like larger objects exerting gravitational influence over smaller bodies. Leaders need to know when they reach this point of controlled chaos. If integration is the next event, a leader must understand how to use the energy of anticipation and anxiety for forward progress. If disintegration is the anticipated outcome, the leader must have a contingency plan and response management strategies in place to mitigate the loss."

Jason nodded slowly and sipped his coffee. This was a lot to take in.

"I'm sure you have some other things to get done today, so let's bring this conversation home. You've seen how these ideas apply to your living. The way I see it, in life, there will be only two dramatic change events. Did you look up 2 Corinthians 5:17?"

"I did." Jason pulled up the scripture on his smartphone. "Paul tells us in his second letter to the church at Corinth that if anyone is in Christ, that person is a new creation. The old is gone, the new has come ... Interesting. Never saw this before."

"What's that?"

"At conversion, which I guess you'd say is the first dramatic change event in our lives, there is both integration to being a new creation and disintegration of the old man nature. Sure you're not a theologian?"

"I'm sure. Anything else?"

"The second dramatic change will come as Paul tells us in his first letter to the Corinthians: in a flash, when Christ comes again, we'll all be changed."

"Nicely done, Jason. The hard part of living is the deep change and changes that come between those two significant

Q.

*Does that explain
anything about
where you're at?*

events—the beginning of our new life in Christ and the beginning of the eschaton—God's reign after the return of Christ. That middle part's where joyful and ugly living occurs. So in between new birth and the death of death, our life is secure, but that space is critical for our living. In that living we have the opportunity for deep change and changes."

Jason exhaled as though he'd just finished a marathon. "Okay, one more aha and I'm out of here. Here's my takeaway. Deep change, I believe, has to do with discovering, restoring and growing the soul-mass so I no longer want to sin. Changes have to do with removing the obstacles—killing the old man—and healthy soul living so I actually don't sin."

"Well done. I've got a suspicion, Jason, that you believe a lot more about your spiritual identity that you like to let on," Lew kidded.

"Okay, Lew. I've got a much better handle on change and control, but we didn't talk that much about trust. Where does it come in to the conversation?"

"Like I said, you are a great listener. We're not done. Hang on and hang in. We'll get to it." Lew put the marker down and took a seat. "But I think that's about enough for today. I'd like you to write down my scribbling on the whiteboard."

"Hey, old tech guy, I'll just take a picture with my smartphone."

"Whatever works for you. Before we meet again, I want you to see Joe Tyler. He's out at Leaventon now. I think you know him."

"I do. I haven't seen him since he crashed and burned. Is he doing okay now?"

"You'll need to find that out for yourself."

Therefore, if anyone is in Christ, the new creation has come: The old has gone, the new is here!

2 Corinthians 5:17

REFLECTION QUESTIONS

1. *Describe a circumstance when you applied changes. What were those changes? What were the outcomes?*

2. *Describe a circumstance when you applied deep change. What were those actions of deep change? What were the outcomes?*

3. *What do you see as steps you need to take in order to regain the organizational soul of your enterprise or leadership responsibility?*

4. *What do you see are obstacles to your personal deep change opportunities?*

5. *What personal or organizational changes have you made you now see require deep change instead?*

6. *In the story, Jason says, "The **quality of my relationship with God** has a lot to do with the **healthiness of my soul**. And, importantly, the healthiness of my soul determines the **quality of my relationships with others**. And, that **increases the density of my core and the gravitational attraction and influence** to those around me. Jason describe a circle of action and response. "How is each piece of the cycle connected to the one before it? If there is not integrity in each connection, how does dysfunction occur?*

CHAPTER 6

Celebrity, Attraction and Radiating Love

LOVE IS THE FORCE OF
gravitational attraction and radiating influence

In your relationships with one another,
have the same mindset as Christ Jesus:
Who, being in very nature God, did not
consider equality with God something
to be used to his own advantage; rather,
he made himself nothing by taking the
very nature of a servant, being made
in human likeness. And being found
in appearance as a man, he humbled
himself by becoming obedient to death—
even death on a cross!

Philippians 2:5–11

"What's going here?" Joe boomed, aiming at intimidation. Joe Tyler, Director of Family Ministries for the multi-site Oak Creek Church, stormed into Lead Pastor Dr. Leo Wood's office.

At six-foot-four and 230 pounds, Joe had once cut an imposing figure. But in the past year, Joe had lost over fifty pounds, making him look like an underinflated toy. Beyond that, his pasty-pale complexion, baggy eyes and exhausted look screamed, "Unhealthy!"

Joe scanned the room. Facing him were Julie, his wife; Robbie, his 20-year-old son; and Sean Williamson, his lifelong friend and co-founder of his NxtGenAlive ministry. His worst fears seemed about to come true.

"Take a seat, Joe," said Leo. "Let me start at the end so it's no surprise, and then we'll work our way through it." Leo took a deep breath and looked Joe in the eye. "You are no longer a part of Oak Creek staff. You have stolen from us through your expense reports, and you've done the same through NxtGenAlive. We know you are seriously addicted to narcotics and have been buying cocaine on the street. And we love you. We are concerned for your life. We want to help. That's the bottom line."

Sean said , "Leo and I have gotten you a spot in a rehab program—"

"What!" Joe roared, slamming his hand on the table. "You did—"

"Joe!" Julie interrupted. "Please listen." This was a moment she had prayed for, for over a year. Yet it was the most fearful moment in their 21-year marriage. Everything was on the line. "Joe, I hope I don't need to convince you of my love and support for you. But you need to know I'm scared to death. I'm afraid of losing you. You are going to die if things don't change. I know your problems—both those in your head and those in your back. I know the pain you are in, and I know your passionate desire to be a part of changing young people's lives for Christ. But you are so far over the line; the only person who can no longer see how far out of control you are is you."

"Julie, you don't understand."

"I understand enough to know we are losing EVERYTHING we've worked and sacrificed for, but the worst part is what's happening to you. You are dying in flesh and spirit. I'm losing you, and it's tearing me up! It's tearing the whole family up."

"Julie, I—"

Julie held up her hand to cut him off and gathered the emotional strength for one last word. "Sweetheart, this is the hardest thing I'll ever say. Your car is parked outside. I've packed a month's worth of clothes in your suitcases. When you leave this room, you aren't coming home. You can do what those who love you have asked and go get well. Or you can go live wherever, associate with your drug-dealing 'friends' and make your life as miserable as you've made it for everyone else. It's your choice."

Joe crossed his arms and looked around the room. "Is that it? I hurt my back in ministry, I struggle to deal with the ever-present pain, and this is what you do? Thank you so much for your kindness and Christian care. You people are brutal. What's come over you?"

"I'm brutal? I'm brutal?" asked Julie, raising her voice for the first time. "No, Joe, I think it's the other way around. You've cheated and stolen from your ministry, thinking you own it. And I'm brutal? You've lied to pastors and to youth, and you haven't thought how let down they will be when you're exposed. And I'm brutal? You've violated the law to get your drugs. You've stolen time, resources and love from our family. You've caused your children to be embarrassed of you. And you think I'm brutal?"

Joe wanted to counter. He opened his mouth, but nothing came out.

It was a 40-minute drive to Leaventon. In the late 1800s and up to the Great Depression of the 1930's, Leaventon was a prosperous manufacturing town. Many old brick structures testified to the former presence of textile mills, shoe factories, furniture manufacturing and tool and die works.

Unfortunately, when the town lost its manufacturing base, the population halved. Then after some seventy years of deep sleep came the technology era. Slowly Leaventon's life returned as consulting and small manufacturing businesses found it a desirable and affordable place for programmers and high-tech start-up entrepreneurs to live. Driving into town, Jason could see evidence of renewed life all around.

I wonder, he thought, *how much of Joe's church reflects what is happening in town ... or in his life?* Jason was looking forward to reconnecting with Joe Tyler. Once a rising Christian superstar with an impressive ministry to youth and families, Joe had fallen from his former glory. Now he was pastoring here in Leaventon.

As he pulled up to the church, Jason noticed it was a traditional-looking church—brick front, white steeple—but everything on the exterior looked freshly updated. Given Joe's history, there was one thing that seemed inconsistent: the building was much smaller than Jason thought would fit Joe's image. He had almost expected laser lights, blaring music and a crowd just waiting for the doors to open to a 5000-seat auditorium.

As Jason walked into the lobby, he noticed it didn't smell

musty, like most churches used once or twice a week. There was the obligatory espresso stand and a lounge area with small tables for conversation. But before Jason could find the office, he heard a loud voice.

"Jason. Jason Cahill. I forgot you lived so close. I should have looked you up. Nice to see you. What's it been, four, five years?"

Joe Tyler followed his booming voice out of the dark auditorium. He'd put on some pounds since they last met, but he still looked like a celebrity: rugged and handsome, with a great smile. Jason was at a loss for words as Joe's strong handshake pulled him into a back-slapping hug. The gregarious and genuine greeting didn't fit with the Joe he knew. Jason expected ingratiating, but distant.

"Let me crank out an espresso for us. What can I get you?"

"Can you brew up a nonfat café mocha, no whip?" asked Jason.

"Got it," said Joe, displaying the skills of an experienced barista.

"Thanks," said Jason.

Joe handed Jason a frothy mocha with a perfect latte art design on the creamy surface. Gingerly letting himself into a dark brown leather chair in the lounge area of the lobby, Joe asked, "So what have you been up to since I last saw you? Last time we met, you were settling into the driver's seat at New Horizons, correct? Did I get the right temperature for you?"

"Well, Joe, the last five years have been intense. I took the wheel and then drove New Horizons through a merger with Family Matters. Things were going pretty well, but we've recently hit some financial speed bumps. We're still doing some really great projects, and I'm sure we'll get over the bumps. Besides that, a new marriage, twin boys, and trying to long-distance co-parent a drama queen from my first marriage, which crashed and burned, not much. And yes, it's perfect—the mocha, that is."

"That's a lot of doing. Didn't know about the divorce. You doing okay?"

"Yeah, it happened a while before we met. But thanks for asking. You'd be surprised how few want to know how I'm really doing. Most just want to know what I'm going to be doing—for them."

"Espresso with a bite, huh?"

"Well, if Lew has talked to you, you can surmise that I've also got my back up against the wall right now as far as New Horizons is concerned."

Joe shook his head. "He just said he wanted us to reconnect. What's going on?"

"Still in the process of figuring that out. I've pushed the staff and my ambition to the edge, and I think the board is concerned I'll give it a kick and watch it drop. Still trying to weigh my options."

"How's your soul in all this?"

"You want to know about that too, huh?"

"Yeah. Look, Jason, I went through the same process with Lew that you're going through, so I know your location. How's your soul?"

"My best answer at this point is that I'm still trying to find it. Funny. Got a Master's in missional leadership, served on a church staff for several years, and never, until my conversations with Lew, did the issue of the condition of my soul ever come up."

"Join the crowd. You're probably wondering how and why the person you knew five years ago ended up here. You're probably wondering how I could have slipped so far to be in such a seemingly small ministry."

Jason looked down at his coffee, a little embarrassed to meet Joe's eyes. "Yeah, the thought did cross my mind. Heard all the rumors. I'm assuming there is a story in there just waiting to get out."

"You're right, there is, and that's why you're here. You probably know some of the story, but here it is as tight as I can make it. Just keep in mind, this really isn't the story. This is just the prologue to the story.

"My first job as youth pastor, we saw youth attendance grow larger than all the adults in the sanctuary. Next church was twice as big as the one before. After two years there I had the materials and system to go national: NxtGenAlive. We created curriculum, sponsored outreach projects throughout the US, and had youth and college-age kids in overseas ministry during Christmas, spring and summer breaks.

"NxtGenAlive was going so strong I resigned my church position to go full-time. I was in constant demand as a speaker. Then Oak Creek called."

"Hard to turn down one of the largest churches in North America," Jason said.

"Right. When they offered me the Family Ministries Director position, I was ready for a little stability. Besides, in one of my stage stunts at a youth rally two years before, I'd injured my back. I still had intense pain, and all the travel aggravated the injury."

"I remember hearing that. You were still dealing with it when we met. Doing okay now?" asked Jason.

"Part of my story," Joe said with a sad smile. "In the first year at Oak Creek, the children's and youth ministries exploded just like before. We wrote new curriculum and sold it through NxtGenAlive, which I continued to run on the side. During that time, the only thing that grew bigger than the ministry was my ego. I really thought God and I made a great team."

He gave a mocking laugh. "Actually, I thought I'd done fairly well on my own. The only thing that grew bigger than my ministry was my ego. I reached a point where I really believed I was responsible for more people at church than the lead pastor or combined staff. I was living the great life. All this time I was popping legal narcotics and muscle relaxants for the back pain."

"I'm afraid I know where this is going," winced Jason.

"Then my life started unraveling. The narcotics became an addiction. I was seeing three orthopedic physicians, none aware of the others, just to get more narcotics. A crisis point came when my doctors started limiting the prescriptions. But I was hooked. I went way over the line and began to buy the drugs on the street. The drugs took care of the pain and mellowed out my manic ambition. Only problem was, I needed more than caffeine to ramp me back up when I needed to be on. So I found people to get me coke and speed. It was a deadly roller coaster. The increased cost for the drugs led to stealing from the church and NxtGenAlive."

Joe paused a moment and closed his eyes, obviously fighting emotion.

"Didn't anyone in your ministries notice?"

"I'm sure they suspected, but between intimidation and awe, nobody was going to risk taking action on the thought. Looking back now, I see a parallel descent into addiction and my toxic relationships. I was increasingly edgy and argumentative, prone to explode and intentionally humiliate anyone who questioned my decisions. I had a growing enemies list within the church. At the same time I desperately needed groupies to feed my ego and quench my insecurity."

"So when I got to know you back then, you were just putting on a show?"

"You got that right. You see, I knew better than anyone else who I really was, and more importantly, who I wasn't. My ego tried to build me up beyond reality, and my insecurity kept listening to the condemning voice of reality, egged on by Satan. I knew we were making an impact on the spiritual front, yet I knew there was a big part of me who was a fake, an impostor. I walked and talked like a pastor, but no one, if they really knew the train wreck I was, should have ever followed me. I was a mess physically, emotionally and spiritually. My problem went deeper than my addiction. I was unable to distinguish between celebrity, coming from a sick human spirit and a wounded soul, and true influence emanating from healthiness—which I probably never had. There was no density to my core."

Joe hesitated, looking for an opportunity to compose. "Can I warm up your mocha?"

"I'm good. Thanks."

"What I didn't realize was, my talent was far larger than my identity. I coasted on my talent without spending any effort in growing a mature identity. I'd turned into a self-gratification engine with no speed governor. Without maturity to control my need for gratification, the temptations of drugs, sex and power through celebrity were incredibly powerful. My crash was going to be from one of the three. There is something primeval and evil going on in that cycle."

"How the mighty have fallen."

"Quoting David from Second Samuel, eh? Fits. Truth be known, I was closer to Saul than David. As time went on the sense of celebrity gave me a feeling of power, power I knew I lacked on my own. It was just that my wife was seeing the train-wreck long before me and was doing everything possible to make sure my crash wasn't going to be from sexual temptation. She joked that there would be a subsequent homicide investigation if anything like that happened. Well, I was never quite sure she was joking."

Jason frowned. "Yeah. Be glad you didn't go there. My first marriage ended with my wife having an affair. I can tell you, the sense of betrayal was devastating. Still is."

"Whoa! I am so sorry. I can only imagine how shattering that would be. Breaking trust is the deepest wound to the soul. You doing okay?"

"Thanks for being concerned. There's been enough time and distance to make it manageable. But, as Lew keeps pointing out, I still have trouble trusting people. However, I think I'm here to hear your story."

"Glad to know you're doing okay, but seeing the other side of broken trust really hurts; I left a lot of wreckage behind. You might wonder, why did both ministries continue to grow? I saw growth as the evidence we were right on—being blessed by God. Unfortunately, we grew only because I was telling people what their human spirits wanted to hear, rather than the truth their souls needed. Simple as that."

"I hear you. So how did it all come crashing down?"

Joe slowly got up from his padded chair. "I got to stretch, or I get stiff. You know, it should have been a police officer taking me to jail for buying controlled substances on the street and conning doctors out of prescriptions. Good grief, those were felonies! Thank goodness it was my wife who pulled the switch."

"I'm hesitant to ask what happened next."

"After an intervention, I crashed. It was really an emotional breakdown. My brain was saying no more of the ego high and self-loathing roller coaster, yet my human spirit wanted the approval rush. While going through rehab, I finally got the back pain under control. Yet, sort of like where you're at, I had no idea what my soul was saying. Hopefully unlike you, I had to deal with the screaming emptiness of my spirit, heart and mind. No voice was getting out of my soul, and the my desperate human spirit was on the edge of losing control."

"So hang on a minute. I keep hearing from Lew and now you about the soul and human spirit, but I'm not sure I get it yet. You really think they have a voice?"

"Great question, Jason. I know for me, the soul has a gentle and quiet voice. It's the sound of love. Never like a clanging cymbal. Never draws attention to itself. Patient, kind and full of the very essence of God himself. If my rebellious spirit would have listened, my soul was speaking godly wisdom and encouragement. But you know, it's hard to hear the voice of God over the screaming sound of self. Helpful?"

"Yeah, thanks. I still need to wrestle with those ideas, but that's enough to go on. So what happened next?"

"After a while, my soul seemed to go completely quiet, and in its quietness, I felt like it began to shrink and become even shallower. In response, I think my human spirit took over, and I went through a dark and lonely time. You may be wondering where the Holy Spirit was in all this. Right where I left him. One thing I've come to realize about the Holy Spirit: like the soul, he's gentle and does his work best when invited."

"Huh, maybe that's why he seems so quiet to me. How did you get back on track?"

"Eventually, a friend put me in touch with Lew, and we began a long process of healing, restoring and growing my soul-mass. Since you're in the middle of the process, no need to go over familiar territory. I ended up working for GoodBrew, starting as a barista. Worked there until my soul had healed and grown enough that I could consider ministry again and get my credentials back. Well, that's my backstory. I truly hope you didn't have to fall as far as I did."

Jason slouched back in his chair. "I don't know, Joe. I feel like I'm still somewhat in free fall."

"Good. That means you're in motion. Don't worry, Lew knows

Q.

Ever been there?

when to pull the ripcord on your parachute."

"Let me get to the heart of what I know you need to know. During my ministry years and up to my intervention, I didn't realize I had a huge hole in my spirituality. I can tell you, celebrity is empty, like a black hole. It will suck the light as well as the air out of any room you enter. It's an addiction. What I've come to understand is that my human spirit desires celebrity because the attention and approval is exactly like a drug. It provided a quick fix, it pumped me up, it made me feel warm and mellow, or it just took away desire and the pressure of doing. Celebrity dangerously rewarded my human spirit, giving me a false and temporary feeling of satisfaction, if not pleasure."

"But it still never satisfies."

"Yes, that's my point. Prescription narcotics are for those in pain. What I didn't realize was how powerfully celebrity falsely fills in the cavity of a wounded and shrunken soul-mass in pain. The facade of my celebrity was a black hole of insecurity and self-loathing. That black hole was never filled."

"I get it. I love the feeling of being in control and making everything run like a well-oiled machine, leaving everyone amazed and impressed. When I get that celebrity feeling, it's like I say to the guy in the mirror, 'See, I'm not the loser you feared I was going to be!' Unfortunately, looks like we both stuck our hands in the gears trying to fill in our emptiness."

"Yes, we are all broken messes. The sooner we get that understanding, the healthier we will be. You're going to have to come to your own awareness, Jason, but here's what I learned about myself. For me, celebrity was about the absence of soul-mass wholeness. I was clueless about what a healthy soul felt like or how it functioned. If you've never been hooked on drugs, you probably don't fully appreciate the contradiction. It's like professional athletes who test positive for marijuana. You give up a multi-million dollar contract so you can smoke pot? Who gets that but another addict?"

Joe sat back down on the edge of the chair. "Following the train wreck, I've had lots of time to think about what I did to myself and others. I failed at the most fundamental level of leadership. Genuine leaders help followers grow their soul-mass. They never leave them dependent. I had become a feel-good dealer as much as a user. I used their talent but didn't have the time nor the interest to invest back into them. Until the intervention I never realized how powerful celebrity falsely fills the void in other people's human spirits. I don't blame anyone but myself, but I know I was also taken advantage of and used by others in this pathetic co-dependency. While I was using them, they were using me."

"What do you mean?"

"I came to the realization there is a significant distinction between a fake, a fan and a follower. A fake pretends to follow, yet lies in wait for an opportunity to rebel and attempt to steal a portion of the empty celebrity. Jealousy and envy, that's the root. Or if you're the celebrity, it's simply using—manipulating—others to get your desperate approval fix.

"Then there's the fan. A fan wants the radiated warmth of association with a celebrity. He's naively unaware there is little substance behind the celebrity facade. I attracted quite a few fakes and fans, and they used me for their own gain as much as I used them."

Jason began to squirm in his chair. "This is not pleasant, Joe. I'm seeing too much of myself in what you're saying."

"Well, join the largest unknown clan in humankind. There is good news in all this. In contrast, a follower wants to acquire the qualities displayed in a person of influence. My problem was, in my toxic state, I was not capable of growing and developing followers. I also realized deeply wounded souls, like I had, cleverly create an illusion of influence. Their influence appears to be substance, but instead is only a distorted reflection of the emptiness within. Like I said, there was no density in my core. Celebrity is attraction without substance in the soul. The pressure pressing in on an empty soul-mass results in an implosion. It often ends suddenly and not well. And I and a long list of others can attest to the 'not well' part."

Joe paused. "Jason, our conversation isn't supposed to be all about me. What are you learning about yourself through this process?"

"Tons. My issues, I'm realizing, surround what I do. I know it's really supposed to be about who I am. But you know what? Show me one ministry, one organization, one institution, one company where leadership really lives out the value that the quality of the soul determines the capacity of the person. Everything I do in life is measured by my works as evidence of my competency instead of a consequence of my integrity. Everything."

"Explain your last statement. I think you're on to something."

"What I see but have difficulty living out is just what James says about faith and works. My works don't validate my faith. My works are a result, the consequence, of my faith. It's as simple as that. I've known the scripture from the time I was in youth group, yet there's this lurking, sick belief that if I show you my works, you'll presume my faith is behind it. You think it's big. I fear it's tiny. It becomes a futile attempt at proof of worth instead of the contented consequence of the worthy One living inside of me."

"Preach it, bro," laughed Joe. "Here's something to consider as you put all this together. Celebrity is a first cousin of works. Most people derive their sense of worth by what they do because works falsely advertise who others think we are. When more than a few people validate a person's works, you've got celebrity."

"Here's a sick truth; I'm far more proud of what I've done for New Horizons than what New Horizons has done as an organization. Shallow, huh?"

"Yeah, and unfortunately, you've got a crowd thinking with you."

"You're right. What I'm coming to realize is that the natural consequence of Adam's curse of toil is merely pride in my own works. From Adam to now, our lives seem justified through the lens of our works. It shouldn't be that way. But, on the other hand, don't you think that if we don't have performance standards, penalties and rewards, the quality of our effort falls apart? I'm still flip-flopping on that point."

"I'm sorry, Jason. I can't sit for long. Do you mind if we walk the halls while we talk?"

"Not at all. I need my ten thousand steps today, anyway," laughed Jason.

"What was your question again?"

"I was asking, or really stating, that if we don't have performance standards, penalties and rewards, don't you think the quality of our effort falls apart?"

"I'm not so sure. What if the quantity and quality of my work, as the worker, was taken as a sign of the respect and trust I have for my employer? Let me put it another way. Here's the bottom line question in all this. How healthy is it for us humans to try and have a grace relationship with God and continually be in a works relationship with other humans?"

Q.

How healthy is it?

"I hate it when what you say feels so right that it also feels like it has to be so wrong."

"Does it have to be wrong? Let me ask, what's your soul-mass saying about this topic?"

"Like I said, most everything in my life up to this point has been validated by my works. I think my human spirit says, 'Feed me! Feed me!'"

"Any idea what your soul may be saying?"

"I would presume it says that Jesus is the bread of life. Consume him. I'm getting the sense my soul always points me to God. Then Satan comes and plays his mind-game, making me fear I'm only as good as my next project. He also reminds me that that last project wasn't that good anyway. In my intellect, I know his accusation isn't true. But something inside me, maybe my human spirit, believes the lie."

"Man, you've got the drama of eternity down well," laughed Joe. "Any idea why that mind-game works so well?"

"It's probably that I have no control over grace. You know

this. I'm sure you've preached on it a hundred times. Grace is a gift instead of an earned reward. You also know the sayings, 'There's no free lunch. Life is what you make it. God helps those who help themselves.' Maybe those sayings are more deadly than I've realized. I've compartmentalized my works and God's grace and fooled myself into thinking they are mutually exclusive."

"So?"

"So probably until I stop judging my value—my worth—on the basis of my works, I can do no different with others. And, if I don't change my mindset of works, I've just reinforced the lie of Satan that, in the end, it's really my works, not the cross, that counts. Only problem is, I'm beginning to understand I'm as addicted to works as you were to drugs."

Joe's outburst of laughter echoed through the hallway.

"I laughed, Jason, not because what you said is funny. What you said is deadly serious. It's just pathetically true that most people who haven't been in full-time ministry think we professionally trained ministers got that truth a long time ago."

Jason paused for a moment. "I'm getting one of those 'aha' moments. Here it is. Every one of us—celebrity or not—stands in the gap between the pride of who we think we are and the shame of who we fear ourselves to be. We continuously fail to grab hold of the true substance of grace. What we desperately want is approval—that someone sees value in us. Yet what we truly need is healthy affirmation. God has already told us who we are. He's told us in actions and words we are so precious that he spared judgment for our own sins by having his son take the punishment for us. We believe it; it's just that we can't accept it. As a result, I call God a liar."

"That's potent preaching, friend. Go on."

"I'm beginning to realize my addictive need for approval and control produced my own form of celebrity. Affirmation validates that something good is present within me. The most powerful affirmation is to validate that God is at work within me. Approval is necessary when I don't have that sense of soul-wholeness or contentment. I've always had a need to fill the sense of emptiness. Yet approval just fed my addiction."

"That's good bad stuff. Can't agree with you more." Joe and Jason's wandering the halls brought them back to the lobby. Joe slowly eased into the brown leather chair and gazed out the window. "Like you, I had a huge desire for approval from people I respected and looked up to. I desperately wanted someone to tell me I wasn't the phony I feared I was. What I really I needed was someone to help me look into my soul-mass and find the woundedness, to allow God to restore and then to grow it in a healthy way. Instead, I had to experience the Principle of Pain. You know what that is?"

"No, but I'm ready to learn it," said Jason.

"I learned this going through treatment. Dependent people—whether that's due to alcohol or other drugs, power or the approval from celebrity, or all of them—don't change behaviors until and unless there is no choice but to change. In other words, change only occurs when the pain of not changing becomes greater than the pain of change. Make sense?"

"More than I'd like to admit. I think I'm living the principle right now. I doubt I would be open to change if not for my board's intervention." Jason shook his head, frowning. "But how do I know when I've really changed and not just made changes? I mean, when did you feel like you were ready to get back into the process of influencing others? You know, to get back into ministry? When did you know you'd really changed?"

"Great questions. Only when I began to deal with my core issues, found in my soul-mass, could I possibly be ready to influence anyone. I'm a recovering narcissistic egomaniac as well as a recovering drug addict. When is an alcoholic ready to just socially drink? When can a narcotic addict be administered narcotics just for pain and not want more? Usually never. When you go over the line, it's not a matter of just stepping back over and determining to not trespass again. You have to understand why you went over the line. I can't just un-remember the high I got from all that adulation."

"I hear you. It's the feeling I get from being in control. Maybe my addiction is being a control freak. Control gives me a sense of power over others and dominance over outcomes. What I'm realizing is that in every dynamic of behavior there are two forces at work within me. One force is a need for and the rush of power. The other force is my fear of failure fueled by my insecure identity. Put those two in the same room, and you've got a person—me—spiraling out of control and yet desperately trying to keep control."

"Great insight. But now you're starting to sound like Lew," Joe laughed. "Let me tell you, the most frightening day of my life was not the day I got outed for my addictions. It was the day I stepped back onto the platform and looked into the faces of people who were expecting me to give them something that would help them better understand scripture, the kingdom of God, Christ in their life and where they fit into community. I realized I didn't have the answers. Perhaps I only had better questions. I finally experienced the awesome responsibility that people's lives could be altered by what I said. Talk about humbling and frightening."

"How did you reconcile that huge burden?"

"The day I was ready was the day when I realized it wasn't up to me to make the audience experience God. My role was simply to be the waiter—to deliver the food, the bread of life. It came with the reconciliation of my soul and human spirit. I realized the more the Spirit of Christ within me flows out of me through a healed soul and a tamed human spirit, the more I could simply be the waiter. I saw that when I started to mess with the recipes, thinking I was the cook, that's when I was in trouble."

"You mentioned reconciling the soul and human spirit. How did that happen?"

Joe leaned forward and winced. "First of all I had to determine who I was going to listen to. As I started to heal, I could begin to distinguish four voices inside of me."

"Sounds more like multiple personalities," smiled Jason.

"Maybe so. Maybe I was becoming crazy for God like I had never been before. I realized my flesh has a voice, as do my human spirit, my soul and the Holy Spirit. I had not been differentiating between the four."

"How did you do that?"

"Simply by asking the question, 'Who's talking here?' In doing so I was able to start discerning the 'Feed me! Feed me!' voice of the flesh, the human spirit's control-based insecurity and the soul's deep yearning for God."

"What did the voice of the Holy Spirit sound like?"

"Conviction, encouragement, grace, empowerment, direction. I don't know, but the Holy Spirit's voice may sound different to each person. You'll need to discover that one for yourself."

Joe paused to let the conversation settle in Jason's mind.

"The next thing I did was begin to differentiate excuses from explanations. Do you know what I mean by that?"

"I think so, but I'm not sure I could explain it."

"I could blame my talent for my problems. I could blame my first senior pastor for rewarding growth from my doing and seemingly caring little for growth of my soul-mass. And, of course, I could blame my pain. In the end, those are excuses for what happened. Excuses demand forgiveness. If I can tell you my sob story and make you feel bad for me, guess what? I'm off the hook. I'm not talking about true, spiritual forgiveness. I'm talking about the 'letting you off the hook and calling it compassion' forgiveness.'"

"Sounds a lot like enabling."

"Exactly. Instead, if I present the circumstances of my life as simply explanations, then these explanations require resolution. These circumstances explain why I made the choice to do whatever, but the choice was still my responsibility. It's all in the way I frame them and you receive them. Once I'm past the blame and excuse game, I'm getting closer to healthiness."

"So taking responsibility was the next step?"

Joe nodded. "My third step was to realize I needed a soul-mentor. Back when I was out of control, no one I knew seemed interested in doing anything with me other than playing a round of golf or talking about sports or how much they were making in the stock market. Looking back, if someone told me I needed a soul-mentor I wouldn't have known what they were talking about."

"Enter Lew and his process?"

"Right. Don't need to tell you much about that. But let me

Q.

How are you dealing with excuses, explanations and blame?

reassure you, since you asked, you are definitely changing, not just making changes. Just based on this conversation, I can see you're a different and better man than you were five years ago."

"Thanks, Joe. Hey, I don't want to take your day, but I want to know how this story is continuing."

Jason asked, "What's different in your ministry now?"

Joe slowly eased himself out of the brown leather chair again. "I've got to walk some more so I don't stiffen up. What's different? This will sound like a cliché, but we are living it out here. What's different is, we are building our faith family one soul at a time."

"You mean the difference is that your church is growing one person at a time?"

"Not really. I mean one soul at a time. I've taken Lew's process and turned it into a practice for our church. We're smaller as a body than you'd expect because when someone decides they want to identify with our community and they want Christ as their Savior, we take that assignment seriously. We explain they will go on a journey of discovering, healing and growing their soul-mass."

"So it's just spiritual formation with a new label?"

"It is. That's all it is. While I was in the process of getting Joe out of Joe, I came to realize how much of what I did wasn't wrong. It just wasn't effective."

"What do you mean? Preaching isn't effective?"

"Don't get me wrong. Growing in and as a community is essential and biblical. But you know this. Until and unless each person who declares Jesus Christ as Lord determines to go on their own journey of spiritual formation, the results have huge potential to be shallow. The challenge, as you know, is that growing as a follower of Christ can't be done exclusively in rows in an auditorium and classrooms. For me, I've chosen not to build our church family from the pulpit. I believe it happens best in coffee shops, cafés, kitchens and family rooms. Then I just reinforce that process from the platform on Sundays."

"That is so basic and sadly refreshingly new. Sad because, don't you think we should have been doing that all along? Instead, so many churches debate whether they should be missional or attractional and are neither. Shouldn't churches simply be intentional? Why isn't the discussion about growing disciples instead of creating magnets or vehicles?"

"My thoughts exactly. We've sidestepped that whole debate. We've determined to build Christ-followers one soul at a time. That is the most inefficient process anyone could ever design. Yet I believe God created us in community and for community, and that means it starts with 'two or more'—not two thousand and more. But I won't take you through all of our steps. That's not what you're here for."

"Can you put it in a package for me? What did you learn?"

"Jason, I just offered you a trace of my past. I'd love to tell you what I've learned, but let me turn it around to face correctly. What have you learned?"

"Now you are sounding like Lew," laughed Jason. Taking a deep breath, he said, "Try this on for size. Number one. Talent does not equal the health of your soul-mass."

"Good. What else?"

"Number two. Talent also doesn't necessarily equal influence."

"I think this is, perhaps, where you are at, Jason. Just because you're talented or even gifted doesn't qualify you to influence others. If you have talent, others trust you way too early in a relationship. The talent of a teacher or speaker is the most volatile of all. You can easily speak into their wants instead of their needs. It's called manipulation. Talent can be a weapon, a tool of utility or an instrument of blessing. Anything else?"

"Number three. If celebrity is greater than your soul-mass, watch out. Collisions are coming. Like we talked about, celebrity is like a narcotic. It feeds all the wrong needs and presses all the wrong buttons. I've got one more."

"Which is?"

"Number four. Celebrity is the reverse reflection of a

shrunken soul-mass. It looks big but is simply overinflated with the hot air of self. The core has no density."

"I represented that comment. Impressive. I think we've spent our time well. Here's the bottom line, Jason, and you clearly demonstrate you're getting it. Celebrity can only be transformed into gravitational influence through the growth of the soul-mass. And only God can heal, restore and grow our soul-mass. My job as the recipient is to desire it to happen. With gravitational attraction, rooted in the soul, there is a counterbalancing radiating love. You don't manufacture it. It's a consequence of the health of your soul. Radiating love is what makes you attractive in the first place. Now isn't that a big discovery! Love. Who would'a thought!" laughed Joe.

"It was great seeing you again, Jason. And I'm glad for both of us that it was under these circumstances. Let's keep in touch. I have some ideas of how New Horizons can perhaps start an initiative in growing soul-mass through the family."

A friend loves at all times, and a brother is born for a time of adversity. One who has unreliable friends soon comes to ruin, but there is a friend who sticks closer than a brother.

Proverbs 1:17; 18:24

REFLECTION QUESTIONS

1. *In the story, Joe Tyler talks about discovering the difference between appreciation, approval and affirmation. What would be your definition of appreciation? How do you feel when you receive words of appreciation? For example, "Thank you John/Sarah for volunteering last night. We so appreciate you."*

2. *What would be your definition of approval? Words of approval sound like this. "The quality of your effort was impressive. You add so much to the value of our team." How do you feel when you hear them? Embarrassed, humbled, prideful or valued?*

3. *What would be your definition of affirmation? When someone affirms what they see as a work inside you coming out, it may sound something like this: "Emily/Tyler, it is clear you are living out the passion of a Godly call and equipping. Just wanted you to know, it shows." Have you ever heard that from someone else? How did you feel? How long did you remember those words?*

4. *Joe said, "I knew we were making an impact on the spiritual front yet I knew there was a big part of me who was a fake; an imposter. I walked and talked like a pastor but no one, if they really knew the train wreck, should have ever wanted to follow me. I was a mess physically, emotionally and spiritually." This is commonly referred to as the impostor syndrome. How do you keep an honest identity? Your life is probably not as dysfunctional as Joe's was. Yet, how do you keep from creating a facade of personal put-togetherness and then living in the fear the true you will be exposed?*

5. *Joe Tyler said, "My problem went deeper than my addiction. I was unable to distinguish between celebrity, coming from a shrunken and sick soul, and true influence emanating from healthiness—which I probably never had. There was no density to my core." How do you build density in your soul-mass?*

CHAPTER 7

Love Still Makes
The World Go 'Round

LOVE IS THE FORCE OF
gravitational attraction and radiating influence

See what great love the Father has lavished on us, that we should be called children of God! And that is what we are! The reason the world does not know us is that it did not know him.

1 John 3:1

C old rain and wind was the weather *du jour*. Stepping into Lew's office, Jason was pleased to see a crackling fire. "Greetings, my friend. Decided to brave the elements, eh?"

"Yeah, thought the exercise would be good for me. Looks like dodging raindrops wasn't the workout I'd planned. Now wet shoes and a drenched coat are my reward. How are you?"

"I'm well, thank you. Grab some hot brew and sit down. I'm eager to hear about your time with Joe."

"Lew, I'm continually amazed, though I guess I shouldn't be, at the number of people you influence. But I don't feel I'm in the same league with them. Talk about a different person than the last time we met."

"Him or you?" Lew got up and added a log to the fire. "I love watching how the souls of those I've spent time with are impacting their world and now yours. What are your thoughts from your time with Joe?"

"My head is still spinning, but I think I'm beginning to comprehend this whole soul-mass thing."

"Good," said Lew as he sat down and began to search for his

pipe in his cardigan pockets.

"Joe spent time explaining his crash. I never realized how much our behavior—okay, my behavior—is driven by a need for approval. I saw in vivid detail how my constant need for approval indicates a deflated and wounded soul. So when the soul-mass is wounded and small, there is a desire for power and control that can come off as celebrity."

"And the converse?"

"When our souls are healthy, we naturally radiate love, and that attracts people to us. Seems so basic and yet fresh. Can I add some of your cocoa to my coffee?"

"Be my guest. I'd say your time was well spent. And how are you doing with your new insight?"

"I'm realizing I have significant work to do on my soul-mass. I've spent too much energy trying to prove my worth by my works. I'm not sure how much I'd be valued if people just knew me as friend. However, I still feel I'm unable or unwilling to trust people that much right now. I know it sounds like my admission of shallowness, but there it is."

Lew paused to pack and light his pipe. "Using an analogy to my oil exploration background, you've been on an expedition to find and drill down to the reservoir deep inside yourself. You've located the source of gravity—your soul-mass. And that's the first part in the truth we're focusing on: influence is the gravitational attraction of one person to another. Let's review what's going on here," said Lew as he got up and walked to the whiteboard.

"As you know, our metaphor for this process is Gravity." Lew wrote on the board.

"And you know and recall from our earlier conversation that gravity is the force of attraction pulling other bodies toward the center of the earth, or toward any other physical body having mass, for that matter."

"Yes, I do recall. It's also a significant force contributing to all celestial objects remaining in a state of equilibrium."

"What you may not recall is that the other force you just mentioned, radiation, is even more pervasive."

"I mentioned radiation?"

"Yes. You said when our souls are healthy they radiate love."

"Oh, I guess I did. I don't usually think of those two words—radiation and radiate—as the same concept. Interesting."

"Let me add radiation and love."

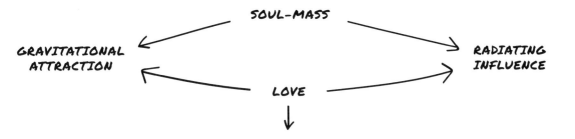

"Consider the fact that between gravity and radiation, all things are in balance. This is the second part in the truth: love radiates through the kingdom of God."

"Like it was in Eden? Until, of course, something like selfishness sent two objects—Adam and Eve—off on a collision course with living." Jason paused to fill his mouth with cocoa-flavored black coffee. "I think you have something going here, Lew. If you like your coffee black, that is."

"This is a good place to center the beginning of our conversation for today. Let me see if I can surmise the essence of your time with Joe. I think you saw that as leaders, we can't make followers. We can't force people to become members of our tribe. Those who follow us do so voluntarily. And followers are drawn by an attraction like the force of gravity resonating from within our souls," said Lew as he patted his chest. "The gravitational force in human relationships is intimacy in progressively powerful forms of attractional love. And here's where I astound you by pointing out the obvious. Radiating love is what keeps collisions from happening. It's the counterbalancing force to gravitational attraction."

"Wow. Joe and I said that? Coming from you it sounds profound. And yes, you got the core of our conversation. But seriously, you really think it's that simple in the real world?"

Lew took a few quick puffs from his pipe. "No, but it should be. This is the difficult part: every person comes into an organization or a relationship with selfish wants. A leader's genius is in reinterpreting and reforming their wants into selfless needs. For example, this can be as simple as an employee development program or as complicated as a growing marriage—the most intricate organization you'll ever belong to.

"Can you give me an example?"

Lew set down his marker and returned to his chair. "Here's one from the workplace. As you know, the concerns of most new employees are about salary, benefits, vacation and quality of their workspace. Over time it's the leader's responsibility and opportunity to shift focus to satisfaction in the quality of their work and encouragement for them to work independently. With the leader's effort, employees come to know their voice is valued and respected. Leaders do that by consistently voicing values of integrity and fair-play and modeling those values."

"Hah, yes, and in the midst of all that, some work actually gets done."

"Speaking of work, I think there was evidence you aren't finished. Looks like some cynic polish still needs to be applied. Seriously, remember, the greatest threat to any enterprise is not enemies from outside. It comes from immature and self-centered behaviors of those within. God help us when these behaviors come from persons we depend on to lead us through times of tension."

"Sometimes, Lew, I'm not sure if I need work or a workover. Either way, you do know how to drill."

"If I get too close to a nerve, let me know," Lew smiled. "Back to topic, have you committed this gravity truth to memory?"

"Yes, I have. Love is the force of gravitational attraction and radiating influence."

"If influence is the gravitational attraction of one person to another and love radiates through the kingdom of God, then let's pull apart this truth like I dissected grasshoppers as a kid on a hot summer afternoon: one leg at a time."

"Considering we're talking about me, that's a disturbing metaphor."

Lew gave a mischievous smile. "It's a simile, but don't worry about it. I presume you learned from your time with Joe there are big-personality people who can draw a crowd. Often we choose to put our small soul-mass under the influence of these people, hoping they will help grow our soul-mass, thinking they are true leaders. It becomes a problem for us when we discover they are only celebrities with small souls as well. Sadly, celebrities with small souls are likely to attract followers with small souls. When things implode, there's the mad scramble to grab what little soul there is to go around—as if it could be shared."

"You have such an uplifting way of describing human nature. But seriously, Lew, that is a significant point for me. I imagine this is why tyrants are so fearsome. They have little souls and must make up for their deficiency with power, fear, greed, manipulation and lies. It's becoming clear to me the soul-mass of true influencers and leaders—the people with larger soul-masses— reveal more goodness. Am I right?"

"Bang, right on, my friend."

A puzzled look crossed Jason's face. "You know, driving back from seeing Joe, something really bugged me. He was different, but I couldn't quite put a label on it. It felt like goodness, but that label is so generic. Then it hit me. He had a humility I don't know I've seen before. Do you think you have to go through humiliation to get to humility?"

"That's one road, if you don't slide into the ditch on the way."

"So where does humility fit into all this we're talking about? It's obviously connected to the scripture you gave me: the powerful one describing the humility of Jesus in Philippians 2."

"Yes, and?"

"I would say it's through a restored and healthy soul like Joe talked about that we're able to live out the selfless example of humility Jesus displayed."

"Good foundation," said Lew.

"You know, I also observed Joe's gravitational attraction is now more effortless. He isn't making his congregation grow by running around the platform with his hair on fire. I'm going to assume it grows because of the condition of his growing soul-mass and the growing soul-mass of those around him. What I now realize is that new sense about Joe is true humility with confidence."

"Very discerning, Jason. I would describe what you saw as confident humility. Strange juxtaposition of words, but you get the meaning?"

"Yes, exactly. To use these terms, I would say Joe radiates love. He has confidence in the source of that love and that also gives him confidence to accept love from others. I didn't sense it before. And that, oh wise teacher, partially completes the third part of the truth: that gravitational attraction and radiating love love are the counterbalancing forces in all relationships."

"You want to explain the partial part?"

"I can now recognize it in others. I'm not sure it's coming out of me, yet."

"*Yet* is a marvelous word. It speaks of expectation. You're putting it together well," said Lew, smiling.

"You know, when Joe was with NxtGenAlive and Oak Creek Church, I wanted to be around him. Back then I felt important by being in his presence. When he wanted to use me, I felt useful. And if he had asked, I was willing to be used. But I never really felt the qualities of radiating love and confident humility from him."

As Jason talked, Lew got up and added **CONFIDENT HUMILITY** to his diagram.

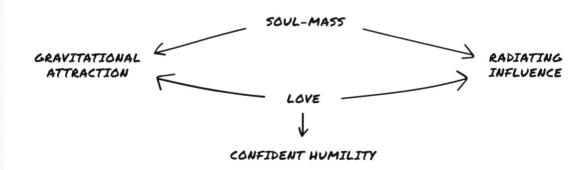

"Good personal insight, Jason. Even with the goodness of gravitational attraction from the soul, without a counterbalancing force of radiating love, collisions will happen."

Jason shook his head. "I now realize how sick a two-way street there is between attraction through celebrity and a small soul-mass. But this time being with Joe was different. I felt inspired and empowered by my conversation with him. Interesting. Hard to put into words, but there was a significant change. When I knew him before, I was in awe of his celebrity. This sounds weird, but you'll know what I mean—now I just want to connect with him again because something inside of him is attractive."

"Let's return to our conversation when we first met. You were uncomfortable with the idea—if I understood your push-back at the time—of having people fall in love with you as a consequence of your gravitational influence. It made you, ah, squirmy."

"You read me pretty well."

"How do you feel now?"

"Not sure. Like I said, I'm good with the radiating part. I really like the confident humility part. And, I enjoy making people feel good about feeling good. And I like connecting with guys like Joe."

"Tell me about the other part—the love that's coming to you."

"Still struggling on a couple of fronts. First of all, guys don't fall in love with guys."

"Really? Did you fall in love with Jesus? He's a guy. Does that seem too romantic? As I recall, the word love is found hundreds of times in the New Testament. But, you know all that, so there's something else I'm suspecting. Let's move past the *bromance* barrier. Is it, perhaps, the high expectations you feel if others fall in love with your soul?"

"I was afraid you were going there," said Jason as he placed both hands on his mug and stared into the dark brown liquid. "I'm a fixer and a doer. I derive satisfaction by being good at what I do, and because of that I help others. What's wrong with that? Are you telling me that being competent isn't good? Just be lovey-dovey and everything will turn out right?" Jason shook his head.

"Consider this, Jason. Perhaps the reason why you squirm

with people falling in love with you is, you feel unworthy of their love. You know all the sin in your life, and they don't. You are uncomfortable because you believe the lie of your unworthiness more than the truth of God's grace. You know the filth, and you feel like a fraud."

Looking up as if caught telling a lie, Jason said, "Thanks. Nailed me again."

"Let me describe a progression that may help make being loved and loving others easier."

Holding his pipe in one hand, Lew wrote **PROPERTIES OF GRAVITATIONAL ATTRACTION AND RADIATION**.

"Here's where it all begins. Love begins with **AWARENESS**." Lew wrote it below **PROPERTIES**.

"Remember the last time someone caught your attention. You became aware of them maybe by hearing them speak, reading an article, hearing their idea or noticing an action. Something made them stand out. You turned your head, in a sense."

"Yeah, I remember noticing a guy in my freshman English class at college. He stood out from the crowd. We got to know each other, and Jim and I have been friends ever since. Joe was the same way."

"That's awareness. As innocent as it seems, that's the beginning of attraction." Lew wrote, **I HAVE BECOME AWARE OF THEIR EXISTENCE**.

"Are you making me feel creepy on purpose?"

"Okay, Jason. You're creeping me out by your thinking I'm creeping you out. How else do you make friends? Or is that part of the problem? You have Fantasy League connections and sports and golfing buddies, but you don't develop a true friendship. Now that's creepy!"

Jason stared back into his coffee mug.

"Next is **CURIOSITY**." Lew wrote it on the white board. "When someone catches my attention, I'm curious. I'm interested. Who are they? What's their story? I want to know more." Lew wrote, **I AM INTRIGUED**.

PROPERTIES OF GRAVITATIONAL ATTRACTION + RADIATION

- AWARENESS: **I HAVE BECOME AWARE OF THEIR EXISTENCE.**
- CURIOSITY: **I AM INTRIGUED.**

"By this time the person has passed the 'sniff test.' There is something about them creating an **APPEAL**." Squeak, squeak, went the marker.

"I guess, if this were romantic attraction, we'd be calling it infatuation? Right? I remember with Emily after I had met her in the eighth grade, it wasn't just hormones. She was appealing. Thinking about her made me feel good."

"You got it. At this point, something is drawing me in. I may not be able to put my finger on it. It could be their appearance, countenance, personality or beliefs. If it's merely empty celebrity, this is when people can get hurt. But if there is substance in the soul, wholesome gravitational attraction is at work. Being around this person brings me enthusiasm, and I enjoy their company. I like how they think and how they live." Lew wrote down, **I HAVE CONFIDENCE IN THIS PERSON'S CAPACITY TO BELIEVE AND LIVE WISELY.**

PROPERTIES OF GRAVITATIONAL ATTRACTION + RADIATION

- AWARENESS: **I HAVE BECOME AWARE OF THEIR EXISTENCE.**
- CURIOSITY: **I AM INTRIGUED.**
- APPEAL: **I HAVE CONFIDENCE IN THIS PERSON'S CAPACITY TO BELIEVE AND LIVE WISELY.**

"Okay, time out," said Jason. "I've seen many shallow people in my short time on earth—and you're probably thinking I'm one of them—and it seems like those who get sucked in to this shallow celebrity mindset think it's more than that. Isn't that where your appeal jumps the tracks? In fact, as I'm thinking about it, that might explain why so many marriages are so miserable. When infatuation wears off and there's nothing underneath to move it forward, the relationship is in trouble. Am I right?"

"No and yes. No, I don't think you're shallow. And yes, you are exactly correct. If true gravitational attraction is as simple as I'm making it look, why are so many people fooled? Why do so many relationships crash and burn?"

"Not sure if that's a rhetorical question or not, Lew, but it gives me a thought about my first marriage to Emily. I needed to connect with a soul more healthy than my own. The problem was, we were both needy, naïve and gullible when we needed to be wise and discerning. We had no experience or wisdom in searching for authenticity in others. It ended with deep wounds." Jason stopped suddenly. Lew's sympathetic look almost sparked tears in Jason.

"Thank you for sharing that. I'm glad to hear you talking through some of those experiences. That's part of healing the wounds."

Jason set his mug down, crossed his arms and stared at the floor.

Rather than pushing deeper, Lew turned and wrote down **INSPIRATION**.

"Jason, this is the moment when another person's presence in your life causes you to do something. I know for me, they add value to my life. I smile more. I feel safe. Their thoughts are empowering and encouraging. Their life provides insight and a model of how I can live my life better. That's influence at work through inspiration. I've been let in to their sphere of communication. We are now engaging in conversation." Lew wrote, **I TRUST THIS PERSON WITH MY THOUGHTS**.

PROPERTIES OF GRAVITATIONAL ATTRACTION + RADIATION

- AWARENESS: **I HAVE BECOME AWARE OF THEIR EXISTENCE.**
- CURIOSITY: **I AM INTRIGUED.**
- APPEAL: **I HAVE CONFIDENCE IN THIS PERSON'S CAPACITY TO BELIEVE AND LIVE WISELY.**
- INSPIRATION: **I TRUST THIS PERSON WITH MY THOUGHTS.**

"Sorry, Lew, for me, this is where your model starts to break down—again. Are you saying I can only be a leader to those I have a personal relationship with?"

"Interesting question. Notice you made an erroneous jump to another track."

"What do you mean?"

Lew shifted his weight standing at the whiteboard. "We were talking about attraction and influence. You started equating that with leaders and leadership. People do it all the time, but the ideas are not synonymous. We'll get to leadership in our next session. Would you care to rephrase your question?"

"I see that. Influence is different than leadership. But if I have to know people—to have a real and personal relationship with them—what about national leaders and significant authors? Don't they influence our thinking and behavior even if we've never met them?"

"Like I said, gravitational influence is a form of progressive love. Relational distance does affect the degree of intimacy. For example, the writings of CS Lewis and Dallas Willard have been significant influences in my life. Never met either of them; never will since they're both dead. Yes, I have been considerably influenced by their writings, true, but I can never be influenced to the degree I would have been, had I been a part of Lewis's Inklings group or a student in Willard's lectures. That would have required intimacy."

"Okay, I get it. There is some kind of relationship, but it's distant. Reading their writings or watching them in a video produces a degree of intellectual intimacy."

"Precisely. Here's a key point, Jason. Only if I can have some connection of intimacy does friendship happen. We talk; we exchange emails; we spend time together. Friendship requires connection, and connection produces intimacy. Let me give you an example. Who did Jesus call his friends in John 15? Let me get this on the board."

FRIENDSHIP INTIMACY

"His disciples."

"Yes, but more specifically, the Twelve. Those who had spent time with him over the course of three incredible years. He ate with them, slept with them, fished with them. He called them his friends. Not colleagues, associates, partners or team members. He called them friends. And then there were Peter, James and John, who were his closest. So Jason, I've got a question for you. Don't answer it now; just think about it. Would your staff call you a true friend? I know there is friendliness, but what about thinking of you as a trusted friend? By what criteria do they decide to let you in? And how mutual is the relationship?"

"Okay, Lew, I won't answer it, but here's a question for you. Can you really be friends with those whom you possess the power to fire, promote and discipline? How does that work?"

"I'll answer that with another question. Do you call your children friends? Now I'm not implying that you relate to your team as a parent, but you've got huge power and responsibility over your children. How does that work? In my view, you can treat employees like family. You don't enable them, and you don't ignore them. You are concerned for their wellbeing, but you don't play favorites. You don't leave them in need. Think about the friends you have. Do you enjoy spending time with them? Do you think of them often? Are you open to their influence in words and action? Do you want to understand their view of life and regularly compare your view to theirs? Here's a key." Lew wrote down, *I TRUST THIS PERSON WITH MY EMOTIONS*.

PROPERTIES OF GRAVITATIONAL ATTRACTION + RADIATION

- AWARENESS: *I HAVE BECOME AWARE OF THEIR EXISTENCE.*
- CURIOSITY: *I AM INTRIGUED.*
- APPEAL: *I HAVE CONFIDENCE IN THIS PERSON'S CAPACITY TO BELIEVE AND LIVE WISELY.*
- INSPIRATION: *I TRUST THIS PERSON WITH MY THOUGHTS.*
- FRIENDSHIP-INTIMACY: *I TRUST THIS PERSON WITH MY EMOTIONS.*

"Even though love is the core of everything we're talking about, I don't think I need to spend a huge amount of time on it." Lew wrote **LOVE** on the whiteboard. "We both know there is sexual love, brotherly love and then the love of God to us. We know, and I'm sure you've preached enough sermons on it, that God's love is the kind of love we want to radiate. My belief is, that kind of love can only come through a healthy soul-mass, which means a disciplined human spirit, an open channel for the Holy Spirit to work, and a restored soul. Anything less than that produces an addictive form of love, far from a model of unconditional."

Lew paused to look directly at Jason. "Love is the essential element found in the force of attraction, the counterbalancing force of radiation. We are attracted to people with large souls. Those same large souls radiate the identical core element of influence: love. It starts as gravitational attraction and refines to a Radiating Love like the Father loves,"

"Got it. I feel like a lot of pieces are starting to come together."

"Excellent. What is the puzzle starting to look like?"

"Here's where I think you're going: When I'm," Jason did the air quotes motion with his fingers, "'*in love*' with another human, I am willing to allow this person to influence me at my very core, my soul. By choice, I am unprotected in my emotions and my identity. I allow them to experience me without filters, lenses and lies. I place no expectations on their performance or their response. How's that?"

"That's a powerful insight, but I sensed a little hesitation. Care to elaborate?"

"What I just told you is what I believe. But there's a gap between belief and living it out. The biggest problem I have is in trusting others at that level. I get it. I just don't feel like I want to risk it. Does that make sense?"

Lew lifted his coffee mug, as if to toast Jason's success. "Jason, you've just described an excellent distinction between belief, faith and trust. You believe with your mind. You have faith in your heart, but your trust is perhaps rooted in your soul. If the soul isn't healthy, trust is either absent or distorted and malformed.

Love is an excursion into trust. As I truly love someone, I am committed to their life and their unreserved influence in my life. Our friendship requires no explanations."

Putting down his mug, Lew wrote, *I TRUST THEM WITHOUT CONDITIONS*, after **LOVE**. "This is the often-missed element of love. I don't require it to be reciprocal. I love to the extent I'm capable at the moment. The other person graciously receives that love and returns love at the level they are capable of in that moment. No conditions. No expectations."

PROPERTIES OF GRAVITATIONAL ATTRACTION + RADIATION

- AWARENESS: *I HAVE BECOME AWARE OF THEIR EXISTENCE.*
- CURIOSITY: *I AM INTRIGUED.*
- APPEAL: *I HAVE CONFIDENCE IN THIS PERSON'S CAPACITY TO BELIEVE AND LIVE WISELY.*
- INSPIRATION: *I TRUST THIS PERSON WITH MY THOUGHTS.*
- FRIENDSHIP-INTIMACY: *I TRUST THIS PERSON WITH MY EMOTIONS.*
- LOVE: *I TRUST THEM WITHOUT CONDITIONS.*

"Lew, I'm beginning to realize gravitational attraction is both an exhilarating and humbling experience. To think someone else sees something of value in me starts a sick track in me. *Yes, but you don't know how pathetic I really am.* But as we—I—mature as individuals and leaders, we recognize this gravitational attraction for what it truly is."

"Which is?"

"Love coming from a healthy soul-mass. It's God's love."

Lew put the marker down and returned to his chair. "Jason, you are coming to realize that loving others and being loved is a wonderful burden of expectation and responsibility. Genuine gravitational attraction comes from the substance of the soul, and in the soul, we find progressive forms of love. Gravitational attraction draws others into a team to accomplish mission and purpose. In return, it enriches those within our sphere of influence. These are accomplishments unattainable on our own.

"By the way, since we've spent a fair amount of time talking about love, what about this 'falling in love' pushback you've got. Any better insight?" asked Lew as he adjusted his glasses.

"You sure know how to bulldoze over an objection. I get it. Until I'm willing to see the goodness of Christ transforming me, I'm unable to allow people to truly love me. If I don't allow people to love me for who I am then I've limited my gravitational attraction and my radiating influence–both containing the property of love. Maybe it's because I really don't believe or have complete faith that deep down in my heart God loves me unconditionally. I like the idea of unconditional love. It's just that maybe I don't fully embrace it."

"Maybe, Jason? Is that a rhetorical 'maybe,' or is that a self-statement?"

"Maybe. Look, Lew, I get the fact my love is not my works. My works are an expression of my love, not proof. I get that. It's merely consequence. Like you said, evidence. Because if I don't get that, I don't get the humility of Christ Paul spoke to in the letter to the Church at Philippi. I'm realizing how much of my life I've tried to prove my worth through my works. Doesn't work for God and probably doesn't work for people in my life either."

"Good work. Oops," laughed Lew. "I meant, good faith."

"Nice play on words. Listen, you've dredged up some underlying issues I am beginning to see revolve around trust and control and works and grace and a feeling of unworthiness."

"Gentlemen, methinks we've arrived at the core."

"I'm feeling the heat and the pressure from your drilling project. Can we pick this up next time?"

"Of course. This is a good stopping place. Take heart; you are making great progress."

"Really, Lew? That's nice to hear. Since this is my one and only pass through this pipeline, I have no idea how long it is and how fast I'm going."

"Well, you are a quick learner, and your insecure arrogance

belies a lot of your developing self-clarity."

"Ah, is that a compliment? I'll take it as one, since I'm trying to get in touch with my soul and allow it to heal. Thank you, I think."

"Definitely a compliment. But you look a little down. What's going on?"

"Just reflecting on my role as a long-distance father. I have a daughter who needs to hear this more than the story of the birds and the bees, which she's too old for now anyway.

"Timing and opportunity, my friend. Make them your friends. I think we've beat this gravity truth to the ground. So let's give some space and time for you to reflect on what we've talked about. Next session is going to be on Leaders and Leading. Here's the next truth: Leadership is the craft of a leader. Oh, and by the way, I've got several scriptures I want you to meditate on. They are Proverbs 29:2, Luke 22:26, Matthew 20:26 and Hebrews 13:17. I've texted them to you. Also, when you're ready for our next meeting, text me ahead of time. I've got someone I want you to talk with. It's been a great session."

Jason got up, realizing he was stiff from sitting so long, and put on his coat. "Thanks for your usual fire hose. It's been good."

Watch what God does, and then you do it, like children who learn proper behavior from their parents. Mostly what God does is love you. Keep company with him and learn a life of love. Observe how Christ loved us. His love was not cautious but extravagant. He didn't love in order to get something from us but to give everything of himself to us. Love like that.

Ephesians 5:1–2 (The Message)

REFLECTION QUESTIONS

1. *At this point in your life, how would you rate the influence (attraction and radiation) of your soul-mass? Insignificant, Small, Medium or Substantial. How do you know? How much is a sense of false humility playing into your answer? How much is pride?*

2. *Name three people who are **aware** of your presence. What are you doing that they would even be aware of your existence?*

3. *Name three people who are **curious** about you. What is it about you that creates curiosity?*

4. *Name three people who find you **appealing**. Why would they have confidence in your capacity to believe and live wisely?*

5. *Name three people who find you a source of **encouragement**. What is it causing them to trust you with their thoughts?*

6. *Name three people whose **friendship** is so secure you would trust them with your emotions.*

7. *Name three people who **love** so deeply that they trust you without conditions. They know, without question, you will always act in their best interests.*

8. *What are you doing or not doing to increase your gravitational influence on these 18 people?*

9. *What is your take on the 'falling in love' push-back that Jason has? Do you feel the same way? Why or why not? What can you add to that part of the conversation? Do you feel there are barriers of intimacy? If so, why?*

CHAPTER 8

Leaders and Leadership

LEADERSHIP

is the craft of a leader

Not so with you. Instead, whoever wants to become great among you must be your servant.

Matthew 20:26

A strong wind had blown in and blown off most of the oak and maple leaves from the trees lining the stately street, covering the ground with a carpet of yellow and red. Standing on the sidewalk waiting for Jason, Lew noticed a late fall bite was in the air. He was glad he had on his Irish Donegal tweed cap and blue wool jacket.

"Greetings, my friend." Getting in to Jason's Audi TT, Lew let out something between a grunt and a sigh. "Is it me, or are these cars getting lower and tighter?"

"It's you, Lew, and greetings."

"Hello to you too. Sciatica's acting up today. But 'time and tides,' you know. Thanks for making time for lunch. Had some sandwiches delivered from a new shop in town. Always ready for something new."

"Lew, for you the only events I wouldn't rearrange would be an activity with my boys or a date with Sylvia. Where are we headed?"

"Compassion Works! headquarters. We're going to meet Paul Ishii."

"I know Paul! We've worked together on several projects."

"Glad to hear it; that will save a lot of time with the preliminaries. You remember the gravity truth for our session?"

"Yep, it goes like this: Leadership is the craft of a leader."

"What about the scriptures?"

"Which one? You gave me a list."

"How about the Jason Notes version of all of them?"

"Funny you should ask. I have a paraphrase of them. Here's my smartphone. Click on the notes app."

"Mind if I read it out loud?"

"Be my guest."

"Leaders, serve with integrity and live in righteous standing with God. Be the one who rules as a servant. When that happens the people you serve will have confidence in you, and all will rejoice." Lew laughed, "You missed your calling. You should have been a scribe for Moses or Solomon."

"Yes, but then I would have missed all these digs from you. Interesting you would mention Moses. The scriptures you gave me got me on an intensive study of the leadership styles of Moses and Joshua."

"Your heated seat is just what the doctor ordered. You can take the long way to Paul's shop if you want. What'd you find in your search?"

"One, Moses will always be a patriarch of the people of God, but Joshua, a type of Christ, had the spirit of leadership in him. God spoke directly to Moses and told him that."

"So what does all that mean for you?"

"I think it's fascinating to see that it took one kind of leader—a patriarch—to bring people *out* of their slavery. It required another type of leader to bring them *into* their promise."

"That's deep. Sure you haven't been preaching on the side? And who are you? Patriarch or leader?"

"Good question. Maybe a little of both."

Located in the warehouse area of town, CW! was a regional resourcing agency for local food banks and street ministries. It also served as a resourcing and response group for everything from a house or apartment fire to a regional natural disaster.

Lew and Jason walked up a flight of stairs to the second-floor office. "Hello, Consuela," said Lew before the receptionist could even look up.

"Mr. Merton, what a pleasant surprise. Are you here to see Paul?"

"Yes, thank you. But please tell me how Miguel is doing since his surgery."

"Thanks for asking, Mr. Merton. We feel so blessed. He's walking again, gaining strength, and the doctor says he should be ready for rehab in another week."

"Marvelous. I know this has been a hard time for you and your family. That was a horrible accident Miguel was in. I'm glad to hear you're moving in a positive direction."

"We are, and thank you for your connections. I don't know if we'd been able to experience all these miracles had you not been a part of this."

"That's sweet of you to say that. Truly, it's been my privilege. God has blessed me with a group of friends who desire nothing more than to be of help."

Turning to see his old friend walking down the hall, Lew shouted out, "Paul, you old fart, you're looking as good as ever!"

Lew's loud greeting triggered an embarrassed blush in Jason.

"Great to see you too, my friend," said Paul as they embraced. "How've you been?"

"Good and busy. I've been having a great time getting to know Jason. He told me on the way over that you two have worked together on some projects."

"We have. Jason, it's great to see you again too," said Paul as they shook hands. "How have you been?"

"Good, thanks. And because you know Lew well, you know this has been a fascinating *journey* for me."

Lew groaned at the emphasis. "Oh good grief! This *journey* thing is going viral."

"Sorry, Lew, couldn't help it. It has been a process as well as a great journey. I am learning so much about myself and how I relate to others."

"Well, that's the plan, isn't it, Lew?" Paul clapped Lew on the back.

"Sure is. So let's get started." Lew held up some bags he'd carried in. "I've got lunch. You got a room where we can talk?"

"I reserved the conference room. Knowing you, Lew, I thought you might want to use a whiteboard," Paul joked.

They entered the conference room, and Lew let out a gasp. "Paul, I can't believe you! Put me in a room with a whiteboard and no markers, and you've got a man in serious anxiety." He set down the lunch bags and, with a smirk, reached into his jacket pocket. "Fortunately, I came prepared."

As they settled in around the conference table and began unwrapping the sandwiches, Lew looked at Jason. "I know you've worked with Paul, but you probably don't know his whole story. Paul, can you give Jason an overview?"

"Roger. Here's the résumé version. Graduated from the Air Force Academy. Served in Iraq and a few covert places in the Middle East we don't talk about. After 20+ years, I felt there was something more and took retirement. Went to work for RJ Metals as a liaison to the Air Force on a new cross-platform fighter jet. Ten years later, I found myself at the C-level, as Executive Vice President for Operations, somewhat frustrated and quickly burning out."

"What was causing it?" Jason asked.

"What I experienced was a great company, highly committed to quality and performance, grinding up great people like a human mill, and I was the miller. I wondered how it could be different."

"And I'm guessing that's when you met Lew," Jason said.

Paul nodded. "We started through this whole gravitational attraction, influence and soul-mass process. I quickly came to the realization that my suspicions were correct: I was part of the problem. Here's the key thing for me. I was doing a fantastic job of managing and was completely failing as a leader." Paul looked at

Lew. "You know, engineers tend to do that, don't they?"

"Yes, we do." Lew slowly nodded his head. "I'm proud of the accomplishments from those times but certainly not proud now of what it cost in human energy."

Paul finished a bite of his sandwich and continued. "Through the process I was able to make a fairly quick turnaround in my managing and leading style, and the outcomes were satisfying and substantive. But I felt I needed a change, even though I wasn't quite ready to leave RJ Metals. Fortunately, the company wasn't ready to let me go. I had been volunteering for CW!. They wanted me to come on full time as their volunteer coordinator, so I negotiated a sweet deal with RJM. Their charity commitment inspired them to create a loaned executive program, which meant I could work half-time for RJM as an internal consultant, and they would pay me to work the other half with Compassion Works!."

"'Sweet deal' is right!" Jason said.

"At CW! I had the encouragement of the CEO to apply what I was learning from Lew—what you're learning now." Paul pointed at Lew with his sandwich. "Jason, the results are phenomenal, and I have the joy of taking little credit for it. It's all this guy's process. Our volunteers even have buttons that say, *Trust the Process.*"

Lew smiled with that kind of satisfied grin, as if someone had complimented him on some intricate model he had built. "You're very kind, Paul. I'm honored and pleased to have played a role. Now how about we get to the subject matter at hand. What are your big 'ahas' from the process you went through?"

Paul put down the sandwich and wiped his hands. "Let me borrow your markers for a minute, Lew." He walked to the whiteboard and wrote out **MANAGING**. "Let's start with managing first. That's what we all do exceptionally well. I got all the leadership training you would expect in the Air Force, and it was good. The problem came in assessment. I was continually evaluated on how well I managed, not how well I led. Over time, without thinking about it, I became the consummate manager. Don't get me wrong, there's nothing incorrect with managing— following procedure and hitting the marks. It's essential and keeps everyone safe and predictable. I call it the hygiene work of getting things done." Paul wrote **MANAGING** and **HYGIENE** and connected an arrow between the two.

"Hygiene is keeping the toilets clean and the floors swept. It's not glamorous work, but it is essential. Keeps systems from getting yucky. When I was in charge of the 23rd Air Force Command, we provided special operations command and control, intelligence, and reach back support forces to deployed air commanders for execution of assigned missions. You think protocol was prime? Protocol intentionally limits you to few options to prevent unintended consequences.

"However, when you get out of those kind of critical environments, you're never able to move people forward beyond the constraints of their job description or task assignment. Follow the book, and hit the mark."

"But isn't hitting the mark a good thing?"

"Don't get me wrong, that's critically important in any organization, but that is not leading. Managing only makes sure you've properly navigated the past to the present. On the other hand, leading takes people and an organization they are a part of to the future. See the difference?"

"How did you integrate managing and leading?" asked Jason.

"It took a while. I didn't fully comprehend it until late in my career. A lot of my Air Force training was to faithfully follow the plan we trained for until it created a subconscious routine. That was a crisis-react model. That, to me, is a good example of the value of managing. We practiced until we could do it brain-dead. Then came reality, when the real world didn't follow anticipated plans. That's when we were ready for crisis-respond. That's knowing your team, knowing strengths and knowing the routine so well we were able to improvise with confidence. That's operational flexibility, and now we're getting close to leadership."

"Thanks, Paul. This makes total sense with what Lew was saying a few weeks ago about continuous and discontinuous change," said Jason. "Very helpful."

Lew beamed. "You remembered. Continuous change responds best to management. Discontinuous change unfolds best in an environment of leadership."

Paul nodded. "Eventually, with Lew's help, I came to realize my true job with RJ Metals and Compassion Works! was to be a force of influence—a leader—not just the keeper of procedure—a manager. While I had responsibility for a quality product, I was unintentionally not taking care of our human assets who made our quality product. Unfortunately, it took a while for that to sink in. Be aware, Jason, the best you can expect from managing is control. Only through leading can you really be an influence. Let me chart out what I mean."

Paul added to the chart he started.

MANAGING → HYGENE → CONTROL → GROUP → PRESENT

LEADING → INFLUENCE → TRUST → TRIBE → FUTURE

Paul sat down and finished his sandwich.

"As I went through this gravity journey, I began to see I was looking at so many things as if there were scotomas. You know what a scotoma is?"

"No, and I know I'm going to find out." Jason smiled.

"A scotoma is a blind spot. We all have two of them. It's where the optic nerve bundles connect with the retina. The brain compensates for that portion absent of rods and cones and creates the sense that the blind spot isn't there. We do it in life as well. We look at a situation and don't see a part of it, or if we do, what we see can take different forms, all seeming real. Our brain does not tolerate ambiguity and will create wholeness, even when it's not there."

"Is that why there are questions regarding the reliability of eyewitness testimony?"

"Exactly. Here's another example. You remember when you bought a plug of Bazooka bubble gum, and you got a riddle or a word game on the inside wrapper? As a kid, my brother and I would ride our bikes down to Fujiya Market. It was one of those now almost-vanished neighborhood stores. Mrs. Nishimura loved to see us come by. Anyway, I remember one of those pictures inside the wrapper was of an old hag. However, if I looked at her long enough, the picture clicked and took the form of a beautiful Victorian woman. That's also a scotoma. Our brain sees something one way, and then, blink!, that one thing becomes another. Here's a key. Scotomas are also leader dysfunctions. The leader thinks a particular view is helping them lead, when, in fact, it's doing just the opposite. Let me share with you several scotomas I've discovered in my life. They may be the same for you.

"Early in my Air Force career, I attended a seminar where Edwin Friedman was the speaker. In full disclosure, I discovered several of these scotomas in myself because of his talk. Unfortunately, it took most of my adult life to understand the truths. The first blind spot, or leader dysfunction, I had was the belief that to be a good leader I had to be at the front of the pack, solving all the problems."

Paul got up, went to the whiteboard and wrote **DYSFUNCTIONS OF LEADERS**. He then wrote, **1. CONTROL—DECISION MAKER**. "In reality, my job, as I now look back, was to make sure my staff were focused on solving problems. My true job was to make sure the solutions fit the vision, purpose and values of the enterprise. However, at the time I thought it was all up to me. As long as I thought I needed to make all the decisions, I was really reflecting my lack of confidence in my team. Of course, that also reflected a deep insecurity in me. If I weren't making all the decisions, my team wouldn't see me as being in charge. As we both know, the reverse is true. Blink!" Paul then drew three arrows going from **CONTROL—DECISION MAKER** to **LACK OF CONFIDENCE, NEED FOR RECOGNITION**, and **INSECURITY**. I think I'm doing it differently now at CW!. Sure hope so."

Lew smiled. "You are. Don't ever have a doubt about that."

"Thanks, Lew. Always the encourager." Paul held up his hand, palm forward. "If this side is a leader who thinks he or she must make all the decisions and thus have a deluded sense they are in control—" He flipped his hand. "—the backside of that is allowing immaturity to rule." Paul wrote, **2. IMMATURITY**.

DYSFUNCTIONS OF LEADERS

LACK OF CONFIDENCE

(1) CONTROL—DECISION MAKER → NEED FOR RECOGNITION

(2) IMMATURITY → INSECURITY

"I've now realized the greatest threat to any organization lies in weak leaders who allow an organization to adapt to its immature members while the person in charge is still trying to micro-manage. You will never get the best solutions from control management or immaturity. The genius of leadership is in knowing when to lead by being out front and when to lead by cheering, asking questions and prodding the team forward."

"Wait a minute, Paul. Can you give me an example of what you mean? I think I represent the first part of that last comment."

"Let's say you asked one of your service teams to complete a time-sensitive project and they're on track to miss the deadline due to turf-wars, over-planning, bickering and poor collaborative communication. In frustration, and due to collective immaturity, you take over the project, burn the midnight oil and deliver the project with minutes to spare."

"You got a GoPro camera hidden in my office? I think you made your point."

Lew let out a belly laugh. "Paul, I feel an amen coming on, but I'll restrain myself. Can't tell you the number of times at Banner Oil I tried to fix other staff members' problems caused by their immaturity. Then there were those caused by my own immaturity. I've got the scars from both."

Paul continued. "Well, Lew, it sounds like you've traveled the same road as Jason and I. I know you'll both agree with me when I say I am deeply disturbed and yet not surprised how much immaturity linked with impotent power rules businesses, churches and politics. We all recognize the integrity of an enterprise can be no greater than the lived-out integrity and maturity of its leader. Where the blind spot comes in is, we believe we're being tolerant and fair-minded and paying attention to detail, but we're completely failing as leaders."

"Wait a minute, Paul," said Jason putting his hands up. "When the team is acting immature, you aren't saying I just step back and let the chaos rule, are you?"

"Good point. No. What I'm saying is, you don't react to their immaturity. Let me ask you. What would you do?"

"As I'm growing through my time with Lew, I'd say, first, I don't get dragged into their immaturity. Second, I encourage the team by demonstrating and illustrating mature behavior. Third, I call it out when I see it, one-on-one, with a timeline for change. I think the last thing is, I'd let staff know if there is dysfunction in the team. Then I'd make resources available to resolve it and, if necessary due to timelines, make the decision—but not do the work."

"Good thinking, listening and learning," said Paul "But what do you do if the source of the immaturity is you?"

"Ouch. I haven't used these tools in the past, but I presume that's where periodic 360-degree assessments, climate surveys and team building coaching come in. Obviously, having a mentor like Lew is key."

"Here's another one." Paul stepped back to the whiteboard and wrote, **3. PEACEKEEPING**.

DYSFUNCTIONS OF LEADERS

1. CONTROL- DECISION MAKER → LACK OF CONFIDENCE
→ NEED FOR RECOGNITION
→ INSECURITY

2. IMMATURITY

3. PEACEKEEPING

"Attempts at peacekeeping by the leader lead to the third scotoma. I've discovered a contented organization can only be found in that brief moment before all hell breaks loose. What fosters a culture of rewarding the immature malcontents is that we tend to promote and reward the soothers and the peacekeeping managers over those who have learned to use the tension of personalities for greater productivity and creativity. In my experience, peacekeeping is the contagion of organizational unhealthiness." Paul looked back at the whiteboard and tapped, **PEACEKEEPING**.

"Wait a minute." Jason had a thought he didn't want to pass by. "Jesus said peacemakers are blessed. Are you saying that's not true?"

"No, I said peacekeepers, not peacemakers. Huge difference. Besides, my take on that is, I believe Jesus was talking about making peace with God. Beyond that, tension is not the absence of peace. It's in the loss of trust where you find the absence of peace—on earth. The way I look at it, peacekeeping is managing. Peacemaking is leadership. The reality is, there is far more peacekeeping in most dysfunctional organizations than tyranny. Don't get me wrong, both are destructive.

"When peacekeeping falls short, then enters another scotoma. It's the belief that when we encounter problems, all we need to do is try harder and get more information." Paul wrote, **4 TRY HARDER**, and, **5. MORE DATA**.

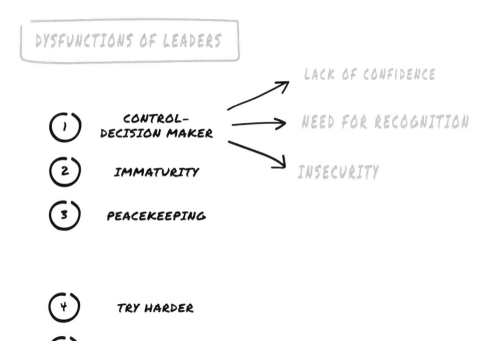

DYSFUNCTIONS OF LEADERS

1. CONTROL-DECISION MAKER
2. IMMATURITY
3. PEACEKEEPING
4. TRY HARDER
5. MORE DATA

LACK OF CONFIDENCE

NEED FOR RECOGNITION

INSECURITY

"Let me explain what I mean. As North Americans, our culture is to build and fix. That's our frontier cultural legend. It's just that some problems should not and cannot be fixed."

Jason furrowed his eyebrows and narrowed his eyelids, putting a puzzled look on his face. "Hold on. Some problems shouldn't be solved? Can you give me an example?"

"Certainly, although each of these is up for argument. But for example, in the work we do, we work toward eliminating poverty.

Yet Jesus said the poor would be with us always. We'll always have violence—whether that's in the home or on the street. We'll always have alcohol and other drug abuse as a way to anesthetize difficult situations and poor decisions and as a way to greedily make money on the backs of the desperate. It's a part of our brokenness outside of Christ. In my opinion, Presidents Johnson and Nixon should never had declared war on poverty and drugs. They are unwinnable wars, and it becomes political jingoism when we think we can win."

Lew put up a hand. "Permit me to interrupt you, Paul, and tell both of you a story I think perfectly illustrates this point, particularly of trying to get more data. I don't think either of you have heard this one. Abraham Wald was a mathematician who fled Hungary on the heels of the Nazi occupation. He landed in England and went to work for the US Army Air Force, studying the flak and bullet damage from returning aircraft to determine where to add armor to best protect the bombers while on bombing raids. Wald made a composite map of a B-17 fuselage showing where the bombers took the most hits. He then recommended the Air Force place armor where there were no holes. You could predict the initial reaction to such a contradictory idea. Yet Wald persisted and made his point. The reasoning? Bombers and crew who never made it home sustained damage in the unmarked areas. These were their most vulnerable points on the aircraft. All the bullet and flak holes on bombers that made it home were irrelevant because the bombers survived. Sometimes we look for data in all the wrong places. Or we take data and make all the wrong assumptions and interpretations.

"What I've come to realize is, successful projects succeed for a multitude of reasons, many unrelated to or in spite of a leader's effort. Sometimes we waste time and effort patching up the survivors while ignoring the most vulnerable who never made it home. This story has helped me to look for the most vulnerable places in any project or team. Often, they aren't where you'd first expect."

"Man, I hate it when my recent past comes flashing before my eyes," said Jason as he tapped his fist to his forehead. "One of the things I'm beginning to realize as a recovering control freak is that I use data as a tool of my control."

Paul nodded. "Data is dangerous when not contained within boundaries. Too often in my search for certitude—derived from data, information and options—I focused on *trailing* indicators, not *leading* indicators. Not a good thing when we're trying to keep ahead of China on aircraft technology."

"Why haven't I seen that before? To manage, I just need to know my trailing indicators. But to lead, I've got to know what my leading indicators are saying as well as my trailing indicators."

Paul smiled. "You're right on, Jason."

"Remember the other scripture I gave for today about Joshua?" Lew interjected. "Where Joshua first showed up in the Bible in a big way was as a part of a team of twelve sent to spy out the land God had promised them. Ten saw it by exaggerating their trailing indicators. 'We are too few. They are too big. They have fortified cities.' Joshua and Caleb saw it from the perspective of leading indicators—the promise of God. Land flowing with milk and honey and luscious fruit.

"Any ideas on how that looks at New Horizons?" asked Lew.

"I see budget data, month-end reports, most staff meetings and 90 percent of the board agenda keying off trailing indicators."

Lew raised his eyebrows, dropped his chin and peered over his eyeglasses. "Kind of like standing aft on a ship, looking at the wake and navigating over the horizon, huh?"

"Okay, so check me out. Leading indicators at New Horizons would be anticipated caseload, staffing potential to meet that caseload, contingency plans, budget trends and predictions and new funding resources. Right?"

"Exactly," said Paul, turning back to the whiteboard. "If you, as the leader, spend your time and effort focusing on leading indicators, it will keep you from the sixth scotoma, Meddling."

Lew scooted back his chair. "Gentlemen, if you would excuse me, I need a break. When we come back, I think it would be good for Jason to sum up where we've been as we wrap up the last two scotomas. It's two isn't it, Paul?"

"Yes and yes."

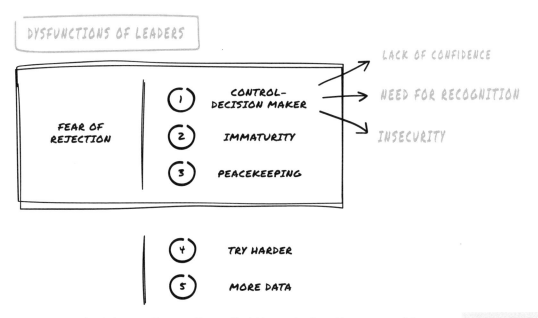

"Okay, Jason, so where were we?" asked Lew.

"I feel like a student in a one-room schoolhouse with two of the best teachers in the region. As I see it, the first three scotomas represent extreme unhealthiness. The leader is insecure and thinks managing by not making mistakes is leading. That's being a control freak and making all the decisions. Problem is, both the leader and the team are immature in their identity and practices."

"Good listening, let me put that on the board." smiled Paul. "You mention that a fear is at the root. Do you think that was a fear of failure?"

DYSFUNCTIONS OF LEADERS

LACK OF CONFIDENCE

NEED FOR RECOGNITION

INSECURITY

FEAR OF REJECTION

1 CONTROL–DECISION MAKER

2 IMMATURITY

3 PEACEKEEPING

4 TRY HARDER

5 MORE DATA

"I don't know. For me those first three dysfunctions were driven more by my fear of rejection. It was the sick addiction to approval that I needed. Sure, I was afraid of failure, but I think that came out in the next two dysfunctions."

"How was that?" asked Paul.

"Almost as great as my fear of rejection was my fear of failure. That's where I tried harder, drove harder, became irritated and demanding as I needed more data to make sure I wasn't going to be wrong. Because if I was wrong, then I'd also lose relationship. Complex, huh?"

"Aren't we all," interjected Lew, delighted to see two of his protégés discovering truth without his effort.

Paul added, **FEAR OF FAILURE** to the left of the dysfunctions of Try Harder and More Data.

"That leads the person in the responsibility seat to dive into work, ignoring the dysfunction by trying harder and looking for more data to justify a failing strategy. I guess you could call that looking for success in all the wrong places."

"I think you've got two more dysfunctions, if I'm not mistaken," prodded Lew, trying to keep the conversation moving. "Could you bring your chart up to date?"

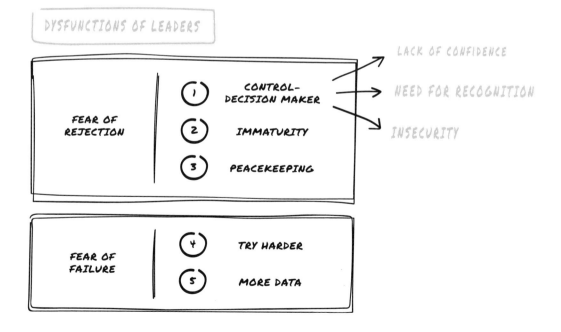

"You're right, Lew; there are two more scotomas of dysfunction. As I try harder and search for more data, the motivation is to find the reason for our problems outside of me as the leader."

"And can I assume there is a fear behind those as well?" offered Jason.

"Yes, good observation. And the last two are examples of what creatures do when the aircraft is going down. When we, as a team, catch the whiff of failure, we start creating enemies to deflect blame and concoct stories of self-justification, leading to the next scotoma of leader dysfunction—Meddling."

"Are you going to give an example, Paul?" asked Jason.

"Yes. I found in my own experience that the key to leader presence instead of manager presence is the ability to maintain objective distance. At RJ Metals, in the beginning, I couldn't keep my fingers out of what we were doing. The worse we did, the more I got into the detail. I thought I was contributing great ideas. After all, I was in charge. I was hired for my technical capacity, right? I loved what I did, and I wanted so badly to be a part of the projects with the operational team. The problem was, I was the leader. The more I kept my fingers in the project, the less ownership the team had and the less view I had of the big picture."

Paul wrote, **MEDDLING**, on the whiteboard.

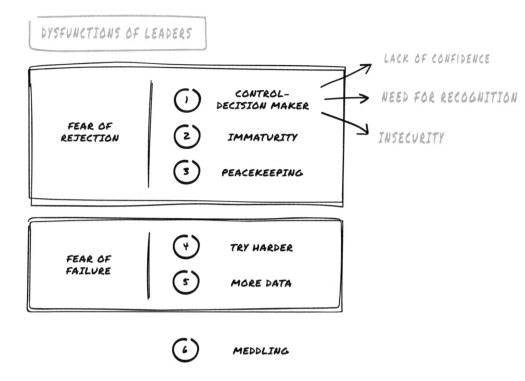

DYSFUNCTIONS OF LEADERS

LACK OF CONFIDENCE

NEED FOR RECOGNITION

INSECURITY

FEAR OF REJECTION

1. CONTROL-DECISION MAKER
2. IMMATURITY
3. PEACEKEEPING

FEAR OF FAILURE

4. TRY HARDER
5. MORE DATA

6. MEDDLING

"How is this different from the Control-Decision maker blind spot?" asked Jason.

"The motivation is different. With Meddling, at least for me, it was a fear of irrelevance and my lack of tangible significance."

Jason finished his soda as he pondered that thought. "I still don't see the difference between that and a fear of rejection. Help me out."

"Permit me to tell you about the last dysfunction of leaders, and then I'll explain. My meddling came out of my identity being tied to the significance of the product rather than the people I was responsible for. I don't know about you, but when I build something, I feel useful. In the past, I had to have my fingers into the business to feel useful and important, and that always leads to meddling."

"How did you get past that one?"

"Interestingly, by learning to ask powerful questions. Not the, *Did you think about this?* and *What about that,* all the while meddling and insulting their intelligence and ability at the same time. Instead, I learned how to ask probing and growth questions like, *Tell me how you got to this point. What did you learn in the process? What can we leverage as* we go forward in other projects? *What questions and ideas didn't make the final stage? Why was that? What are some ways we can approach this from a different angle? How can I help you?* These questions demonstrated my curiosity and interest in the person, not the product. These are the questions that test the depth of a team's thinking, not questioning whether they have any great thoughts.

"My role as leader means never letting go of the big question, *'How does this contribute to our purpose and our mission?'* See the difference?" Paul stepped back from the board. "When I meddle, I want to get back to my old role as cook instead of being responsible for the quality of the dining experience. Make sense?"

"More than you want to know, Paul. More than you want to know," said Jason, slowly shaking his head.

"If control, immaturity, peacekeeping, trying harder, getting more data, or meddling don't render me impotent as a leader, I have one more. It's **GROUP THINK—TOGETHERNESS**." Paul wrote it on the whiteboard.

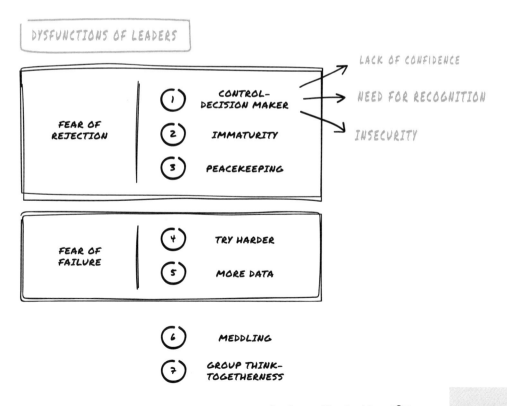

"I'm going to need an explanation of that one too," said Jason.

"When a leader is insecure in his own sense of presence and identity—in other words, suffering from small-soul syndrome—the best way to feel secure is to get others to agree with you and make it a mutual admiration society."

"Sounds a lot like celebrity."

"Group think-togetherness feeds celebrity. I can only be a celebrity to those who blindly follow and drink my Kool-Aid. Keep in mind, if I'm a leader, I have positional, economic and relational power over you. As a leader, if I'm insecure, then you as a team member are also insecure in that relationship. What happens? I get you to agree with me whether you really do or not. It's too risky for you to challenge the completeness of my thought. I can exercise my power. Group think is not the only problem of most organizations; it's leader think as well."

"What's the fear category?"

"I think it's irrelevance. The fear of irrelevance is the withdrawal sickness of celebrity. The way I counteract that is to begin the manipulation dance of getting everyone into lock-step with my ideas. The best way to do that is to trick everyone to think they are the outsiders and they are heretics."

"Man, you're scaring me and nailing me. But don't you think it's important that you and your team all have the same beliefs?"

"Great question. On the key mission, purpose and values points, of course shared beliefs are critical. But this is also where diversity of view reflects respect for the person and keeps mission from becoming unintended dogma. Respect should be the foundation to ask questions, not dictate answers. If I don't properly respond to questions and challenges about who we are and how we're doing our business, we're going down a very dangerous road."

"So, Paul, how do you bring divergent questions and ideas into group conversation?"

"Great question. Here's how I do it. When someone comes off the wall with an idea or a thought, I have two questions. One should be for that person to explain how that thought fits into or properly challenges our foundational purpose, vision and mission."

"And the second question is?"

"I simply ask the person to describe how our doing business would look if we incorporated that thought or question. It's what I call relational jujitsu. I use the power of the person's concern and use it as energy. I can either go head-to-head, or I can capitalize on their concern to find a better solution."

Lew spoke up. "Can I jump in here, Paul? In any enterprise, and I personally think that includes church, doubt has an important place. Not at the head of the table, but at the table of discussion. When I become doctrinaire in my beliefs, I better be absolutely correct on all points. Know anyone like that? I sure don't."

"Even my esteemed friend, Lew, here, gets it wrong every once in a while," laughed Paul as he poked at Lew.

Lew smiled and nodded. "This blind spot of herding is all too common. In times of tension, the tendency of a team is to draw together in fear of being left outside the pen when the gates are closed. Here's the apparent contradiction in the dysfunctions of meddling and group think. While the team is reacting to the fear of irrelevance, stepping outside the pen is what the leader needs to do. In times of tension, great leaders find time to make distance from the team in order to have a clear view."

Jason was eager to add his thought. "Jesus did that on several occasions—made distance, that is. We have to be so careful because at times the wisdom of collective leadership tends to reflect the lowest acceptable common denominator— the practical rather than the ideal. In other words, if we're not careful, the need to pull together for comfort and then squelch any contrary thought or opinion makes us collectively more stupid. Re-read the gospels from the point of view of the disciples as a growing team. They failed to get Jesus' teachings more often than they did get them until after the crucifixion. It took Christ's reappearance and the evidence and presence of the Holy Spirit for the reality to sink in. Think about this. What would be different today if Jesus had relied on the disciples' advice? Scary thought, huh?"

Paul pointed the marker at Jason. "Exactly. In times of tension the effective leader actually promotes differentiation rather than collective consensus. In other words, leaders who feel drawn to consensus will possibly increase the likelihood the decision will be disastrous. Don't misunderstand: wise counsel is essential. But leading through counselors is disastrous. Do you see the difference? Sometimes the effective leader must become contrarian. That can only happen with a high level of mutual respect and trust."

Paul wrote **FEAR OF IRRELEVANCE** on the chart, handed the markers back to Lew and sat down. "Those are the times when leading, by intention, gets very, very lonely. There you are, Jason. The seven dysfunctions of a leader."

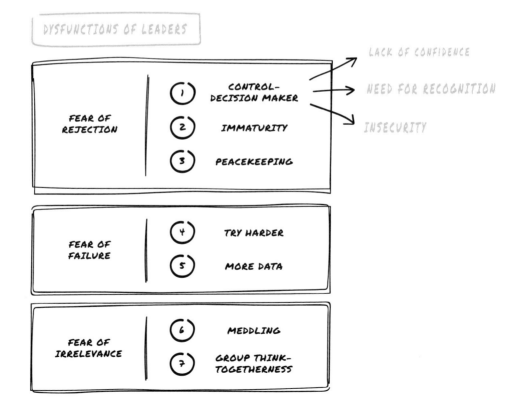

"Paul, can I add two thoughts to your list?" asked Jason, more as a statement than a question. "First, I'm seeing, like Wald, that I should be doing the opposite in each of these areas."

"Explain."

"In response to my fear of rejection, I need to become more bold in my relationships while building an even stronger environment of trust."

"What about the fear of failure?" asked Lew, smiling at Jason's deep realizations.

"I need to confront the fear with taking more risks that could result in failure. I've got to learn to put armor on the plane while it's in flight."

"And your fear of being isolated and alone?"

"For me, it's getting used to being alone. Not lonely. Alone. I've got to become as comfortable being with me as I am with others."

Lew smiled, contented with seeing growth in his friend. "Good thoughts, Jason. In my experience, God usually doesn't speak to me in a crowd. That still, small voice needs solitude. A good discipline to cultivate."

Paul looked at his watch. "One last thing before we wrap up this conversation on leaders and leadership. I don't think we should ever forget who accomplishes the true work of mission and purpose. Its followers. Leaders are essential, but it's followers who change the world. Here at Compassion Works!, I'm responsible for over 400 volunteers. I have no power over them. We pay them nothing. How am I able to get them to respond to a natural disaster, to come in for training on their own time and to become trainers themselves? Why do they do what they do? Because they believe in a cause and they trust me to help make that cause their experience. Simple as that.

"Jason, I hope this has been helpful to you. I know you got a boatload of information, and I said more information doesn't solve problems. And it won't. The only way you are going to solve problems is when you internalize what we've talked about and allow your soul to take in what's been nourishment for it to grow while disciplining your human spirit. That growth produces

Q.

What are your leader dysfunctions and fears?

integrity, and in the end, gravitational influence is about the integrity and health of your soul."

Paul smiled, "I'm quite sure that's not the first time you heard that about your soul and human spirit. It won't be the last either."

As the three walked out of the conference room, Lew put his hand on Paul's shoulder. "Paul, thanks so much for taking the time to meet with us today. You take care," said Lew.

"You as well. And, Jason, take care of my friend here, and don't let him get himself into any more trouble than he already is in. Okay?" Paul laughed as he teased with Lew. "I am looking forward to finding more ways we can partner with New Horizons as you continue to be a visionary leader for it."

And David shepherded them with integrity of heart; with skillful hands he led them

Psalm 78:72

REFLECTION QUESTIONS

1. *In your responsibilities at work, what percent of the day are you leading and what percent are you managing? What about your home or ministry responsibilities? Are those percentages achieving the results you want?*

2. *Using Abraham Wald's discovery, describe an experience where you now see you failed to focus on protecting the most vulnerable parts of a project or team. What were the consequences?*

3. *Paul Ishii talks about the scotomas of leader dysfunction. In his first grouping were three dysfunctions centering around the fear of rejection. In your experiences, describe how a fear of rejection of you as a person or your ideas leads to control and needing to be the decision maker. How does a lack of confidence, a need for recognition and/or insecurity play into that dysfunction?*

4. *How does the immaturity of the team or the leader feed a fear of rejection? What have you found to be the consequence of leader or team immaturity?*

5. *What in your experience is an example of how a fear of rejection leading to peacekeeping behaviors resulted in dysfunction?*

6. *When the team isn't performing well and there is a fear of failure in your mind and/or the team's, describe how trying harder and trying to gain more data has actually produced the failure you feared.*

7. *Describe a personal experience or an observed situation where you've seen the fear of irrelevance result in meddling or group-think.*

CHAPTER 9

Defining
Leaders

LEADERSHIP
is the craft of a leader

*Have confidence in your leaders and
submit to their authority, because
they keep watch over you as those who
must give an account. Do this so that
their work will be a joy, not a burden,
for that would be of no benefit to you.*

Hebrews 13:17

J ason turned into the parking lot of Lew's office. "I've
worked with Paul, but I didn't know his background and
the depth of his understanding of leading. Lew, I need a
little more of your time."

"Sure. Come on in." As they stepped into Lew's office, Lew
asked, "What's on your mind?"

"Still processing. I guess the big one is how significant it is
for a leader to lead and not just manage or, worse yet, manage
and think it's leading."

"I agree," said Lew brewing a fresh mug of coffee. While
waiting for the mug to fill, he slipped on his cardigan, searched for
his pipe and found it in the left pocket. "What else?"

"I'm thinking of your story about Abraham Wald and
merging it with how contrarian a leader Jesus was and how
contrarian Jesus expects us to live."

"For instance?"

"You know what I mean: he said, 'Do you want a life? Lose it.
Want to be rich? Give all your possessions away. You want to be
first? Be last. You want to rule? Serve.' After our time with Paul,

that is making more sense. Like Wald discovered, perhaps our most vulnerable spiritual spots are where we least suspect and expect them."

"Interesting point," said Lew as he sat in his favorite green chair, found his tobacco humidor and filled the pipe bowl. "How do you think Paul might be applying that idea?"

"All of us seek for or after a leader. I know I do. It's our human nature. What the principle says and I'm now really beginning to get is, when we find a leader, we progressively fall in love with that person. What I missed was understanding that as followers, we too are in some relationship of influence. We aren't only takers; we desire to contribute too as we learn under the influence of a leader. That means as leaders and followers, we operate from a position of mutual trust. Followers allow leaders to ignite emotions, passions and drive while encouraging beliefs. What I knew but didn't really live out was that if I, as a leader, violate that bond of trust, the wound goes deep, to the soul."

Jason noticed that Lew was drifting into his contemplative zone: he had lit his pipe, grabbed his coffee with a touch of cocoa power, and leaned back in his chair.

"My friend, here's my understanding of the nature of a leader. First of all, and you know this already, leaders have the capacity to touch, enrich or wound the mystical essence called our souls. So above all else, leaders must be spiritually centered and protectors of the mass of our souls. To do that we've got to be settled. We have to have come to a place of influence having resolved the questions of our personal identity and meaning in relationships before we go too far into the lives of others. I think what helps is to possess three mindsets all at the same time. Yes, I suggest you write this down or, if you must, type it into your tablet or smartphone or whatever you brought in."

Lew set his pipe down on the ceramic pipe holder, adjusted his round tortoise-shell glasses and held up his left thumb. "First is to have the mindset of a servant. As you know, in Jesus' time servants were at the bottom of the social ladder. Lower than slaves. Servants were day laborers and had no protection of the household, as a slave would have. Often they were paying off a debt with their servitude. As a Christ-following leader, we are servants to Christ and to the cause and the people we willingly serve. With a mindset of a servant, we realize we have no rights and a debt so great it can never be repaid, and yet it has been cancelled nonetheless."

Lew then held up his thumb and index finger. "Second, another mindset is that of a slave. The concept of one human owned as chattel by another is repugnant and evil. Yet the mindset of a spiritual slave is altogether different. Like the slave of ancient days, we have given over our personal liberty to act independently. We choose instead to become slaves of righteousness. To be a slave is to be committed for life—not only to God but also to those we serve. In the context of leadership, to become a slave is to have an attitude that our life is not our own. Remember Romans 6:22? *But now that you have been set free from sin and have become slaves of God, the benefit you reap leads to holiness, and the result is eternal life.* Leaders who willingly choose to be slaves of righteousness add value to all relationships without expectation of return."

Lew then held up his thumb, index and middle fingers. "The third mindset as leaders is, we are stewards of the process of righteous behavior. Core to knowing the mindset of a steward is understanding the role of trust. A steward acts in the stead of the owner. Stewards manage in trust the great resources of the master's estate. Paul the Apostle, also in Romans, said not only are we slaves to righteousness, we are also instruments of righteousness. There is a process of righteous influence, and as leaders, we are keepers and practitioners of that process. Leaders are in some sense the stewards of the followers' tender souls.

"Here's a thought to consider. As stewards of the process we are also agents of glue: both adhesive and cohesive."

"Please explain, Lew, as I know you will."

"You see, as leaders, we are the cohesive glue holding together diverse people with diverse passions and desires and directions. Leaders keep the dynamics of diversity—the very energy pushing outwards—bound together through the systematic reinforcement of shared values and beliefs and a unified purpose and mission. That's cohesion. Yet, as leaders, we are also adhesive agents. We bind together our tribe of followers through the sticky nature of our personal character, personality, and capacity to express love. Our stickiness spreads among the tribe, and they too become agents of glue. Remember the fourth gravity truth?"

"I do. Leadership is the leader's craft."

"So like in any craft or trade, the quality of the workmanship defines the identity of the worker. A good carpenter is not a good carpenter because of sincerity or even goodness of heart. A worker of wood has the reputation of a good carpenter because the quality of the craft is good. So it is with leaders. We want and—even more so—need leaders to be of good character. However, having a caring and pure heart does not make a leader with impact. It is the practiced craft of leadership, including the quality of goodness, making a leader effective."

Jason felt like Lew wanted him to add something, but all he could think of was, "You're right."

Lew got up from his couch and went to the whiteboard. "Here's all you need to know. One warning. It will take a lifetime to live it out." Lew wrote, **LEADERSHIP IS A PERSONAL CALLING AND A COMMITMENT TO GOODNESS AND PERSONAL GROWTH.** He put five bullet points underneath and sat down. Lew picked up his pipe, stoked the smoldering fibers with a couple of fast draws and slowly blew out the smoke.

Jason broke the silence. "You say leadership is a personal calling. Do you mean like being called into pastoral ministry?"

"Not quite. To me it seems leadership is not a selective calling. I think when you accept Christ into your life, you also accept the call of influence. It comes as a package. Then as you marry, have children, become a worker, and become a supervisor, you are exercising the power of God in you through the Holy Spirit."

"Okay, I get it. Some are called to be leaders of two and some, 2000, yet for all, our vocation is influence."

"Exactly. How many you influence is irrelevant. The fact is, if you are a Christian, you are called to influence and leadership. Then it gets real personal. A personal calling is a centered, seeking, clear personal identity in the soul revealed through the Holy Spirit. As you seek, you will find what it is you are to do to influence others for the kingdom of God."

Lew pointed his pipe towards the whiteboard. "Second is this commitment to goodness. If your soul-mass is increasing your evidence of goodness—which is really the goodness of God—it means you have to be committed to growing your soul-mass."

"I would presume that is an example of the transforming work of the Holy Spirit."

"You are presuming correctly. For me, a commitment to goodness is evidenced in Christ-like behavior—which is my authenticity—due to Christ-like nature—which is my genuineness—as a slave to righteousness. Sound familiar?"

"Yeah, we talked about this earlier—slave, servant, steward. You don't behave to be Christ-like. Rather, because you are Christ-like, you behave that way. It's the difference between effort and evidence. Between content and consequence. It's the faith and works paradigm that James addressed in his letter."

"Exactly. Now, the third element is like the second. It is a commitment to personal growth. We owe it to those who influence us to continue to become more Christ-like in how we serve. Growth is the effort. Goodness is the evidence."

Lew got up and walked to the whiteboard. "Okay, that's what's going on inside the leader. What's the output? Let me give you the briefest version I can. An effective leader ..." Lew picked up a dry-erase and began filling in the bullets.

LEADERSHIP IS A PERSONAL CALLING AND A COMMITMENT TO GOODNESS AND PERSONAL GROWTH. AN EFFECTIVE LEADER:

- **CULTIVATES A SHARED VISION,**

"That means the leader has a focus and a sense of destiny—personal and organizational—leading to intentional effort."

- **INVESTS IN LOVING RELATIONSHIPS,**

"The orientation of the leader as a servant is to energize people for ministry and community rather than use them for selfish objectives. Remember, this is about *being* in relationship, not *doing* relationship."

- **CREATES AND MAINTAINS OPTIMUM ENVIRONMENTS,**

"Like Moses, the leader uses the toolbox of influence. What would be some tools that come to your mind?"

"You know, Lew, in my experience it would be tools like the properties of insight and vision."

"How does that work for you, the leader?"

"To me, insight involves the ability to anticipate the thoughts and thinking process of another. Vision, of course, is having the big view of why we're doing what we're doing and reminding the team of it."

"Anything else in the toolbox?"

"I think a leader needs to be flexible—unlike my past several years. I'm beginning to realize the more I have a clear vision, the more pathways I see to get there. I also feel leaders must always be in submission."

"To what or whom?"

"Of course, to Christ, but also to overseers like my board. I think we also need the attitude of a servant, like you said, toward those we lead and toward the constituency we serve. I think what feeds accountability is the openness to disclose or reveal who you really are and to give and receive feedback without defensiveness."

"That's an impressive list."

"Oh, two other things come to mind. The ability to successfully resolve conflicts and to actually embrace healthy conflict as a way to get the best out of the team. As I'm discovering with your help, good friend, I need to utilize the system of gravitational attraction and influence to keep the diverse people gathering for a common purpose moving in the same direction."

"Good processing. And as we've discovered, one way the leader does this best is by asking powerful questions."

- **FOSTERS VIRTUOUS PRACTICES**

"The leader does this by having well-grounded values, systematizing and reflecting godly virtue and thus reflecting the mind of Christ. Virtuous practices flow from a healthy soul. And finally:"

- **EMPOWERS TEAMS TO SUCCESSFULLY TOLERATE, EMBRACE, NAVIGATE AND ARBITRATE SURPRISE, TENSION AND PARADOX.**

"The leader influences and empowers team members through trust-building and personal development to have the confidence to respond to any number of scenarios with confidence and clarity."

Lew put the marker down, went back to his chair and picked up his pipe. "Jason, sometime when you have time, take the words, *tolerate, embrace, navigate* and *arbitrate* and factor them off of *surprise, tension* and *paradox*. In other words what would tolerating surprise look like? What would navigating paradox or tension look like? How would you arbitrate surprise or tension? You get the picture? As you draw on your experience and acquired knowledge and draw in more, ruminate and regurgitate it over and again."

"Thanks for the earthy analogy."

"My pleasure. So where are you at?"

"Man, Lew, where to start? Here's a few really big pieces. I think of Jesus' words. One is from Luke, I think it's 12:48, *From*

everyone who has been given much, much will be demanded; and from the one who has been entrusted with much, much more will be asked.
The other is from John in chapter 15, where Jesus talks about his relationship with the disciples, and he says, *Greater love has no one than this: to lay down one's life for one's friends.* Bottom line for me—to be a leader is very costly, and like you said, it first has to be about me so that I can make it not about me.

"In that light, influence through my leadership is my personal calling. I can only accomplish that with an internal quality of goodness and personal growth. If I'm effective, I've infected others with my personal vision made possible through investing in relationships grown in optimum environments. The lubricant of caring relationships in optimum environments is through fostering and modeling virtuous practices so that people are better able to tolerate, embrace, navigate and arbitrate surprise, tension and paradox."

"Wow. That was a brain-full. You got it. Now spend the rest of your life making it real." Lew paused, looked at Jason with a slight smile. "Can I make a personal observation?"

"Sure."

"When we first started meeting, you appeared to be mad at God as well as the Church. You felt your trust had been violated in both places. Your cynicism is transforming. You are more open to talk about the things of God without a sarcastic dig. It's sounding more and more like not only do you have the scripture but the scripture has you. Nice to see a work in progress."

Jason replied, "Thanks for the observation. If we were calling this a journey, I'd say that was a milepost checkpoint."

"Are you ever going to let that one go?" Lew laughed.

"Seriously, Lew, I think we—I—need to be reminded that as leaders we do life together. This isn't a transactional relationship. It's got to be a transformational relationship, eventually leading to an empowering relationship. The 'duh' on this one is that leadership requires relationships. Building relationships for shared vision, purpose and culture is our craft. Our craft mark as an effective leader is the formation and reformation of organizational and individual purpose. It happens in the context of doing life together."

"Excellent processing. Anything else?"

"One more thing—and this isn't the last; it's only the last one I can think of right now—is that when we lead well, we add value to the community we serve in many different ways. When you put leadership into the context of craft, it creates great pictures."

"Such as?"

"Such as effective leadership leaving its maker's mark. It's not a logo or even the initials or name of a leader. I think the craft mark of effective leadership, like I said, is relationships: it's an increased value in everything the craft of the leader touches."

"Let me interrupt, Jason. In your mind, what does that craft mark look like?"

"Organizations are stronger and healthier. They look out instead of in. They look to the future instead of the past. They are growing in numbers and in impact. We see the value of effective leadership in the stability of ordered chaos. The value of good leadership is people attracted to the kingdom of God. The craft mark is people."

"You are so right on. In the end it's not the programs we've built that make the difference; it's our influencing opportunity."

"I remember a wise and older seminary professor I had—older but probably no wiser than you—who told me about intaglio."

"You mean the printing process?"

"Yes. As you probably know, it's the family of printing and printmaking technique in which the image is incised into a surface, and the incised line or sunken area holds the ink. It is the direct opposite of a relief print, where the ink is on a raised surface. Is that not what describes the process of spiritual formation? How often we want a relief print of Jesus who conforms to our image, when God's intention is that we should be incised with the *imago Christo*. Then the sunken area can hold the ink: his blood for my redemption."

"Well, well. Sounds like you *have* been listening."

With a smile of satisfaction, Lew said, "Very good, Jason. It's obvious you are extracting the gold from our time together and integrating it with your foundation of others who influenced you. Methinks you are not as cynical as you would like to appear."

"Back to drilling, huh? Thanks, Lew. Coming from you, that means a lot. Okay, just one more big 'aha,' and that's the last for today. Too often, I've equated leadership to the one leading many. Yet as I'm seeing, the numbers who seem to follow can't be the sole measure of leadership. As the influence of a leader increases due to growing soul-mass, the imago Christo, the reach of that leader, expands."

"Well, well. Sounds like you have been listening."

With a smile of deep affection, Jason teased. "Listen, oh great soul mentor, you are helping me see that the true craft mark of leadership is found in the quality of my effort. It's in the utility of my leader tools and proportional to the size and density of my soul-mass. And it's found in the satisfaction of those served.

"Can't say it often enough: my time with you has added value to my life. For the first time in a long time, I'm beginning to see the opportunity of contentment in my life. Thanks."

"Jason, you have no idea how much those words bring joy to me. If you get it, you'll live it. You know, for many years I too had a skewed view of leadership. I thought of it as the one leading the many. In reality it is one leading one, repeated as many times as I've got the capacity to influence—and no more."

Lew pointed his pipe at Jason and said, "But in the end, like you said, the only true measure of our leader craft is lives changing for the better because of our influence. It happens in business when the prosperity of the community enlarges due to the presence of godly business leaders faithfully executing their craft. It happens in government when the community is safer and more secure because government leaders were faithful stewards of their legislative mandates. It happens in schools because a teacher cares about the future security and potential of each child they teach. It happens in places of worship because spiritual leaders care for the living while remaining focused on life. That is the measure of effective leadership: the craft of a leader."

"That's really good, Lew. I hope you put it into a book at some time."

"I'm moving in that direction. Speaking about direction, fill me in on your developing insight on followers falling in love with the leader as a condition of gravitational influence."

"I was afraid you weren't going to let me off the hook."

"And?"

"And here's where I'm at on that. My pushback took me to the same spot as the rest of my issues."

"Which is?"

"Which is, my identity was rooted in my works. Challenge my works, you challenge my identity. But because I had control over what I did—my talent, creativity and personality—I felt I had control over my identity. Am I making sense?"

"Feels like you're going in circles but I'm with you. So far, so good. Keep going."

"Up until that Saturday board meeting knocked the props out from under my feet, I thought I had a pretty good handle on who I was, what I did well and the satisfaction I gained from having that sense of security. Yet, deep down inside, I didn't feel that secure. I knew I didn't think as nice as I talked. Behind closed doors and behind people's backs, there were times when I wasn't proud or pleased with my behavior. I'm not sure if I should put this in the present or past tense, since there are still times I feel that way. A phony and an imposter."

"Very insightful, but be careful how aggressively you beat on yourself. If you overheard someone on your team telling a stranger how much they loved you as a friend and leader, how would you feel?"

"Embarrassed and certainly unworthy."

"Here's a part of your homework for our upcoming meetings. I want you to think, meditate and pray about why it is you feel unworthy rather than just undisciplined. And if you've concluded that a changed life is the craft mark of a leader, shouldn't that start with you? Of course you are unworthy to stand before God, the Father, on your own. But you are a worthy child of God. You're the preacher; you know what I'm talking about."

Jason knew Lew was speaking truth he had known for a long time. And he found it interesting how much he was fighting it.

"Our next gravity truth is: LEADERS are defined by their gravitational attraction and radiating influence. Also, before our next conversation I want you to give Jim Oliver a call. I'll text you his number. Tell him you're on the Gravity project, and I suggested you find a time to meet. Jim is an expert on influence and power, since he's Governor Wilson Barlow's Chief of Staff. Call me after you meet, and we'll process the session."

But select capable men from all the people—men who fear God, trustworthy men who hate dishonest gain—and appoint them as officials over thousands, hundreds, fifties and tens.

Exodus 18:21

REFLECTION QUESTIONS

1. *Thinking about the three mindsets of slave, servant, steward, describe when your leading looks like the work of a slave to righteousness. When does it look like when you are a servant to all? How would you describe the differences? What are you doing in your steward identity to be a steward of the process?*

2. *As you reflect on the first part of Lew's definition of leadership, "Leadership is a personal calling and commitment to goodness and personal growth," do you see your role of influence in a specific setting as a calling? If it is a calling, explain what you understand it to be.*

3. *What are evidences in your life of a commitment to goodness and personal growth?*

4. *As a leader/influencer (parent, manager, minister), do you understand the shared vision? What is it?*

5. *What are some examples of investing in loving relationship?*

6. *How do you "create and maintain optimum environments?"*

7. *What are some examples of fostering virtuous practices?*

8. *How are you empowering your influence team to successfully tolerate, embrace, navigate and arbitrate surprise, tension and paradox?*

CHAPTER 10

Influence
and Power

LEADERS ARE
DEFINED BY THEIR
gravitational attraction and radiating influence

Those who walk righteously and speak
what is right, who reject gain from
extortion and keep their hands from
accepting bribes, who stop their ears
against plots of murder and shut their
eyes against contemplating evil—
they are the ones who will dwell on
the heights, whose refuge will be the
mountain fortress. Their bread will be
supplied, and water will not fail them.

Isaiah 33:15–16

"I don't get it, Barlow! I'm the speaker of the house; you're the minority whip, and you're pushing me around like I'm on an ice rink. What kind of power do you have over these legislators?"

Jim Oliver had asked for a meeting at the "D Street House." It was owned by a group of successful Christian business owners. Located two blocks from the Capitol, the two-story Georgian house was used as a neutral place for people to meet outside the bright lights of television reporters and the tweets of freelance bloggers and journalists.

Wilson Barlow was a former litigator with a law firm representing some of the largest oil companies in the U.S. Leaving the high-intensity environment of corporate law, Wilson had returned to his home state, run for a legislative seat and been elected now for his third term.

"Jim, I understand your frustration. A lot of people are expecting you to bring home your party's agenda, and it isn't happening the way you and your party leadership want."

"You bet they're frustrated! And the pressure is on me to

wield the power of the majority party. We're off the record, so tell me, what do you have over the people on my side of the aisle?"

"I'm not sure if I should be flattered or insulted."

"What do you mean?"

"I should be flattered you think I have some power of compulsion or fear or irresistible charm I could dangle over our colleagues. I should be insulted you think I would stoop to that level of coercion. The truth is, I have neither irresistible power nor charm. What I exercise is gravitational attraction and influence."

"Care to fill me in, or is this one of your party's secrets?"

"No power and no secrets, Jim."

"Then what is this ... this gravity or whatever you call it? Are you going weird on me?"

"I'm having lunch with an old friend from my oil days, Lew Merton. I think he can explain it better than I do. I won't buy your vote, so how about your lunch tomorrow?"

"I'm intrigued. How could I not be there?"

Although Jason had lived the state capital for most of his adult life, it had been years since he'd been inside the capitol building. Walking up the steps, he remembered how impressive the building was. Located on a hill overlooking the city, the Capitol was impressive: all granite on the outside, capped by a graceful dome reminiscent of St. Paul's Cathedral in London. Inside, marble was everywhere. The grand staircases, steps and walls were clad in a gray-white marble, while the columns were made of imported pink Italian marble. Contrasting with the stone were gilded light ornaments and chandeliers and massive murals depicting the state's history. The voices of visitors and workers on different floors opening to the rotunda created an echoing din, making any one conversation indistinguishable from another.

Jason had never been in the governor's office. Up to this point in life, there was neither a need nor an opportunity. Politics and government was not the direction Jason intended to go. Through the years, Jason had become cynical about politics, following the same path of his growing cynicism for most other systems, and so he stayed out of the political scene locally and at the state level as well. All the political game-playing, not unlike union negotiations, seemed like war in ultra-slow motion. Instead, Jason focused on doing work where he could see a direct outcome.

On the middle floor stood an open double doorway. Gold leaf on an acid-etched transom window read, "Governor's Office." Inside the cavernous reception room sat a state police cadet at what normally would be the receptionist's desk.

"Sir, may I assist you?"

"Yes, I have an appointment with Mr. Oliver, the Governor's Chief of Staff." *Oh good grief,* thought Jason. *I don't need to tell them who Mr. Oliver is.*

"May I have your name and some identification, please?" The cadet typed something on his computer. "Mr. Oliver will be out shortly, Mr. Cahill. I see he's expecting you. Please feel free to look around. There is coffee in the far corner if you'd like some."

The massive reception room did exactly what it was designed to do—impress visitors. The raised panel wainscoting was oak with a rich green fabric wall covering that reached at least 16 feet to the ceiling. The plaster cove molding jutted out at least 14 inches with elaborate figures of the state flower and state tree woven into the design. The reception area was a museum in itself. There was the ceremonial blanket given to one of the first governors to commemorate the first of a long string of broken promises and agreements with the Native American tribe who had inhabited the very grounds where the capitol complex now sat. There were bowls and figurines given by foreign dignitaries through the years, the usual collection of awards, commemorations and honorary this-and-thats.

This is all very interesting yet somewhat meaningless because there's little that speaks to the character of the people of the state, thought Jason. *Looks like it only speaks to the magnificence of the office of governor. Oh, well. That's politics, I guess,* Jason mused.

Just as Jason was getting comfortable in a leather couch, a warm, friendly and energetic voice called out, "Mr. Cahill, I'm Jim

Oliver. I only have a few minutes between meetings, but come back to my office and let's talk about your Lew assignment."

It was coming from a man about 5' 10", slightly rotund, with a ruddy complexion and a shock of red-gray hair needing a lot of mousse to keep it in place. He looked like a throw-back to the 90's: wing-tip shoes, argyle socks, pin-striped pants, a Brooks Bros. blue striped shirt and suspenders. All that wrapped a flesh-engine running just below the redline.

The fast-paced walk back to Jim's office seemed like a taxi ride in lower Manhattan. Jim began to engage Jason in conversation, only to be constantly interrupted by staffers who had a brief question or Jim introducing Jason: "Hey, I want you to meet my new friend!"

Jim's office wouldn't soon be on the cover of *Tidy Government Offices Monthly*. There was a pile of legislative bills to the left of Jim's desk, binders from various commissions and study committees on the right. The office looked just like Jim—churning and on the edge of combustion. Jim offered Jason a burgundy leather high-backed chair after moving a two-inch binder from the seat. Jim sat in the chair's twin, moving another binder to the side so he could fit in. The chairs seemed a little out of place. These were the kind you'd relax in with a cup of coffee for slow, meandering conversation. Jim's energy didn't seem to allow for that kind of relaxation.

As Jim pulled out his smartphone and texted his admin not to interrupt, he said, "I see you got some coffee from the reception room. Let me know if I can get you anything." Before Jason could think of anything else to order, Jim was on to the next topic.

"So glad to meet you, Jason. And I'm so glad you've connected with Lew. Love that guy! I've been through the process, and so I know where you're at. I can presume you'd reached a crisis in your capacity to be effective. Most people don't come to Lew unless they're in crisis mode. I'm the *Influence versus Power* guy in your journey. I know the gravity truth well. LEADERS are defined by their gravitational attraction and radiating influence."

"You're right, Mr. Oliver. I guess you could say I'm going

through some turbulent times at work, so I appreciate your taking the time to talk with me."

"Feel the power?"

"I'm sorry, Mr. Oliver. I'm not following you?"

"First of all, it's Jim. Mr. Oliver is my father. Second, coming up the steps to the capitol building, you see the massive dome, the ornate brass doors, the marble steps and walls, the massive artwork, the ornamental ostentation—all designed for a single purpose. Same one the Romans had in their architecture. Same one the ancient Christian church had after Constantine. All this stuff is designed to show you, the little people, and the state's enemies, how powerful we are. This isn't to create influence. It's about power. We do it by architecture. Then we do it by laws, traditions, functionaries and what I call the rules of engagement. We do it by hiring enforcement officers and compliance specialists. I could go on for hours. In fact I do. I'm an adjunct professor at the state university on power, politics and the process of governing. But let me get to the point for you and what Lew wants you to see in your time with me. You know my title, Governor's Chief of Staff. But what do you think I really do?"

"I guess I'd call you The Fixer or maybe The Collaborator. You're the lubricant allowing the governor to get his job done."

Jim gave out a belly-laugh and slapped Jason on the knee. "You, my friend, are very insightful. If you ever get tired of directing a nonprofit, I've got some work for you in a very large and truly nonprofit: state government. So, Jason, let's take your metaphor of a lubricant and run with it a bit. What's the nature of my oil?"

"Power?"

"You are 100 percent WRONG!" Jim exclaimed in a loud voice.

Jason reflexively hunched down and looked toward the door, feeling self-conscious that staffers in other rooms may have overheard and thought he was being lectured and called out.

"Don't feel bad. Common mistake. Too common, in fact. I've come to realize the hard way that power is highly unstable as a lubricant. It'll explode like nitroglycerin if not treated gently. Like

Q.

What is your lubricant of leadership?

the nitro in dynamite, the longer you keep it, the more unstable it gets—until the slightest jar, and KER-BOOM!" Jim's eyes lit up, and his arms flew into the air as if an explosion had happened under his chair.

"The truth is, my lubricating oil isn't power. It's influence. I am the arbiter of influence. Governor Barlow has all the power he needs. He's leading the majority party in the House, most of the populous counties have office holders in our party and there are enough laws, commissions, executive orders and appointments to keep him in power for a long time.

"But the governor has determined that is not going to be his base. Sounds crazy, huh? I know, and we've had enough pundits tell us we're foolish to even think otherwise. But here's his governing philosophy: to rule from power means you have to possess something other people want or need. Freedom, land, wealth, prosperity through jobs, armies and loyalty are some of the accoutrements of power. And, of course, in a democratic society, votes and money also represent the currency, the exchange for those elements of power. Every politician I know is holding office because they love either the feeling of power or the sense they can actually accomplish something good. And, trust me, Jason. Run as fast as you can from the politician who thinks or promises you they can serve you better if they only had a little more power."

"If I may re-ask your question: what do you see as your role?"

"I like that. You won't leave a question incompletely answered. Here's my job description in a nutshell: I'm here to help Governor Barlow keep his feet firmly planted on the side of influence instead of power. Power is simple, and it's seductive. And if I don't keep a vigilant eye on keeping our course on the influence track, I've failed the governor. Simple job description. I just wish the day was as simple as my task!"

"I know what you mean," said Jason.

"Good. Now let me back up a bit. Here's a little history to put this whole story in perspective. A number of years ago Governor Barlow was a litigator for a major law firm out of Houston, Texas. In the process of negotiation for a drilling project, he and Lew connected. I think Lew was with Banner Oil or Energon at the time. Anyway, they struck up a friendship, and in due course Lew *infected* Wilson with his Principle of Gravitational Attraction and Influence. Ever since then, Wilson has never conducted business the same way."

"It's a good infection."

Jim smiled. "That it is."

"How did you get connected to Governor Barlow?"

"Well, Wilson and I became friends when we both served in the legislature—young hotshots in opposing parties. I was Speaker of the House, and he was the minority whip for his caucus. First few times we met, we went head-to-head on bills, and each time, even though he was in the minority party, he was able to gather the votes from both sides, put in workable amendments and get the bill to the floor. He was running circles around me, and I was the guy who supposedly held the power."

"From what I've seen, he's pretty good at that."

"You know what really bugged me? People respected Wilson. They flocked around him, asked his opinion. I couldn't figure out what he had over them. Yes, he was handsome and all, but charm only gets you so far in the bloody pit of politics. People were attracted to him. I couldn't put my finger on it, and it bugged me. One day I decided to meet with him off-campus.

"Following that meeting, he introduced me to Lew over lunch. Wilson shared about how the Principle of Gravitational Attraction and Influence had radically changed his view of influence and leadership. Now look what happened. I'm serving Wilson today. Who would have thought?" As another belly-laugh exploded, Jim's phone alarm buzzed. "Hey, we're running up the clock, and I haven't even got to the meat yet. Come with me; I think we can wrap up your assignment in about fifteen more minutes."

Jim jumped up from his chair, moved to a door built into the wall and wainscoting, knocked and opened it at the same time. It was the governor's office, and there was the imposing Wilson Barlow sitting at a massive, intricately carved oak and walnut desk in a room the size of a cottage. The governor looked up from his computer screen and swiveled his chair to face them. A warm smile lit up his face, and in a deep and resonant voice he said, "Jim, I see you have our special guest with you." His voice had a gentle but booming quality to it, the disciplined voice of a public speaker.

"Governor, I'd like you to meet our new friend, Jason Cahill. Jason is the Executive Director of New Horizons. I know you're familiar with them for their outreach to strengthen foster parenting programs in the region. Jason is spending time with Lew, so you know why he's here. I just told him for all the power you now possess as governor, you've taken a completely different approach to moving the state's agenda forward."

Reaching out his giant hand, the envy of any basketball player or pianist, Governor Barlow said, "Good to meet you Jason." Barlow motioned him to a chair in front of the massive desk. "Have a seat, please." He turned back to Jim. "Jim, could you go greet our next visitors and keep them occupied for a few minutes?"

Jim nodded. As he ducked back into his own office, he said, "Welcome to the fellowship, Jason. I look forward to spending more time with you as you put all the pieces of the principle together. I find it amazing how many different expressions of the same principle I find."

"So, Jason, you're here on your Gravity journey, and this is the Influence station. You've seen all my power decorations. What do you think? Jim didn't show you the vault where the vast collection of power chips is stored, did he?" Wilson laughed.

"Um, no, Governor, sir."

"Out in the hall, it's Governor. In here it's just Wilson, please. Believe me, the vault is massive, but we intentionally don't count the chips in it. Instead, let me tell you how I've chosen to get governance done. It's as simple as this. If I want to accomplish my agenda through power, I must possess something you want, and you must possess something I want. Then I've got to go into my chip vault, make a withdrawal and pay you. Make sense so far?"

"My life is just passing before my eyes."

"You too, huh? The problem with power is that it's a transaction—a transaction for *wants*, remember that. If I'm not watchful and the withdrawals are greater than the replenishment through power favors, I could be in a power vacuum. Power requires me to spend enough to get what I want, so I often don't get stronger because I'm trying to leverage power by paying with power. When I base my sense of protection on my power and I feel I'm losing it, I get desperate. Then you just don't know what I might do. And there, my friend, is about 4,000 years of history."

"It sounds a little ugly. Kind of medieval," offered Jason.

"It is, and it is. When you have some time, reread Niccolò Machiavelli's *The Prince*. Look at it in terms of how his ideas would play out today, when you can't physically annihilate your enemies, but you can render them impotent. But that's another rabbit-trail." Rising from his chair, Wilson walked over and sat on the corner of his desk. His towering six-foot, four-inch figure exuded power by his mere presence. Governor Barlow continued, "So if I want to retain power, I have to gain more power in the process. The basic rule is, whoever possesses the most power possesses the agenda."

"Do you think it will ever change? I mean, the way power works?"

"I truly hope so. Yet, through the millennia, no civilized culture has been able to keep the power balance for long. Even the Roman Empire collapsed because of a power deficit. By the way, game theory says conflict starts from an insecurity of power, not having too much. Nations don't start wars because they have power. It's because they need power or are afraid someone else is going use their power first. But here's the point of this long speech: if America ever ceases to be regarded as a great nation with a great culture, it won't be because we've lost our power, it will be because we've lost our capacity to influence—our capacity to be and do good. Can you see the difference between power and influence?"

"Well, with power, I have to continuously make sure I have

enough. I guess I can gain that power by making you weaker—by taking or breaking your power. But with influence ... do I try to make you more influential?"

"Sure 'nuff. And there's the key to how I govern. If I'm going to leverage my influence, which is the key to governance, it is to help make you more influential as well. My job is to make sure you are continually growing stronger in influence. If I want my agenda accomplished through influence, I must give away something you need, not what you want. And at some point our relationship, our alliance, becomes mutually supportive. Most politicians and business leaders confuse their wants with their needs. Either that or they have a clear understanding and intentionally use what they think you want to gain power for themselves."

"Pardon me for appearing bold, but isn't that naïve to think you could be mutually supportive to those who politically oppose you?"

"I hope so. This is how it works. If I am able to anticipate your objective *need*, and then work with you to freely give it to you, it empowers you to be more free, more prosperous, more healthy. It's not that complicated. If I toy with your fundamental needs, I've got rebellion around the corner. But if I anticipate your needs, we have a strong alliance. And that means I must anticipate your needs possibly before you are even fully aware of them, or they've transmigrated into subjective wants. Here's the key: because of that, as a leader, I've gained the capacity to bless others and not to hoard power. Power always leaks, and I must constantly find ways to replenish the supply. On the other hand, influence grows without direct action by me. The more I give away, the more I have. The more I focus my concerns on you, the more influence I gain. Influence, in my book, means I anticipate your needs, seek to provide for those needs and empower you to repeat the process. You could say that influence is like a refined instrument—surgical or musical."

"Wait a minute. If you just start giving people their needs for nothing, won't they take advantage of you?"

Governor Barlow held up his hands in a defensive gesture. "Yes, yes, I know. I understand your concern, but you must understand there is a difference between being naïve and being gullible."

"And that is?"

"Being naïve, in my book, is taking risks while believing in the best for and from others. It's not being stupid or clueless. It's just unaffected simplicity. Wise as a serpent, innocent as a dove. Now, being gullible is another matter. It means you haven't counted the costs ahead of time. In the end, you may take advantage of my openness, but my influence allows you to be less self-centered than you usually are. Sometimes in politics like in the oil fields, it's not about the best thing. It's often about the possible thing. If it's possible to get you to act less selfishly, I consider that a win. The healthiest organizations are ones whose vision and purpose is beyond just self-protection. When you belong to something bigger than yourself, it allows for generosity incapable of being attained individually. That's the fundamental principle of collective association at any level. Neighborhood associations, local government, unions and, yes, even special interest groups. That's what New Horizons is at its core, right?"

"But does it really work? Can you keep people with different visions and different wants working together simply through shared influence?"

"I believe so. We've established influence is far more sustainable than power. Let me give you an example. Long ago, I came to realize that the power of political office was much like a narcotic. I call it OPM. You know, Other People's Money. While I was a young legislator, I realized I could be a very effective dealer of OPM. Once I got a constituency hooked on my OPM, I could get them to do what I needed because I too had an addiction— the ego massage of feeling important as their dealer. The only problem was, my addicts continually wanted more OPM, and when they demanded more than I could provide, they had a hissy- fit and challenged my authority and the source of their power. That conflict challenged my addictive need to feel important, and you can see how the vicious cycle spun. You never want to be in the same room with two people with desperate addictions.

"Jason, when I pick up the phone or I look someone in the

Q.

Who is dependent on your OPM?

eye and ask them to do something, they will only respond in one of two ways. One is out of fear and awe for the power they think I possess. The other is, they will respond because they believe in me, my perceived goodness and our shared cause. What do you think gets more long-term traction?"

The governor leaned forward, and the intensity of his voice and expression intimidated Jason a little. "I'm in my third term as governor. Do you think being governor is the fulfillment of my competence and ambition? Why do you think the voters keep sending me back? Is it the OPM fix I can drop into a legislative district, or is it something else? Here's a peek under the hood to see my engine. Because of the intensity and unpredictability of each day I govern, I've broken my philosophy of influence into three pieces.

"First is vision. I have a vision for the people of this state. I don't need this office to make it happen. But being governor facilitates that vision. My vision is bigger than this office, and yet in humility I understand this office is bigger than my vision. But in that gap, come hell or high water, I will work my heart out to bring about the change I believe I have the influence to make happen. I might not be elected for the next term, but I will still continue to do what I believe in. I don't make decisions to get elected. I make decisions because I *am* elected.

"Second is to continue to mature—to grow my integrity. To be honest, that's the greatest challenge. You have no idea how easy it is to simply motivate and manipulate those I'm responsible for because of the chair I'm sitting in. That includes my agency directors, staff, and constituency. I believe the true mark of influence is not in what gets accomplished. Rather it is in whether greater virtue and integrity is demonstrated by those who identify with the organization, the cause or the constituency. Then, accomplishments are the consequences of an enterprise of integrity, not the end goals. Does that make sense, Jason?"

"Yes and no, It's similar to the 'works as a consequence of

faith' conclusion we've come up with over the past couple of weeks. But I think what you've said is so rare from someone in your career. Refreshing, but rare. I've got to take more time to process it."

"It may be rare, but I think there's no other way to do this job. You see, as governor, I don't want people to expect me to have integrity. I need for them to *know* I have integrity. In times of tension, and believe you me, the art of governing is always in a state of tension, the most essential role of a leader is to possess self-clarity—I know who I am and I act true to that understanding."

"Let me see if I'm tracking with you, ah, Wilson. I'm sorry, it's almost impossible to call you by your first name."

"I understand. It's a sign of respect. But if I expect you to call me Governor, then I need to call you Mr. Cahill, in respect for what you do as well. You were asking if you were tracking with me?"

"Yes. You said you've been elected with the power of office and position but you've chosen to govern through influence instead—with vision, integrity and something else."

Wilson leaned forward from his perch on the corner of the desk. "Jason, I know you're a Christ-follower; otherwise you wouldn't be meeting with Lew. So here's my third principle of influence. Like in Jesus' parable, I believe in sowing, and I believe in reaping. I just don't believe they are necessarily directly connected. As governor and as a person, I sow, and I expect and anticipate reaping. But here's the key point: I don't sow with the ulterior motive of reaping. Does that make sense? Because I sow, others may reap. As a result, change happens, and people do something because of that change. Here's the crucial point: I have little control over the direction of that change—and that's what makes influence so powerful.

"Here's the bottom line, and then I've got some people waiting for me who've been very patient with my schedule. My influence does not reside in my title. It resides in my soul. Not in my willful spirit or the power of this office. My influence is a radiating force of love and is the root, the origin, of trust. You have influence when you have trust. And when people trust you, you've got influence."

Wilson rose from the corner of his desk, signaling that the conversation was ending. "Here's my admonition to you, and when you tell your kids and grandkids about meeting the governor of the state, tell them I told you this: if you want to make a difference in this world, allow people to fall under your influence. Let them fall in love with the goodness of your soul. You know gravity is that attractional pull of one object to another. Gravitational influence is one of the most powerful forces on earth. Your gravitational attraction and influence emanates from the spiritual mass whose center is the soul. I learned that from my time with Lew. I hope that truth becomes yours as well."

Jason nodded, feeling child-like without feeling childish in the presence of a truly effective leader.

"Governor, ah, Wilson, sir, I know your time is packed today, but can I ask you one question? I understand what you've said, but how do you find balance? How do you center yourself so you aren't operating from your power seat?"

"Thank you, Jason, for going to the heart of the issue. Short answer. I'm never sure. That's why I have Jim as my right hand. You need trustworthy friends like Jim to give you unvarnished feedback and to watch your back. He has little power, and we try to keep it that way. His only power is in advising me on policy issues and controlling, or influencing may be a better term, my schedule and appointments.

"The other reason is, I continually center my soul in Jesus Christ. I know, in some circles that's not politically correct today, but that's who I am. If I can make my governance internally all about me, then I'm free, externally, to make it *not* all about me. Make sense? I fully realize the integrity of this state, while I am governor, rests with my integrity as a person. If I want the people of this state to be more generous, more serving, less bickering, it starts with me. That, in a nutshell, is gravitational influence as I've come to live it out."

Wilson stretched out his right hand, putting his left hand on

Jason's shoulder. It was a nice way to get Jason out of his chair and moving towards the door. "Thank you for coming today, Jason, so that I can be reminded of why I sit in this chair. I need to hear this as much as you do. Take care."

As Jason exited the door, he felt a massive hand on his back. "Jason, one last thought. If you really want to understand the nature of influence, you must determine to understand the nature of God. The passage in the Bible inspiring and bringing me to my knees is out of Philippians, I think. I'm probably going to butcher it up but essentially it says that Jesus, a part of the Trinity, didn't assert his claim of equality with God the Father. Instead, he dropped his heavenly power, took on the form of a servant to be just like us for a time until he was humiliated by dying on a cross made for criminals. This, I believe, is the essence of influence. Out the door, to the right and you'll be back in the reception room."

"And," Wilson called out down the hallway, "greet Lew for me when you next meet."

Driving back to his office, Jason struggled with all he'd heard. He was awed at being able to spend time with the governor of the state and was blown away by his good heart. *So that's what true influence feels like when combined with a charismatic personality,* he thought. *It is possible to have a large soul-mass and still be able move large numbers of people to action without abusing their commitment.* Jason felt some scales of cynicism beginning to drop.

He who forms the mountains, who creates the wind, and who reveals his thoughts to mankind, who turns dawn to darkness, and treads on the heights of the earth— the LORD God Almighty is his name.

Amos 4:13

REFLECTION QUESTIONS

1. *Governor Barlow said, "To rule from power means you have to possess something other people want or need." How would you distinguish a want from a need? How does exercising power to meet needs create influence?*

2. *Describe an evidence of the use of influence instead of power that you've seen in the recent past. It could be a personal experience or one you read about in the media.*

3. *Describe examples where you've experienced the consequence of OPM addiction.*

4. *Make a list of the 'power chips' you own as it relates to your family, your ministry and your work. Next list how those 'power chips' can be turned into influence by anticipating needs.*

5. *Seriously, how realistic is Governor Barlow's theory of influence in real life? What makes it realistic? What makes it unrealistic?*

6. *How do you, personally, find balance between the power you possess and the influence you can exert?*

7. *Wilson said to Jason, "If you really want to understand the nature of influence, you must determine to understand the nature of God." What do you understand he meant by that?*

CHAPTER 11

Influence and
the Perception
of Power

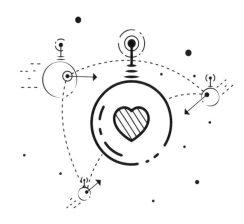

LEADERS ARE
DEFINED BY THEIR
gravitational attraction and radiating influence

The God of Israel spoke, the Rock of
Israel said to me: "When one rules over
people in righteousness, when he rules
in the fear of God, he is like the light
of morning at sunrise on a cloudless
morning, like the brightness after rain
that brings grass from the earth."

2 Samuel 23:3–4

G *ood thing I remembered to bring my scarf,* thought Jason, as he briskly walked to Lew's. There was an wintry chill in the air. Daylight was getting shorter. Winter had taken up residence and was making its presence known. Dark clouds and chilling wind at 4:30 in the afternoon made the day feel dark and dreary.

"Lew, you there?" Jason called as he walked up to Lew's partially open door.

"Come on in, Jason. Chelsea had to leave early to take her sister to the doctor. Grab a cup of coffee on a chilly day." Lew chuckled. "You'd be doing that yourself anyway even if Chelsea were here."

As Jason carried a little too full cup of coffee to his chair, Lew stood by his whiteboard.

"This is beginning to feel like a hideaway, Lew. A safe hideaway."

"Glad it feels that way. Let's get started. We're at the fifth truth of gravity." Lew scribbled on the board, **LEADERS ARE DEFINED BY THEIR GRAVITATIONAL ATTRACTION AND RADIATING**

INFLUENCE.

Lew walked back to his desk, sat down, leaned back in his vintage oak swivel desk chair, put his hands behind his head, and said, "Tell me about your time with Jim and the governor. What did you discover?"

"Now, that was a meeting to remember. From reading the comments of all his critics floating in the media, I didn't expect to meet a man of such substance. Thanks for the opportunity. You know, what struck me was how natural Governor Barlow was as he related his soul-centeredness to the source of his influence. I've never heard a politician speak of ignoring power in order to achieve influence. You taught him well."

"Jim and Wilson. I didn't teach either of them much. After all, I'm not a teacher; I'm a pitcher. They just caught a lot of things, and I'm hoping the same is happening with you. So let's see what you've caught. What did you think of Jim?"

"He and Governor Barlow make a great team. And to think they were political opponents at one point. Gives me hope that politics hasn't been completely ruined by power, selfishness and greed."

"That's great, Jason. I knew it would be a great experience. It renews my faith and my belief in this intangible trek we're on. I too love to experience the evidence of our beliefs. Your next assignment will be to take a deep dive into the soul. Why do you think I wanted you to talk to Jim first?"

"I don't know. I've been trying to get my head around that, and I can't quite get the clue."

"What did Jim say he was?"

"Well, I said he was a lubricant for Governor Barlow. He liked that metaphor, and he also said he was an arbiter of influence."

"You listen well. And what did you go away realizing?"

"That Jim could be a very powerful person. In a sense, Jim is the power behind the throne. He controls the governor's agenda and who gets to see him. It's obvious Jim tries very hard to leverage the governor's influence to accomplish Wilson's vision. I guess here's the big aha for me from that: influence perceived as power is often more powerful than sheer power."

"Any insights on your insight?"

Jason's brow furrowed as he thought. "Okay, Lew. I don't know if this was your intention but here's a couple of concepts that really hung in my head. I'm not sure how they'll all fit into your paradigm of influence."

"Lay them out, and let's see if they adhere."

"I found fascinating Governor Barlow's analogy of other people's money as a currency of power. I thought it was disturbing, yet true: the addiction that comes with heroin and other narcotics seems remarkably similar to the addiction to other people's money. We know it happens in government. I see how that can happen in churches as well. Scary thought. Pastors, executives, business owners, even nonprofit leaders. I now see I am always the steward of other people's money, and I can use it as healing medicine or as a destructive substance of abuse. Methinks I had been snorting a little of my stash."

"What else?"

"The perception of power has to have tangible evidence. I never realized I perceived the buildings, the trappings, the titles and the possession of OPM as necessary illustrations of power. I remember when I was at Continental Beverage, the top floor, largest corner office and of course a private bathroom were non-negotiables of being in charge. If you didn't have those perks of power, who was going to know you were in charge? Seems a little shallow now."

"Jason, you have no idea how hard Jim and his staff work to make sure people have an accurate perception of the governor. It goes way beyond dressing the set, if you will, of the governor's office for him to look powerful. It's a strange enigma of life. Someone who has the trappings of power but puts no value on them appears even more powerful. So after talking with Wilson, what do you think soul-centeredness means?"

"Well, that wasn't the first pitch I expected, but I should have known, Mr. Soul-mentor, that's exactly where you'd go. Starting with the basics: I believe there is a soul as much as I believe there is God. As we've walked through these gravity truths, I've seen more clearly the centrality of our soul in everything we think and do. I really appreciate you providing me with living examples. You know, what I've noticed too: it's not just them. Like with Joe and Paul, it's the impact on the people around them. When I say that, it sounds so elementary, yet I can't believe how much of the elementary I've become insensitive to over time."

"And could you see the soul-centeredness in Jim and Wilson?"

"It was obvious, and it was refreshing to experience two leaders with uniquely different versions of gravitational attractiveness and to see it wasn't just celebrity in either of them."

Lew got up, went back to the whiteboard and wrote **SOUL-CENTEREDNESS**. He then drew a vertical line to the right of the word. On the other side he wrote **SELF-CENTEREDNESS**.

SOUL-CENTEREDNESS | SELF-CENTEREDNESS

"Any observations about the opposite, self-centeredness?"

"I think there's a difference between self-centeredness and selfishness, but I'm not sure I can articulate the difference."

"I think it was CS Lewis who made the distinction. He said we're all selfish. We eat to survive, we sleep to refresh and we engage in sex to procreate. Those are all fairly selfish behaviors. None in the proper context is bad. But when that selfishness turns to self-gratification at the expense of others, control at the cost of other people's freedom of expression or self-preservation as an act of cowardice, then evil has entered the scene. Follow?"

Q.
Follow?

"Where were you when I needed to know this the first time?"

"Right here. Perhaps you weren't looking for me. Let's get back to your visit to the marble palace."

"I like your dark humor, Lew."

Lew wrote down **STEWARD**. On the other side he wrote **CONTROL**.

SOUL-CENTEREDNESS	SELF-CENTEREDNESS
STEWARD	CONTROL

"Steward—now that's a useful word. You probably caught that both Jim and Wilson enjoy history, particularly Ancient Rome. So if Jim were living in the first century Roman Empire, what role would he have? He'd be a steward, wouldn't he? He would have been entrusted to manage the landowner's assets. And what does the parable of the talents Jesus taught tell us about stewards' responsibility?"

"As stewards we are to grow and multiply the assets of the leader or master of the household."

"And Jesus was primarily referring to spiritual assets, but what assets does Jim manage?"

Jason almost answered, but then he hesitated. He drained his now-lukewarm coffee in one gulp as a chance to think. Finally, he said, "Based on our conversation topic, I know the right answer is influence. But I'm not sure how to get there. It still feels like he manages power. Help me out, Lew."

Lew nodded, looking at the word **STEWARD** on the board. "Good answer to a tricky question. It is influence. However, there is a very fine distinction here, so I want to be sure you catch it. Jim, as steward of the governor's estate, preserves the assets of power, which are like the land and tangible wealth of our first-century Roman governor. Jim protects the land from being squandered, drained of its potential resource or swindled away. He protects the orchards and vineyards from pestilence and pilferage. But what does he manage and grow? And let's bring this analogy back into this century. For Jim, as the governor's steward, what is the fruit and grain produced from the land?"

"Influence?"

"Exactly."

"I think I'm beginning to get the picture. I preserve the power

I have. And at opportune times, I take advantage to increase the power of our assets, in a sense to assure the greatest yields from the fields for the storehouse. Maybe like I did with the merger of Family Matters and New Horizons. But in the end, how I make progress is through leveraging my influence, my capacity to increase the harvest, not my power. That's how the people get fed."

Lew couldn't help but smiling. "Great catch, Jason. Now here's a curveball you might struggle with. Think of influence as a precursor or an extension—probably both—of trust. If I'm a leader, I own my power. It's tangible, I can count it and I can show it to others as an act of intimidation or a display of wealth or assurance. In other words, my power rests in what I own."

Lew put down his marker and sat opposite Jason in the green leather chair. "On the other hand, my influence rests in this intangible quality I choose to call gravitational attraction and influence. In reality, it is a form of mutually progressive intimacy—in other words, love." Lew stopped and laughed. "When we talked about it earlier, you got a little squirmy. Obviously attraction, intimacy and love are not common terms found in the lexicon of leadership. Yet that is the basis of the Principle. To be an effective leader requires others to fall in love with you. And to be an effective spiritual leader requires people to not only fall in love with you, but also to fall more in love with Jesus."

Jason glanced at his empty coffee mug. There was nothing to hide behind this time.

Lew leaned forward in his chair, pushed his glasses back up on his nose and steepled his fingers. "Jason, people follow either, one, out of fear or greed because of tangible elements of power, what you own; or, two, out of love because of who you are. In other words, they follow because of your gravitational attraction and influence. They will follow you because they fear you or because they believe in your goodness, your cause and your capacity to be all they need you to be."

Lew seemed to be waiting. Jason took the silence as a cue to speak. "I think that's what I've been running from. I've believed in what I can do, but I'm really uncomfortable with people believing in me simply for who I am."

"Why do you think that might be?"

"I guess I don't trust others because I am not sure I trust myself. My track record as a person is marked with disappointments and 'woulda, coulda, shoulda's.' I started off as a promising business leader, then an up-and-coming pastor with a lovely family, and suddenly I found myself with a failed marriage and a career and reputation in shambles. The church I loved and people I sacrificed for turned their backs on me. Now just as I've rebuilt my life and career, I am starting to see the warning signs of impending doom again. I'm having a hard time trusting in anyone, and so I'm relying more and more on my efforts to validate my worth. And it's all unraveling. The harder I try to prove my value by what I do, the more friction and failure I experience. I feel like I'm on the edge of catastrophic failure, and my influence tank is on empty."

"I'm going to cut you off there. Did you notice you were changing the subject? You started drilling for the trust issue but ended up hitting the 'value of works' topic again." Lew's face had a sympathetic but determined look. "Let me bring us back on target. What I hear you saying, my friend, is you're all in for Jesus, but transformation hasn't really happened. Otherwise the living you're experiencing wouldn't be in such conflict with the life you'd like others to think you have, would it? It sounds like you believe in the concept of the indwelling power of Christ through the Holy Spirit; you just don't believe it's happening for you, right now. Am I right?"

Jason, uncomfortable with Lew's intensity, could feel his face flushing and his breathing rate increasing. "Yes and no. I told you I've got some work to do on figuring out the whole trust package. I don't have a good frame of reference. The reality is, my experience with trust and my belief in trust aren't on the same track."

"So you just want a little bit of Jesus, but not enough that you lose your illusion of control. You are waving the Jesus flag as you see him go by, but you are not willing to walk with him. Afraid of where he might take you? Am I right? I know you're not a fake. So are you a Jesus fan or a Jesus follower?"

"Ouch. Listen, Lew. You've become my friend, and I appreciate your willingness to press me as far as you are. But you're pushing into areas I don't think I'm ready to explore right now. I've got to think about all that you've been saying."

Lew felt Jason was on the edge of a breakthrough and continued to press. "Jason, I have a question for you. What do you call people who have power but have no influence?"

"Bullies?"

"Yes. I have another name too. I call them tyrants. I think, too often, in order to be politically polite, we like to color the nouns of life in shades of gray. But not in this case. For me, there are only two categories of people who have sway over the lives of others. They are either tyrants, or they are true leaders. Leaders exercise their stewardship of power through influence. Tyrants control through fear, greed, enemy-hatred and shared fame or spoils. Tyrants appeal to people desperately seeking for identity and unable to look beyond their own distorted reflection. What appears to be influence in tyrants is merely the reflection of an emptiness within."

Jason could feel an angry defensiveness rising within. "Talk about going for the jugular. You think I'm a tyrant? First you question my commitment, and now I'm a tyrant?"

"Of course I don't see you as a tyrant. I didn't mean to imply that. I apologize. I see a man who desperately wants to serve people. It's just that I think you're pushing in the wrong direction, Jason. But whether you're a tyrant or not isn't the point. It's not even the point if others think you are but just haven't found the label yet. Can I share with you what I think is the point?"

"Please do, as long as you don't jab your point into my eye."

"For a number of reasons, when you first came to me, you had lost most of your influence at New Horizons. I think we can agree the root was a deeply wounded soul in need of restoration. And because it was wounded, it affected your identity and your abilities—particularly your capacity to believe in and act for goodness. I've seen significant growth, but is it possible your sense of being is still deeply wounded? And is it possible you are still trying to make up for it by your doing—that even going through this process with me is an act of doing to cover that wound?"

"Listen, Lew, if I didn't think you cared about me, I could get upset. Actually, I am anyway. You are pushing into my life like no one has done before. If I didn't know you cared for me and felt you were getting close to truth I would rather not admit, I would chuck this whole process and walk out."

"Good thought. If you didn't think I cared, believe me, this would be a very dangerous place, and you would be right to leave. But since you know I do care, look at the situation from this angle: you are pushing back because I'm hitting on truth. Sometimes the densest rock is the layer protecting the oil field. What are we spending time together for if it's not to get past the surface issues and get down to the soul issues? From my perspective, you're probably pushing back because my drilling is getting close to your core mass."

Jason took a deep breath and exhaled. He closed his eyes and nodded. "I'm sorry, Lew. You're right. It's just that I've never let myself get to this vulnerable level before. There have been a few times I wanted to open up to somebody, but it's hard. I don't know if it's a lack of trust, my own unwillingness to be honest and face reality, or what. At this point, it's a little more than unnerving."

"Let's stop here for a moment and survey the field. Right now you're looking back at all your trust issues, and you have little foundation for going forward. I get that. But your leader effectiveness—as a person of influence with a tribe of followers—will only increase in proportion to the size of your soul-mass. You can't trust others if you aren't able to trust God through your soul. And people won't trust you until and unless your trust of them radiates out from your soul. In other words, you've got to start finding a way to trust God, trust others and become a trustworthy person. Key to that, I think, is learning to trust yourself through your soul, which is your window to God. Make sense?"

"It makes sense at some level and is overwhelming at

another. I've got to slow down here. This is rocking my foundation. I do need to reflect on what you're saying. Let me see if I'm getting the point of this gravity truth. You're saying my influence, which is rooted in who I am, is really rooted in my soul-mass. And that's what draws people to me, not my abilities and what I know? It's not what I can do for them, to them or even with them. It's that I possess gravitational attraction.

"I think I hear you saying—and I'm having a hard time processing it right at the moment—if my gravitational influence, my soul-mass, is not the origin of change and changes I initiate with others, then I'm acting like a tyrant, and that makes me untrustworthy. Is that what you're telling me?"

"That's what you are telling you, Jason, and that's the key. Let's just say I think you are moving in the right direction. I'm glad you're uncomfortable. It's a signal learning is taking place. Jason, we've talked about this before. You've heard this before, and you'll hear it again, I'm sure, before we're through. It's got to be about you so it doesn't have to be about you. If you don't develop, grow and become more Christ-like, then you're going to be what you presently are—why you came to me in the first place—a stumbling block for others. You've got to find your identity in your life before you can lose it in Christ's identity. Here's the point of our time together. You can't lose something you don't own."

"You know, driving back from the governor's office, I was perplexed at how much power Governor Barlow has but says he chooses not to use. That's interesting. It seems like the force of power is in how little you choose to use instead of what doesn't get used. That's a fascinating contradiction I'm still trying to get my head around."

"Perhaps like, if you want to be first, be last. If you want life, lose it. If you want to lead, serve?" asked Lew with a smile.

"Ah, yes. Just like those."

"And what does that say about you?"

"Well, in thinking of contradictions, I'm realizing I've based my career, my reputation and to a certain degree, the failure of my first marriage, on what I have done. Yet I've determined I won't fail again; I will do anything to avoid that. Yet, I'm afraid I'm building a second marriage on the same principle. It's the old definition of insanity—you know, doing the same thing and expecting different results."

"And?"

"Apparently, I'm still convinced that if you want something, you have to work and work hard for it. The fruit of that effort will come as a result."

"But?"

"But what I believe and what I've experienced are two different realities. Lew, I hope you know what you're doing because I feel like I'm standing in a cabin hanging over a cliff with a drop of a thousand feet, and you're starting to pull the floorboards out, one by one.

Lew smiled. "And?"

"Okay, fine: And I'm realizing whatever creativity, ambition, vision and head-smarts I've got, that's not what makes me influential or successful. I want to inspire people to do great acts of service, be a great husband and father, and I've thought all along that if people would just follow through on the energy of my abilities and talents we could accomplish anything."

"And?"

"And I now see that people will only follow great ideas for a short time. Eventually it has to be about the integrity of the leader, my integrity not just in conduct but integrity as a structure. I've got to be built or rebuilt in such a way that I don't crack and shatter at the first blow. I'm also beginning to realize I can't base my security on a floorboard labeled *Bright* or *Ambitious* or *Resourceful,* I'm beginning to see that integrity is like a bell. The influence of the bell is in its tone. The quality of its tone is not in who rings the bell or even in where it is hung. A bell with integrity of tone calls people to safety, prayer or the order of the day and resonates because it's been made well. It rings true. I'm coming to realize at a deeper level a truth I've always known.

"Which is?"

"That integrity is found in what you call my soul-mass."

"And?" Lew smiled at Jason's suddenly incredulous expression. "Just kidding. No more *ands*. Seriously, that's a powerful insight. I think God has revealed a potent truth to you." Lew went back to the whiteboard. "So sum up my scribbling for me."

"Well, like Governor Barlow's, any perceived power I have is due to how close I get to the center of my soul-mass. And even though I need to protect the power I have, any sustainable fruit from that power comes from my influence. How's that for starters?"

"Excellent. And..."

"I thought you said no more *ands*. And I should see my role more as a steward of my soul-centered influence rather than just a protector of my self-centered power."

"You, my friend, are on roll. Keep going."

"Here's where I've got more work to do. I realize my identity is not defined by how much power I possess. I am realizing that is a false sense of security. It's elusive. Rather it comes from the health of my soul and radiates out through the influence I cast or spread or whatever. It's just that old habits die slowly. The area I'm struggling with is coming to grips with owning the reality that my influence is found in the integrity of my being, not in the quality or effectiveness of my doing. I get it, but I don't yet own it."

"Don't worry, Jason, you will. That's a lot to process. Before you get away, let's return to the 'falling in love with you' conversation we've been having. Did you see how Governor Barlow has intentionally deflected the power option? Why is he so effective?"

"People love him."

"And you want to be effective like Governor Barlow but are unwilling to accept the love from the people you serve? How does that work? It's pretty clear: because they love him, they trust him and respect him. Right? He's a keeper of the tender trust of others. Is that burden what scares you?"

"Yes, it is, and thank you so much for making that frightening responsibility more real than I've felt before. You really have fun doing this to me, don't you?"

"Not sure that's a statement or an accusation. However, guilty on all counts, your Honor, but only because I know you're going to grow from it. Let's stop here for today."

"Thank goodness. I'm ready to come up for air. That was intense, and I've got a lot to process."

"Rightly so, my friend. We've spent a lot of time talking around the soul and soul-mass. Next time we meet, we're going to dive deeper into the murky waters to discover how being more aware of your soul-mass increases your capacity to be an instrument of righteousness to the people you touch and serve. We're down to gravity truth six. You got it on your phone?"

"Yep. Our capacity to influence resides within the intertwined influences of the soul and the spirit of man—our soul-mass—and the Spirit of God."

"Good. I also want you to go back and look at Matthew 9:17, because what we're going to be looking at is that new wineskin Jesus talked about."

"Got it. I'll be ready to stretch, so I don't burst again. Thanks for being my friend and pressing in while I'm pushing back. I trust you, friend."

"Trust and friend used in the same sentence? Seriously, I'll treasure that. See you soon."

Neither do people pour new wine into old wineskins. If they do, the skins will burst; the wine will run out, and the wineskins will be ruined. No, they pour new wine into new wineskins, and both are preserved.

Matthew 9:17

REFLECTION QUESTIONS

1. *Think of a person in your life experiences whom you'd now describe as a tyrant. This isn't a judgmental label. Rather a description of their style of getting other people to follow them. What were their behaviors making them appear to be a tyrant?*

2. *Think of a person in your life experiences whom you'd now describe as an influencer. What are/were their behaviors making them appear to be an influencer?*

3. *Jason said, "Lew, I think that's what I've been running from. I've believed in what I can do but I'm really uncomfortable with people believing in me simply for who I am." Can you identify with Jason? In what ways? How do you change your 'value proposition' from doing to being?*

4. *How does your doing provide a substitute for your need to trust others?*

CHAPTER 12

What is Soul–Mass?

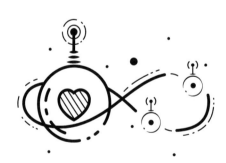

SOUL–MASS AND THE SPIRIT OF GOD

determine influence

You have searched me, LORD, and you know me. You know when I sit and when I rise; you perceive my thoughts from afar. You discern my going out and my lying down; you are familiar with all my ways. Before a word is on my tongue you, LORD, know it completely. Search me, God, and know my heart; test me and know my anxious thoughts. See if there is any offensive way in me, and lead me in the way everlasting.

Psalm 139

S lipping out of the warm heated seats of his Audi, Jason felt the biting chill. Winter had not only gained its foothold, it was burrowing in, signaling cold, blustery, wet, snowy days for at least two more months. It had been a month since he had last met with Lew, and Jason had immersed himself in every book he could find on the soul. His Amazon account had worked overtime. He was apprehensive as he slowly climbed the stairs to the now-familiar second-floor office.

For several months, I've talked with Lew and his friends about the soul and soul-mass. It isn't like it was a foreign subject. I was paid to be a minister of the soul. But back then, it just wasn't familiar. So abstract. Inside himself, Jason knew he hadn't really intentionally ministered to anyone's soul-mass. Strangely, in his apprehension there was also a strong feeling of expectation. *It's a truth I've known all along. The source of my problems and my future lie in my being able to connect with my soul and the rest of my spirituality. Maybe that finally happens today.*

"Come on in and warm up, my friend," said Lew as he rose from his oak desk to give a man-hug to Jason.

Jason had grown to love this man who had poured time and wisdom into his life. *What an example of gravitational influence,* he thought.

Jason walked straight from the two-slap man-hug to the Keurig to prepare a mug of Bon Café coffee. "If possession is 9/10 of the law, is this mug mine now?" Jason laughed as he hoisted the empty mug.

"Hi, Jason," It was clearly the voice of Chelsea.

Jason was taken aback. Chelsea sat on the leather couch, legs tucked up in a yoga-like fold. He hadn't seen her when he came in. He felt most safe with just Lew. "Well, hello yourself. Looks like you're settling in to be a part of the conversation today. By the way, don't do Pogo's unless you want their all-you-can-eat special to sit in your stomach for three days."

"Ha! That's funny. I was joking when I mentioned Pogo's."

"Hope you don't mind, Jason. I asked Chelsea to join us today as we talk about soul-mass," said Lew, waiting for his turn to refresh his coffee. "You may have the impression she was working on her final project at university on mentoring. Well, sort of. Actually, it's on the soul and how the soul becomes lived out in a person's spirituality—or not. Mentoring is simply a vehicle for that to occur."

"I'm impressed. Have you decided yet to include me in your research as one of your prized mounted specimens?"

"I'm not done, so you can tell me where to stick the pin to mount you. But seriously, Jason, the progress Lew and I have seen in you needs to be shared. You can be pleased and not self-conscious of your progress."

"Thanks. That's encouraging, and being serious for a moment, it means a lot."

"If you're comfortable with me being here, I would consider it a privilege to add anything of value to the conversation."

Jason pulled his mug off of the coffee machine. "Next?"

"Jason, I wouldn't have asked Chelsea to be here if I didn't think you'd be helped. She's a great resource, and I don't think anything we talk about is not for her ears too. Sound fair?"

"Ah, sure," said Jason, not fully comfortable with drilling as deep as he expected with another person in the room. He was uncomfortable letting down all the walls to a woman who wasn't his wife. Catching that thought, Jason realized he had been transparent with Chelsea after his meeting with Alisha Bishop. *She has a talent in disarming the 'uptight' in me,* he thought. *She's really good at what she does and maybe even trustworthy. For the first time in a long time, I'm allowing someone else in the room besides Lew to have control. Huh, I wonder if this is what progress feels like.*

Lew set down his mug of coffee by the Keurig and picked up a marker. "Well, let's get this drilling platform operational. I want you two to help me. This is going to be a deep drilling session, so we need to keep on track. Here are the four points we need to accomplish today." Lew turned to the whiteboard and wrote:

1. DEFINE SOUL-MASS AND ITS COMPONENTS,
2. DEFINE THEIR PURPOSE,
3. EXPLAIN HOW THAT RELATES TO INFLUENCE AND LEADERSHIP
4. SHOW THAT RELATIONSHIP IN JASON'S LIFE AND CHARACTER

Lew took a swallow of coffee, walked over to his favorite green chair, settled in and cleared his throat. "So with that, let's start where everything starts—with Adam and Eve. Since the beginning of recorded time, we've understood we are not just flesh, blood, bones and sinew. Scripture is clear, a soul and human spirit exist, as well as our sin nature or spiritual flesh, if you will. Yet—and this is a mystery—God chose to veil our understanding of the what-where-how of our soul nature. How these three elements coexist and yet maintain separate identities is even less clear than the mystery of the Trinity. That's why I call it our soul-mass."

"Soul-mass. The more I'm studying the soul and human spirit, the more I like the term," said Jason, balancing his coffee and tablet and settling into the vacant leather chair. "It takes this somewhat mysterious inner me and keeps it an integrated unit."

"Hah," laughed Chelsea. "When you get a chance, explain the 'somewhat' part of mysterious."

"Okay. How's this for 'somewhat mysterious': it's interesting the soul and human spirit are mentioned over 400 times in the Bible. I think we think it's mysterious because we just haven't explored the concepts that deeply."

"Good point," said Lew

"What are you finding," asked Chelsea.

"I'm beginning to see a fundamental truth even more clearly."

"Which is?"

"The Word of God comes to life when I see it playing out in my life. Best way to know God is to experience him at work in my life and my living. Then as I read scripture, I have a frame of reference to process my experience. Going back and exploring with a specific purpose in mind—drilling for soul-mass—has shown me things in the Bible I never realized were there."

Lew jumped back into the conversation. "You've just discovered how adults learn best. But that's for another time. Here's my experience, Jason. When I finally got down to what matters, it's knowing God in all three persons, through the three aspects of my person: flesh—physical and spiritual—my human spirit and soul. Keep going."

"I'm thinking, Lew, of what you've said since we first started meeting."

"And that is?"

"That this has to be about me so it can *not* be about me."

Chelsea nodded. "Good point, Jason. One thing I keep in mind as I go through my own self-discovery process: I can't understand myself if I only listen to myself. It's like creating a definition for a word by using that word in the definition. It just loops. If I truly want to know myself, I must know God first."

"Know self, know God, know self. For once circular logic makes sense."

"Okay, you two, help me keep on track so we can finish my first point before midnight. Jason, what was your take on the sixth gravity truth?"

"I think it's basically that our spirituality resides within the intertwined influences of the soul, the spirit of man and the Spirit of God. Our soul-mass is the source and the container of our gravitational influence. It's obvious to me, to use your drilling analogies, Lew, that our soul-mass is the core of our being and our identity. Also, something you said the last time we met sparked a huge aha about the new wineskin."

Lew leaned forward and rubbed his hands together. "Okay, lay it on us."

"I think the Apostle Paul, of all the New Testament writers, really understood our spiritual nature."

Chelsea grinned. "You mean, for example, First Thessalonians 5:23?"

"I ... yes, that's exactly the verse I was thinking of," said Jason unable to keep a surprised look off of his face.

"As you recall, he said, *May God himself, the God of peace, sanctify you through and through. May your whole spirit, soul and body be kept blameless at the coming of our Lord Jesus Christ.* You think the key phrase is 'our whole spirit, soul and body,'" said Chelsea, unable to hide a prideful smirk.

"Ha, well aren't you the grandstander? And, yes, it is. I think that has to be our construct for understanding our spiritual makeup—body, soul and human spirit. That's what we take on our, ahem, *journey* through life. Right, Lew?"

"Okay, friends, I think we've run the *journey* joke into the ground. Jason, for a guy who at one point said he didn't know much about the soul, you're on your way to making good sense. Finish the insight you had."

"Thanks. As we've been talking, there's this intersection of the tangible here-and-now with the spiritual. As you recall, Jesus said no one pours new wine into old wineskins. Otherwise, he said, the new wine will burst the old skins. What if we called this intersection—this container of our soul-mass—a wineskin?"

"Wow, that's original," snarked Chelsea. Then she caught herself, "No, really, I don't mean to make light of your thought.

That is original, and it connects my imagination with my comprehension. Good work."

"I think that was an 'atta boy,'" said Lew. "Better take it as it is, Jason, since, in my experience, they don't come too often."

"Allow me to continue. In this new wineskin are the blended ingredients of human spirit and soul. But there is this drama taking place. The human spirit—the old man—has to give up its rule to the Holy Spirit in order to become the new man. The Holy Spirit is waiting to empower this new creation but only if the will of the human spirit willingly hands over control. It's really the drama of the ages. Anyway, that works for me. How about you guys?"

"That's a great way of framing it." said Chelsea, getting up to refresh her coffee. "Jason, can I make a fresh cup for you?"

"If this wasn't such a serious conversation, I'd give you a jab about fixing me coffee," Jason volleyed back.

"Sounds like you just did," cracked Chelsea.

Ignoring the friendly jibing, Lew said, "Keep going, Jason. You are on a roll."

"Thanks. Like I was saying, let's place the properties of the immortal soul and the temporal spirit of man into this one wineskin." Jason cupped his hands. "This soul-mass is the soul as well as the will, heart and mind of our human spirit. That's our old wineskin. To that we add the Spirit of Christ on conversion, and a new wineskin is made."

"That's good stuff," said Chelsea. "I agree. What I've experienced is, out of a renewed and healthy soul-mass flows new dignity, identity and capacity for selfless love. Great picture. This new wineskin is a vessel filled with various expressions of love—loving God, loving one another and loving self like Jesus said: *'Love the Lord your God with all your heart and with all your soul and with all your mind.'* And the second commandment, he said, is like it: *'Love your neighbor as yourself.'*"

"For being a relative newbie to Christianity, you know your scripture, Chelsea. You've done your homework."

"I think that's a compliment. Thanks, Jason. It doesn't take a research project for me to know that selfless loving attitudes and behaviors are at the heart of gravitational influence. And it's really hard to be selfless, which is essential to loving others, when you don't love yourself."

"I've told my teenage daughter, Sydney, on more than one occasion there is a huge difference between loving yourself and being in love with self. What I'm finally beginning to grasp is that I haven't been demonstrating that in my own life. How do I expect her to believe it's true?"

"It's not too late, Jason. Trust me, from experience, it's never too late," sighed Chelsea.

Lew continued, "Let's do a lab experiment on this new wineskin of yours, Jason. Either of you dissect a frog in high school biology?"

"We aren't going there, if that's the point of your question," said Chelsea, screwing up her face.

"Don't worry, just an analogy. My point is, when you dissected the frog, you teased out the nerve from the muscle and pulled out the blood vessels. You could see the parts, but each individual part didn't make the frog. Even with all this together, the frog certainly didn't jump off the table. So it is with our flesh and soul-mass. We know there are spiritual blood vessels, nerves, muscles and connective tissues. They all must be connected for the spiritual and the natural man to jump. All the parts, working in a living organism, make a frog. So it is with the human spirit and soul of the wineskin and the ever-roguish spiritual and tangible flesh. Let's try to remember that as we dissect this spiritual organism. We'll try to tease these things apart a little, but unlike biology lab, let's not get hung up on anatomical labels when we really don't completely understand what we're looking at."

Jason nodded. "Good thought. Trying to categorize and define something as mysterious as our spiritual nature is so abstract. That's helpful."

Lew leaned back in his chair and steepled his fingers. "Let's start with the soul, Jason. What are you finding?"

"Got a day? All the reading and reflection has sparked dormant thoughts. I don't know about you two, but I'm realizing the soul has all the gentleness of God."

"How so?" asked Chelsea.

"You know in 1 Corinthians 13, when Paul talks about love? As I re-read that chapter, I saw the soul right in the middle of his discourse."

"In what way?" asked Lew.

"I saw he was describing God's love as it flowed through me. I saw the soul as a wellspring of genuine love. I know, I know. Love is the core of your gravitational principle, which centers on the soul-mass, but I guess I'm a little slow in putting all the connections together."

Q.

How is love at the center?

"Keep going, my friend. Looks like the drill bit has been sharpened," laughed Lew.

"Well, the soul is quiet. I'm coming to realize it's my human spirit that's yelling like a demanding teen, not my soul. I'm also realizing in that passage that my soul is patient to the point of injury. It's kind and humble. I see the reason why I know so little about my soul is that by its very nature it isn't going to press into places and conversations where it hasn't been invited. It doesn't demand its own way—which is probably why it wounds so easily. Envy and boasting and pride come from the human spirit. Certainly not the soul. Never saw the connection between love and the soul until now."

"Boom! Right before our eyes a theologian is born!" laughed Lew. "Actually, good thought. I won't give you a laundry list of scripture references, but here's what I know about the composition of the soul to add to your insight from the Corinthian love chapter. It's tender and innocent. It's capable of deep joy and rejoicing as well as anguish, bitterness, sorrow, torment and weariness. However, the soul is not a being, so it doesn't think, or reason. The soul does not have a mind. It just is. And certainly, then, it doesn't scheme and devise. It's the heart and mind of the human spirit where that occurs. I don't find reference that the soul is evil or scheming or filled with murderous hate."

"I was seeing the same thing, Lew. What I found, without going academic on you two, is that there are only a few references to soulish behaviors, but when they are mentioned, it's in the context of the behaviors of the inner man and not so much a characterization of the soul."

"Good point. I agree. I think those evil descriptions are reserved for the extremes of our spiritual flesh. Let me go back up to the board, and we'll capture our collective thoughts. What else do we know about the soul? Speak it out, and I'll put it on the board. Do we all agree the soul is immortal?"

"I would add to immortal the sense that God created the soul, and the soul will return to God for judgment. Also, it's immaterial in that it is our spiritual nature, not of this world. That's an easy one," added Jason.

"Easy-peasy. Yeah, right." Chelsea repositioned her legs on the couch. "How come it's taken us 2000 years, and we still don't fully get it? There are tremendous implications for each of those ideas, although diving into them might not be helpful for today's conversation. The way I get my head around the soul is to see it like a quinoa grain, very small and seemingly insignificant. If you grind it into flour, it is nutritious. But if you soak the seeds for two hours, they germinate, and the seed germ begins to release powerful micro-nutrients and enzymes not fully present in the flour. For me, that's the way of the soul when energized by the Holy Spirit."

"Helpful picture. What about the human spirit? What do we know about it?"

Jason took a gulp of his coffee. "Another big aha is that—and this actually came from Dallas Willard—my heart and mind and particularly my will, are merely different facet reflections of the same thing: my selfish human spirit.

Lew smiled. "Now, that's an interesting hypothesis. How do those parts fit together in the living organism we're examining?"

"You know, as we dissect this soul-mass, here's how I see the functions. Check me out, and see if I'm tracking correctly. The human spirit is the direct connection to the conscious awareness of our flesh. How much of our thoughts and emotions are purely biological and how much are spiritual is not clear to me or anyone I've read or talked with.

"What we do know is that as we become one with Christ, we have God's Holy Spirit at work within us. It is the Spirit of Christ, the Holy Spirit of God, who talks for us to the Father and talks with us with Christ. I'm thinking of where the Bible says that we don't know what we ought to pray for, but the Spirit himself intercedes for us through wordless groans. At the same time the Spirit knows us and the condition of our soul and intercedes for us according to God's will, not our will, which comes from our flesh through our human spirit."

"You've used your time between sessions very well, my friend. Keep going."

"I wonder if there is a part of the human spirit wanting goodness? It seems like there is sometimes. Tell you what. I'll answer my own question. Most often, I think, even that version of goodness is merely a desire to *feel* good about *doing* good. Left to ourselves—human spirit and flesh—we can't be trusted any more than a dog can, left alone in a kitchen with a steak on the counter. We commit violations of God's law because, as we all agree, we can't be good for more than a moment on our own. We are *nearly* hopeless addicts of self. I say nearly because God won't let anyone go without a fight."

"Nice," added Chelsea, settling back on the couch while balancing a fresh cup of tea. "Thanks for adding that glimmer of hope at the end."

"Here's how I see this being tied into a package," interjected Lew. "We've talked about the soul and the human spirit. The only thing that creates this sustainable gravitational influence coming from our soul-mass is the power of God's Holy Spirit. You know Paul's often-quoted plea in Romans chapter 7, as he describes this continuous battle of will and desire. He says, in essence, "Can anyone help me?" Then he answers his own question by stating, "Only Jesus." What's he talking about? Obviously it's the battle between his human spirit and the opportunity of a fully restored soul, wholly yielded to the graceful love of Christ and the power of Christ's Spirit."

"Humm? Makes me wonder if we could have gotten to this conclusion more quickly," said Chelsea.

"Not everyone's brain moves at your speed, Chelsea. Some of us are on the spiritual milk diet. So what we're saying," Jason continued, "is that the soul is life. The flesh is where our living takes place, and the human spirit is where living and life integrate."

"I wasn't aware I said that," said Lew, "but that sounds really good."

Lew looked longingly at his pipe in his cardigan pocket.

"Gentlemen," offered Chelsea. "I have a premonition that in a minute the air will be filled with the rich fragrance of a burnt sock."

Lew laughed. "Subtlety doesn't become you, Miss Chelsea. I'll refrain. Would you move us to point number two, the purpose of soul-mass."

"Thought you'd never ask," laughed Chelsea. "As we've already seen, somewhere wedged in the intersection of the soul, our human spirit and the conscious awareness of our spiritual flesh resides our identity."

"Chelsea, can I interrupt?" asked Jason.

"I think you just did," laughed Lew. "And since our time is about and for you, go for it."

"I just got a picture of what you're talking about." Jason went to the whiteboard and drew three overlapping circles.

"Imagine three overlapping circles labeled soul, human spirit and flesh, and what if the overlapping area of those three circles is where our sense of self resides—our true identity. And what if, through the restorative work of the Holy Spirit, the three circles come closer together? See what happens? The closer the circles are to each other, the greater the overlapping space. Is that, perhaps where and when we experience a greater sense of wholeness and peace?"

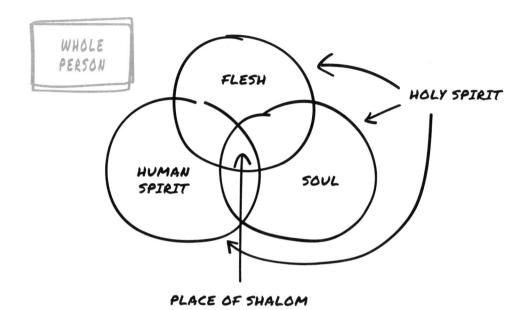

WHOLE PERSON

FLESH

HOLY SPIRIT

HUMAN SPIRIT

SOUL

PLACE OF SHALOM

"You're making a great point. Continue," prodded Lew.

"In that case, the work of the Holy Spirit is to produce convergence, alignment and integrity."

Lew smiled. "Care to explain—in a hundred words or less?"

"The way I'm envisioning it, the Holy Spirit presses in our circles of human spirit, flesh and soul. As that happens the overlapping area enlarges. That is convergence."

"What about alignment?" asked Chelsea.

"I see the Holy Spirit forming the flesh, the human spirit and the soul into the characteristics of a holy and whole person. That's alignment. He aligns us with Christ. The integrity piece is the balance, harmony and order occurring in the complete system of the flesh, the human spirit and the soul. Integrity or soundness allows the complete soul-mass to function as a healthy whole."

"That's potent, Jason," added Chelsea. "And what if that overlapping center is the place of *shalom?*"

"Explain your thought, Chelsea," said Lew.

"As you know, *shalom* is the Hebrew word for peace, yet in its original sense it has a deeper meaning—one of completeness, wholeness and well-being. It's in an attitude of *shalom* where real living takes place."

"Like, 'it is well with my soul'?" said Jason.

Lew looked at Jason and then Chelsea and then down in deep thought. He sighed deeply before he spoke. "This is special. Let's pause for a minute and breathe that understanding into our innermost being. This is a holy moment."

After a few minutes of reflection, Lew got up from his chair and went to the whiteboard. "This will be good review of our discussion up to this point." Lew wrote **SOUL–MASS/WINESKIN PROPERTIES**, and completed the diagram.

Q.

Is shalom the cry of your soul?

SOUL-MASS / WINESKIN PROPERTIES		
SOUL	HUMAN SPIRIT / WILL	HOLY SPIRIT

"Let me turn this back to you, Jason. How are you going to protect your soul from self-inflicted wounds, elbows from friends and subtle attacks from the Enemy?"

"I don't have a clue. What I do know is the soul—no, let me own what I say, my soul—is wounded and desperately desiring to be made whole. Through nothing more than benign neglect, I've allowed my soul to be beaten up between Satan on one side and my self-willed spirit and deformed self-identity on the other. For many reasons I don't fully comprehend, God allows my soul to be defenseless."

"And who do you think protects your soul? Any thoughts?"

"In a perfect world it should be my human spirit. But in an imperfect world ruined by sin, instead of being the servant-protector of my soul, my human spirit is a selfish bully always demanding its way. It follows its own will and ceases to be my soul's keeper."

"Let me see if I can add to that," offered Chelsea. "The way I look at it, the soul needs more than a keeper. The soul needs a protector. Like you said, the soul is intentionally defenseless. For example, when Jesus says to turn the other cheek when someone offends us, where do you think that response comes from? The flesh says, 'Attack.' The human spirit says, 'Hold a grudge and get even. The soul quietly says, 'Get real,' but the other two shout it down."

"Okay. You've stated the problem and the need for something more than a keeper. What do you see as that protector?" pressed Jason.

"To me there is only one source strong or powerful enough to fight off the devil and his minions. It's the Holy Spirit. The human spirit—the old man—gives rule over to the Spirit of God—the Spirit of Christ. There is nothing inside of us other than God strong enough to protect our souls from attack."

Lew turned back to the whiteboard. "Good processing, friends. Let me capture what I think you're saying and what I'm hearing."

SOUL-MASS / WINESKIN PROPERTIES

SOUL	HUMAN SPIRIT / WILL	HOLY SPIRIT
· IMMORTAL	· IMMATERIAL/MORTAL	· ETERNAL
· ABOUT LIFE	· ABOUT LIVING	· ABOUT ATERNITY
· NEEDS A PROTECTOR	· IS AN ATTACKER	· PEACEMAKER

"There's more to come," said Lew with a satisfied grin. Then he got an impish twinkle in his eye. "I'm thinking as you're talking that my soul is like this metaphor that, I'm sure, will offend Chelsea, the cat woman, and delight Jason, the dog guy. Imagine our soul is like a golden retriever. It's kind, gentle, faithful and there to reflect its master, the Lord God Almighty. Unfortunately, the soul has been dispatched to serve a selfish charge—the soul keeper, the human spirit—for a season. The retriever can be easily hurt with a strong word or a slap on the nose. But this faithful dog is naïve to the motives of its temporary and often devious keeper. The soul-dog, this golden retriever, longs for contentment and peace and desperately wants to faithfully serve his master, yet it's often ignored, abused and left unprotected."

Chelsea could anticipate what was coming next as Lew continued. "On the other hand, the human spirit—made up of the will, mind and heart—is like a Siamese cat. It's essentially self-focused and self-serving. The spirit does not want a master. It thinks it *is* the master. Yet the spirit has little idea how badly it needs a master as well—the Spirit of God. And all the while, the human spirit looks at the soul and purrs, 'If I were thirty pounds heavier, I could eat you, soul!'"

Lew laughed at his own story and then continued, "Here's the thing to remember. While the flesh can be trained, it is wild at the core. The human spirit can be trained and tamed, but it too is always wild at its core, even when the Holy Spirit takes up residence. We know all too well that the will side of the human spirit, if given an inch of independence, will take the proverbial mile. If the human spirit is anything like a cat, you know training has its limits. Here's a contrast that helps me get a handle on this soul-mass package. While the soul is filled with the character of God, the human spirit is filled with selfish control—the bitter Eden fruit from the tree of knowledge. The problem is, selfish control inevitably leads to sin, and then in a demented mind and heart, the human spirit degrades to evil. This is our ever-present battle. Almost everything the human spirit desires and does is to feed the need to be in control, to assure preservation and to feel gratified."

"I mentioned earlier that no one I've read or talked with is clear on this distinction, but where do you two think the flesh comes into all this?" asked Jason. "There is a high-thinking animal creature inside us all. As we think and act, when is it flesh, and when is it spiritual?"

"Jason, when you have a definitive answer to that, I'll visit you as the Dean of the School of Theology at the most esteemed seminary on the planet," laughed Chelsea.

"Not exactly what I was hoping to hear. Well, Lew, what's your flesh animal in this metaphorical menagerie?" asked Jason.

"To me, the animal best describing my biological and spiritual flesh is the bear. A bear's life centers on food and procreation."

Jason laughed and shook his head. "That is funny. Really, though, are we that simple?"

"Yes and no, Jason, and here's my take. Our brain integrates complex ideas, puts them into words we comprehend, merges them with emotions and then searches for clarity and coherency. Clouded in mystery, the brain also integrates the thoughts and emotions of our spiritual heart, mind and soul. What comes out is a mixture of material brain processing and immaterial soul-mass processing."

"Can you give us an example?" asked Jason.

"Certainly. Let me take you back to the Apostle Paul for that answer. He recognized, with even a more limited understanding of human physiology than we, that two agendas were running inside us. He called it the inner man and the outer man. For example, as flesh we can be intelligent, analytical and logical. Yet as spiritual beings, we can be consistently wise. As flesh we can be thoughtful and decent. But again, as spiritual beings we can be constantly compassionate and merciful. See the distinctions?"

"And this works inside me, how?" asked Jason.

"How exactly? Only God knows?" laughed Lew as he turned

his palms up and shrugged his shoulders. "Remember the frog: even with all the parts together, it doesn't jump. We still don't understand how God gives life. And if we did know, would that make a difference? I think where we have to focus is that there is an outer battle of the physical and spiritual human creature and an inner battle in our soul-mass. And heaven waits for the opportunity for the Holy Spirit to rule."

"You know, I'm continually amazed at how little I thought I knew about spirituality, yet I see what I do know gets smaller as I realize how much more there is to understand in my spiritual realm. Speaking of not knowing things, please don't take this wrong, Lew, you being my soul-mentor and all. But why is it necessary to know all this detail, since there's so much we can't really know? I mean, I don't need to know about how fuel injection and propulsion works to drive a car or fly in a plane. I don't mean to say all this is not interesting exploration. But how does this help me with my family and my work?"

Lew smiled and leaned back in his chair. "You know what's coming next, don't you? Why do *you* think it's important or unimportant to know all this detail about soul-mass?"

"I hate it when you do that."

"Yes, and sandwiches are in the fridge. And your thoughts?" asked Lew, raising his eyebrows.

"I can only tell you what I've experienced up to this point. I see how the core of these ideas is valuable. As I'm becoming more aware of my spiritual nature, that awareness is helping me to live each day more intentionally. Being in church all my life has done a good job of making me aware of my sin nature, but there is more to me than a bag of sin."

"You were wondering just a minute ago about the usefulness of knowing about soul-mass, and now you're saying it's helpful. I'm confused," said Lew.

Jason went over to the small fridge and pulled out a C'est le Bon signature sandwich: bacon, turkey, tomato, onion and sauce on a brioche bun. Jason held up his sandwich. "Anyone want one? Look, if I sound a little confused, Lew, it's because I am. This soul-mass topic is abstract and mysterious, and yet, as I'm seeing even more clearly, it's essential for me to realize it's more a part of who I am than my flesh and blood."

"No, thanks, I'm good," said Lew. "I'll be having a late lunch. How are you working through your realization of soul-mass?"

"As I'm becoming more soul-mass aware, I'm starting to use a simple question as I maintain a conversation with myself. I'm asking, who's talking here? Is it the voice of survival, my flesh; the voice of control, my human spirit; or the voice desiring to glorify God, which of course is my soul."

Chelsea slightly cocked her head. "How do you keep the voices straight?"

"Simple. Volume control. I'm becoming more discerning as to what voice is yelling, crying or calling. I just turn the volume down on the voice of self and turn up the volume on the voice of God. Sounds simplistic, but it works for me."

"That's deep and practical and really good, all at the same time. Can I use that?" asked Chelsea. "But where do you think the voice of God comes into this?"

"Great question. And, yes, when I get that Dean's position I'll email you the answer," laughed Jason. "Actually, with the Holy Spirit ruling instead of my human spirit, I believe that the voice of God is echoing through my soul."

"How do you think I would recognize the voice?" asked Lew.

"I should do a Lew and ask you for your answer. But for me it's tone. In my experiences—and frankly, it's been a while—God's voice is gentle. Not always soft, but with the gentle voice of a loving father. When the voice is feeding self, including self-justification, preservation, gratification and control, it's loud and demanding. When it's God's voice, it's sounding less like me. It's not condemning and demeaning. And, importantly, the voice points back to scripture. God doesn't lie about himself or contradict his word."

"My oh my. That is good. Maybe I should pay you for this session!" laughed Lew.

"You paid for the lunch; we'll call it even. This sandwich is really good, by the way. Bill and Marge are certainly back on track." After another bite, Jason added, "Don't you think somewhere inside the flesh of brain, combined with the will, is this little glimmer of hope of finally desiring the Spirit to rule? I've got to believe there is a part of the human conscious awareness and the human spirit that hungers, like the soul, for goodness and decency."

Lew tapped the marker against his palm, thinking. "Interesting thoughts. It's got to be. There is in all his created beings a drawing to the Father, perhaps because somewhere in our souls is the memory of Eden before the Fall."

"'Drawing to the Father' ... You mean like what happens in gravitational attraction?"

Lew looked at Chelsea. "Now there's a guy who's connecting the dots."

"Okay, Lew, you asked to help keep us on track. So allow me to make this about me. You asked how soul-mass relates to influence and leadership. We all know I came to you with the distinct impression I wasn't cutting it as a leader at New Horizons. I think my board members were clear I needed to fix more than my style. I would now agree they were right. I'm motivated and energized by the realization there is more to Jason than I realized. And please, on this question, don't ask me to answer my own question."

Lew turned back to face Jason. "Fair request. I think you now realize our human spirits are hopelessly addicted to self. As we know, addicted people can do horrible things to fill the hunger. The additional problem is, your human spirit desires to be in control of your living, and therein we find the enigma. We've got a dysfunctional addicted human spirit trying to still be in control."

"I could say, I represent that comment, but I'll pass," laughed Jason.

Lew stepped back to the whiteboard. "While you two are finishing your sandwiches, let me fill in a few boxes on our chart."

SOUL-MASS / WINESKIN PROPERTIES

SOUL	HUMAN SPIRIT / WILL	HOLY SPIRIT
• IMMORTAL • ABOUT LIFE • NEEDS A PROTECTOR • TENDER, WOUNDED BUT RESTORABLE, NAIVELY INNOCENT • FILLED WITH THE CHARACTER OF GOD.	• IMMATERIAL/MORTAL • ABOUT LIVING • WILD YET TAMABLE • SELFISH BY ITS NATURE • OBSESSED BY SURVIVAL	• ETERNAL • ABOUT EXPERIENCING GOD • PATIENT, GENTLE, KIND, POWERFUL • FULLY OF THE NATURE, EXPRESSION AND EMBODIMENT OF GOD, THE FATHER, AND CHRIST, THE SON

"It's clear, Jason, you are starting to pick up the fine distinctions to finding your self-integrity in your soul. And to keep us on track, that's the heart of influence."

"You lost me. What's the heart of influence?"

"Isn't it letting the goodness of God flow out through the transformative ongoing work of the Holy Spirit, otherwise known as love and otherwise known as God expressed through Jesus Christ?" said Lew.

"Now there was a mouthful. And right after lunch, no less."

"Allow me to add to that, Lew," Chelsea said, weaving her way back into the conversation. I think the core of our conversation is whether we can be good without the overpowering presence of God in our lives. We know no one is good but God. Jesus said that. However, goodness is different than good. Goodness, as a human quality, comes out in a desire to please God and serve one another. See the contrast? Trying to be good on our own and seeking God's goodness, his righteousness, are two separate things. Oil and water. Don't mix well. I think that's why Jesus said if you want to live, you must die to self. You can't keep the old woman alive and be totally devoted to God. Sound familiar?"

"Yes, it does," said Jason. "However, don't you think that for goodness to be sustainable for more than a brief moment, this soul-mass needs help?"

"You're exactly correct," said Lew, "And if I may add without the question: a human spirit that is subordinated to Christ's Spirit. In my consideration, that's where the will comes in."

"Let me add, Lew," offered Jason as the whole soul-mass concept began to make sense, "it needs a healthy, functioning soul, also empowered by the Holy Spirit, for this soul-mass contained in this wineskin to move beyond its own selfish desires. Am I right?"

"Only to the extent that we are like Saxe's blind men trying to describe an elephant. We are trying to create structure on something that has no structure," said Lew with a smile.

"Gentlemen, here's my take on that," said Chelsea. "Jason, you created this metaphorical vessel—this new wineskin—as the container for our spirituality. Paul refers to it as earthen vessels, clay jars, in his second letter to the Church of Corinth and speaks about it containing a treasure. So what do those vessels hold? It's the fullness of God, expressed through our soul-mass. But when the selfish needs and lusts of the human spirit dominate, our human spirit inflates, squeezing the soul and reducing its capacity. At another point Paul uses the example of a bladder. Self becomes a bladder of hot air, pushing out the fullness, the goodness of God."

Chelsea set down her partially finished sandwich on the coffee table, got up from her comfortable position on the couch and walked to the whiteboard. "The way I see it, the human spirit is a control system capable of thought and possessing insatiable lust. I don't mean just sexual lust. That's a flesh-and-bones drive. The human spirit has passions easily degrading to lusts, reducing the spiritual human's ability to be filled with the Holy Spirit. Mr. Merton, may I have the marker please? Allow me to add a few points."

"I thought you would never ask. Be my guest."

"We've just about filled in the whiteboard, but let me carve out a corner here." She wrote out another chart and checked off the **DISCOVER** column.

"First of all, I think we've more than worked over the discover part."

Lew glanced at his watch and a concerned look came over his face. "Chelsea, I apologize for interrupting your part of our session. The time got away from me. Jason, I scheduled a meeting with another client. They just flew in to meet. I thought I had enough time to fit you in, but I've got to break this session into two parts. Could you come back late this afternoon? I am so sorry, but I jammed my sessions too tight. I want to give adequate time for us to look at growing your soul-mass."

"Not a problem, Lew. I can be here at 4:30, but I need to be home by 6:30. The boys are just starting Cub Scouts tonight. " Jason got up to leave. "Well, you two, this has been a deep and powerful time together. In the meantime I'll go back to the office and clean the oozing brain from the information explosion in my head."

Lew said, "Let me just sum up where we'll be when we start back this afternoon. I had four points I wanted to make sure we covered. First was defining soul-mass. Are we good on that point?"

"As good as a mystery can be made known. Yup."

"Secondly, I wanted you to see the purpose of our spiritual elements. What's your takeaway, Jason?"

"Our flesh, both material and spiritual, is oriented to here-and-now survival and pleasure without any consideration for others or the other elements of our spirituality. Our flesh needs to be subdued, but it will always remain wild. On the other hand, it's our soul-mass that makes us human. It's through the soul-mass that we establish relationship with God. How's that for listening?"

"That's good. Point three was to explain how the soul-mass and our understanding of it relates to influence and leadership. What did you get from that?"

"I'm not ready for my final exam, but it seems to me this is the core of your principle of gravitational attraction and influence. The size, density and health of our soul-mass combined with the empowering work of the Holy Spirit determines our impact on others. Right?"

"Give the man a cupie doll. You hit the target," laughed Chelsea.

"Good. This was a lot, and we'll finish it up this afternoon. Thanks for your flexibility."

"By the way, Jason," said Chelsea, "don't miss that little bit of brain on your earlobe."

Whoever wants to be my disciple must deny themselves and take up their cross and follow me. For whoever wants to save their life will lose it, but whoever loses their life for me will find it. What good will it be for someone to gain the whole world, yet forfeit their soul? Or what can anyone give in exchange for their soul?

Matthew 16:24–26

REFLECTION QUESTIONS

1. *Have you discovered the voice of your soul?*

2. *How do you distinguish the voice of your soul and your self-voice of conscious awareness blended in with your human spirit?*

3. *How is the voice of your soul different and the same as the voice of God?*

4. *How do you see the Holy Spirit changing/growing/enlarging the properties of the soul-mass?*

5. *In looking at the soul qualities list, what one(s) do you feel are most necessary to start your focus? Why have you chosen those?*

CHAPTER 13

Soul–Mass Woundedness

SOUL-MASS AND THE SPIRIT OF GOD

determine influence

My soul yearns for you in the night; in the morning my spirit longs for you. When your judgments come upon the earth, the people of the world learn righteousness.

Isaiah 26:9

J ason came up the stairs to Lew's office a little slower than earlier in the day. *That was a heavy, content-loaded time. I hope I can retain that great information.* He was also pleased that Lew and Chelsea had positively responded to his insights on the new wineskin and the three intersecting circles. *Chelsea's addition in calling it the place of shalom was really good,* he thought. Lew said healing and growing the soul were next. Jason was tired but ready. As he entered Lew's office, Jason noticed Chelsea sitting in her favorite place, curled up on the couch, and Lew in his favorite green chair with his back to the whiteboard.

"I am so sorry for the break from our earlier session," apologized Lew, "I had another pressing issue that couldn't wait. Besides, we needed a little time to come up for air. And that leads me to our beginning to pull all this soul-mass together into something that is understandable for you, Jason. This is a lot for one day, but you will see how important our conversation will be to tie it all together. Grab a mug of coffee and a stale Danish from this morning and settle in."

Jason grabbed the last soggy pastry and settled into his

now-favorite green chair facing the whiteboard. "Lew, I truly love your drilling expeditions where you force me to comprehend and own this deep soul-mass stuff. And Chelsea, you have added great depth and insights. Thanks for the investment of time."

"Truly, my joy, Jason."

"I can see it working at work and at home. But do me a favor. It's late, I'm tired and I know you've got a point. Put it out quickly, and then let me sort through it. I've got two boys needing some Dad time this afternoon, and I need to reserve some brain energy to be fully engaged with them."

"Fair enough. It's this. As you recall, I had a fourth point for our time on soul-mass. It's showing soul-mass in your life and character. You know, as we've talked about, that fully loving yourself is not possible if your soul-mass isn't healthy and renewed. Self-loathing is the natural end-point when we make living all about us. Sadly, in my experience, self-loathing is so much more common than the evidences of self-love.

"Well, aren't you a messenger of cheery news. Only problem is, you're right," said Jason.

Chelsea stood up. "This is the critical piece, certainly not the only one, but the piece I think that puts this conceptual soul-mass model together. May I, sir?" she asked, nodding to Lew as she walked to the whiteboard.

Jason noticed Chelsea was more serious and subdued than her normal perkiness. She wrote **SOUL-MASS WOUNDEDNESS** on the whiteboard.

"Jason, what do you think wounds the soul?"

"Deep question. One part, I think, is a deformed or malformed identity for who we think we're *not*."

"Interesting. Tell us more."

"I'm coming to realize a—okay, *my*—deformed identity can't protect my soul and may even become the assailant. I vividly know I'm not always good, caring, full of integrity, pure or disciplined. Not only do I act poorly toward others, but I betray myself as well. And I believe this is true for everyone; we all remind ourselves of our failings. Of course those reminders are egged on by Satan, speaking lies of who we aren't. 'You call yourself a

Christian? Look at the pathetic example. If I were Christ, I'd be ashamed of who you aren't!' Recognize the voice? The flip side of that is the self-condemnation for who we think we are, also egged on by Satan. 'I know who you really are. I know what you do and think when you think no one is looking. Shame!' Satan has us on both sides: ridiculing us for who we aren't and prosecuting us for who we are. Therein lies shame, which is truly out of the pit of hell.

"How true," said Chelsea. "Between our own self-inflicted wounds and Satan's condemning poison arrows, no wonder we have wounded souls. Then two more things get added: trauma and significant violations of trust."

"Do you feel comfortable in elaborating on that, Chelsea?" asked Lew.

"I think so." Chelsea hesitated, took a deep sigh and looked into space, not focusing on anything. "When I was 11, I was raped by an older boy in our neighborhood who was babysitting me and my baby brother." She swallowed hard, hesitated and, finding an inner strength, continued. "I can tell you from my experience that when we've been raped, lied to or attacked verbally and physically, our self-protective survival nature is to withdraw so we aren't as vulnerable. We become less open and trusting without some proof of safety. Years of therapy help us get through the trauma, but they don't really help with the withdrawn trust."

"I am so sorry, Chelsea. I can't even imagine what you've gone through." The thought of that happening to her at a young age and thinking about his own daughter, Sydney, brought a lump to Jason's throat.

"Don't try to imagine. It's horrible. Obviously, distrust, shame, fear, panic have all been emotions and wounds in my face for a long time. It wasn't my fault. I know that. But the distance between what I know and what I feel is still great."

"Can I ask how you are getting through it?"

"A lot of therapy, a lot of anger, a lot of tears and, in the last three years, a lot of prayer. And thanks for using the word *getting* and not *got*. You never get through this. It's always with you."

"Whether you're the victim or the victimizer, the burden

Q.

Have you worked through your violations of trust?

must be monstrous. That explains a lot of the conversation I had with Joe Tyler. It's amazing how both of you have been able to take those personal devastations and turn tragedy into a force of goodness."

"It's the same Holy Spirit at work," said Chelsea.

"How was it possible for your soul to become healed?"

"For, me—and I think everyone has to find their own route of restoration—it was a dual process of healing and growing at the same time."

"Please explain."

"For me—and that's all I can say—for me, it started with simply asking Jesus to take away the pain, the anger, the self-loathing and the shame. I also had to forgive my attacker. It was only after becoming a Christ-follower that I understood the power of forgiveness."

"I think it would be helpful for Jason to hear your insight," encouraged Lew.

"For me, forgiving my attacker did nothing to minimize the damage he did to me. What it did do was release me from that hate and shame, so it was no longer sucking life out of me like a leech. Forgiveness was also a breaking of bondage so that my attacker could begin to put his life back together. Importantly, for me, it was so that the Enemy couldn't trap and bind me in hate, shame and destructive anger."

Jason longed to say something to help. "Chelsea, it wasn't your fault. You must know that."

"Of course I do. But my broken heart and my wounded soul heard the lies of Satan. Only Jesus—and simply his name—can break that bondage to the lies. It starts with confession. Not only the confession of guilt if it's there but, importantly, the confession of the love of Christ and the power of the Holy Spirit working through the pain, the shame and the rage.

"Back to your question, Jason, of how did I heal my soul. It seems too simple, but I can find no other way than to do what he asks. Cast my burden on him. Miraculous healing began when I started doing that. And in that process restoration began. Trust me. I know. With that healing I needed to start strengthening and growing my soul to be the healthy vessel it was intended to be. It was only then I was able to begin the process of healing through reconciliation."

"Excuse me, Chelsea, but you were the victim. Who did you need to reconcile with?"

"For me it had to start with God. Eventually it ended with me. For a long time, I didn't trust God. I was young so I couldn't fully process, but deep inside there was a question. 'God, how could you have allowed this to happen to one your innocents?' It wasn't until after my rebellious and angry teen years that I realized my first step of reconciliation was to God."

"How did that happen?"

"I ran into Lew after I started university studies. Literally. I was texting while driving and rear-ended his car. He was so kind. I broke down, he took me to coffee, we started talking and here we are. Lew helped me see that I may never fully understand but I can't base my trust in God on the basis of testing and proving his every step. God is good, or he is not God. I also needed reconciliation with myself.

"I still felt guilty and ashamed from the rape over ten years earlier. I was still beating myself up. I could have fought harder, could have screamed, could have … who knows what? I didn't need to forgive myself. I didn't do anything wrong. What I needed was reconciliation between my human spirit and my soul, and it wasn't happening. My soul-mass was deeply wounded and scarred. My human spirit was angry and somewhere, between my spiritual flesh and my spirit, I was full of hate."

"How did you get healed and restored?"

"Accepting Christ as Lord of my life was the first step. That then opened the door for deep spiritual work. What I began to see was that confession leads to restoration. Restoration leads to forgiveness, and then—and for me, only then—there was room for reconciliation."

"Sorry to interrupt again, Chelsea, but you said something very interesting. You used the word *room*. Can you explain?"

"In my experience, hate, woundedness, fear and shame occupy my wineskin, as you aptly named it, Jason. For me, when those destructive emotions fill me, there is no room for joy, peace, hope, love—the fruit of the Spirit. I had to intentionally expel those destructive emotions, but I could not do it on my own."

"I think I know how, but what was your experience?"

"That's the healing work of Christ within me, empowered by the Holy Spirit. Jesus said, "Cast your burdens on me." I did that in prayer and faith, and from there I finally began to feel whole again. As I've become whole, I am now able to begin to create wholesome relationships. First with me, then my parents and then with those in my close circle of trust."

"I don't know what to say, Chelsea, other than I'm sorry for your pain, and I rejoice in your restored joy."

"Thanks, Jason. We kid around and tease a lot, but what you said is tender and kind."

As Chelsea was walking back to the couch, Lew got up, picked up the marker and stood in silence as he gathered his thoughts. "Most of us are not in a continuous awareness of our spiritual nature. I don't know about you, Jason, but given a lack of focused attention, I think and act like I'm 90 percent material and 10 percent spiritual. We all agree it should be at least the reverse. Actually it should be 0:100 percent. I'm consciously aware of my need to do an identity shift, but I seem to have SADD. You know, Soul Attention Deficit Disorder."

Q.

Know anyone with SADD?

The mood noticeably lightened, and Jason laughed. "That's good, Lew, I can use that."

"As I began this whole Gravity project, I wondered, how do I grow the soul? Can I intentionally have an impact on the quality and integrity of my soul? I believe we all can. The way I see it, here's one way to discipline the human spirit to become a soul protector. I did the original work of discovery, and then Chelsea has been making it into a systematic study. Of course the spiritual disciplines like prayer, reading of scripture, solitude, community and service, among others, are essential for empowering this process.

"With Chelsea's conversation, let me add some notes to the Heal portion of our chart."

SOUL-MASS / WINESKIN INVENTORY

DISCOVER	HEAL	GROW

WILL/HEART-MIND/SPIRIT	SOUL	HUMAN SPIRIT WILL/HEART-MIND	SOUL	WILL/HEART-MIND/SPIRIT	SOUL
VOICE OF SELFISHNESS AND SELF-CENTEREDNESS	VOICE OF GOODNESS	FULL OF ANGER, HATE, UNFORGIVENESS, DENIAL AND FALSE ENEMIES	WOUNDED, AND IN NEED OF HEALING		
WILL-ENERGY		IN NEED OF RESTORATION			
HEART-FEELINGS EMOTIONS					
MIND-CONSCIOUS AWARENESS AND THOUGHTS					

Chelsea chimed in. "Let's move this conversation to 'grow.' I've just sent a list to your tablet, Jason. The focus of my internship has been on these, I call them, *soul qualities.* Here's what I've discovered for me as well as my work, and it might be helpful for you. It's how I got legs on this whole soul thing. As you recall in Philippians, Paul says to fill our minds and to meditate on things that are true, noble, reputable, authentic, compelling and gracious, the best and the beautiful and things worthy of praise. I know you're familiar with the scripture, but have you ever wondered what those things are, anyway? Our answer— and mind you, it's just two people agreeing on one thing—is that we believe those encouragements of behavior are simply those qualities found in scripture. And when you follow them, they don't take you to sin. They are the words of Jesus and those of Peter, Paul and the other writers of the canon under the inspiration of the Holy Spirit. Here's the simple collaborative approach of a younger and a considerably older mind."

"Watch it there, young lady!" Lew laughed. He turned in his chair to directly face Jason. "I don't know about you, but I need lists. I need concrete. I love it when Jesus says for us to be holy because he is holy, but my thought is, 'That's easy for you to say, Jesus, but how does that work for me?' The list, which works for me, are those virtues of the Living Word helping me live out a holy life. Take some time until we have our next meeting and do as Paul suggested in his letter to the church at Philippi—think on these things—and tell me if these help your sense of a growing soul within you. We'd love to hear the product of your work."

"Excuse me, you two," said Jason, leaning in to the conversation. "So you're saying there is a list of soul qualities."

"Oh, they are there," said Lew. "Like Chelsea said, they are the lists and encouragements found all through the New Testament. They are the behaviors that speak to *be*, rather than just *do*."

"Like I said, I just sent the list to your tablet, so you can bring it up if you want," said Chelsea.

"Be sure and note," said Lew, "we've grouped them into seven categories. They are Caring/Loving, Spiritually Centered, Wise, Disciplined, Selfless, Full of Integrity and Pure. I won't go into each one now, but take some time between now and the next time we meet to meditate on the list. Make your prayer, 'Lord, how can this virtue be evident within me?' Importantly, these are not *do's*. Let me repeat that. These are not *do's*. These are the consequences of *be's*. This is the tangible evidence of your being."

SOUL QUALITIES

CARING/LOVING (AGAPE, PHILOS, EROS)

BRAVE

COMPASSIONATE (GRACIOUS)

CONCERNED

GENEROUS/BENEVOLENT

GENTLE

HOSPITABLE

KIND

MERCIFUL

PEACE LOVING/PEACE MAKING/PEACEFUL

GRATEFUL/THANKFUL (INDEBTED)

FORGIVING

SELFLESS

HUMBLE

MEEK

SERVANT-HEARTED

TOLERANT

FULL OF INTEGRITY

COURAGEOUS

FAITHFUL

TRUE/STRAIGHT/ UPRIGHT/GENUINE

HONEST

JUST

ABOVE REPROACH

PURE

INNOCENT

CHASTE

GODLY

SPIRITUALLY CENTERED

HOLY/GODLY (IMPUTED)

RIGHTEOUS (MAN AND GOD-IMPUTED)

GOOD (FULL OF)

PURE HEART (OF A)

FAITH (FULL OF)

WORSHIPFUL/DEVOUT

CONTENT

JOYFUL

WISE

DISCERNING

KNOWLEDGEABLE/ (INFORMATION – (WHAT)

UNDERSTANDING/AWARE – (HOW)

WISE (WHY)

DISCIPLINED

ENDURING/PERSEVERANT

PATIENT/LONGSUFFERING/ FORBEARING

TEMPERATE/SELF-CONTROLLED

SOBER (SERIOUS-MINDED)

STEADFAST

SELF-CONTROLLED

ALERT/ WATCHFUL/VIGILANT

DILIGENT

FRUGAL/RESOURCEFUL OBEDIENT

Lew had an impish grin on his face. "There you are, Jason. A little homework for you."

Jason's brow furrowed. This was not what he had expected.

"What do you mean, there you are? You're going to give me a list of what you call soul qualities and send me out the door and say, 'Good luck'? We've spent all this time together, and it comes down to you giving me a list?"

Lew leaned forward. "What do you want me do, Jason? It's pretty straightforward. Meditate, study, cogitate, pray, be silent, ruminate—whatever. It's not that complicated, so don't make it that way. You want to grow your soul? Feed it. Like I said, don't turn this into a project. Just do it. Period."

"Just about the time I think I'm making progress, you show me my odometer. Not sure how many miles I've come on this—journey."

"Come on, Jason," said Chelsea feeling confident enough in the friendship to push Jason. "You really think you're going to blink your eyes and you're a totally different person? Or Lew is going to wave a magic wand and you're a changed person?"

"Please don't be offended, but that list is too much data. My eyes just glaze over when I read the list and my brain goes, 'NOT ANOTHER LIST!' I wouldn't argue for a moment, Lew, that these are not essential qualities for my soul. These are the change items you and Bill Courtland talk about. But I asked for a glass of orange juice, and you brought me the whole tree!"

"Good point," said Chelsea. "You raise an interesting challenge of learning. Content and context. If the content is greater than the context, your brain is going to reject it. Which yours just did."

"So you noticed, huh?"

"What would you like me to do?" asked Lew. "I can dumb it down and turn it into a cliché if that would make you feel better."

"I know you wouldn't do that if I begged you, friend," said Jason, tempering his tone in the conversation.

"You're right, I wouldn't, but you sense my frustration. You need to understand that my frustration is not with you, the consumer. It's with me, the producer. My challenge is to find a better way to make the quality of the content more acceptable in consumption—in your context—yet not lose the quality of the content."

"Good luck with that, Lew. You do that, and you've just revolutionized Sunday morning!"

"Jason, here's something you can do for me. Take this list with you. Next time we meet, I need—notice I didn't say, I want—I need you to bring me back that list in a form that's been useful to you. Will you do that for me? No instructions. Just make it useful to you in your way. Fair?"

"Fair. You can count on it, Lew. I'm looking forward to the challenge and being able to give back in a small way what you've poured into me. I hope you didn't take offense at my pushback on the list thing. It just seemed overwhelming."

"Thank you. I understand. Perhaps your reaction came out of a sense of work instead of a sense of process. When you've found a process to make this list meaningful for you, send Chelsea an email, and she'll schedule a time for us. Oh, and before you leave, can I have a word with you?"

Chelsea smiled. "That is a clear cue for me to exit stage left. Good session, and thanks for letting me be a part it."

"Thank you, Chelsea. Being able to share your experience so others can grow shows the healing you've experienced," said Jason with a smile.

Lew waited for Chelsea to shut the door.

"What's up, Lew?"

"Where do you think you're at in our process of meeting together?"

"Well, things are going a lot better at work since we first started. I owe a lot to you for helping me through this. Several of the board members have remarked how pleased they are with my progress."

"How so?"

"They said I am much more sensitive to the feelings of others. That tells me I'm more soul-mass aware of others. You've helped me become aware of the influence of my own soul-mass too. Also, there's less tension with my team members, and I've become far more patient and less demanding."

"Any reason you can think of as to why I asked to for you to stay so I could talk with you?"

Jason could feel himself becoming uncomfortable. "No. You obviously have an agenda, but at the moment you're starting to become mysterious. What's up?"

"You're a bright guy. You've picked up on the fine points and deep truths of soul-mass as we've worked our way through this murky marsh."

"So what's your point?"

"Something's missing."

"Really? Look, Lew, let's not make this conversation an Easter egg hunt. It's late in the day, and you've got an agenda for this meeting. Why don't you just come out with it?"

"Okay. There's an elephant in the room. There's something blocking you from making any more forward progress. Until you address it, we've gone about as far as we can. Any ideas what it might be?"

"I can think of a few ideas," said Jason

"Then why are we playing this game of twenty questions? Out with it, man."

"Out with what?"

"Do you remember our conversation in your car about monkey-catching?"

"Yes."

"Are you tired of dragging the pot with your fist inside?"

"Better than having it beaten to a pulp by people you're supposed to trust."

"So you know where I'm going with this conversation, don't you?"

"I was kind of wondering how long it would take to get here."

"Look, Jason. You, like everyone else on this planet, are hopelessly addicted to self. And in that addiction you've created a number of self-inflicted wounds on your soul as well as taking a number of blindside hits from others you didn't see coming. And that's not counting the verbal assault from the Enemy."

"Now it's my turn to play the *and* game. And?"

"Through life, you've had two choices when deep hurts have come your way. One, you could deny everything good about your heritage and personal culture, rebelling by engaging in risky behaviors and risky relationships to anesthetize your hurt and anger. You didn't do that, so you've pulled your tender and bruised soul in as tight as you could—put it in a jar—painted on a pleasant facade and vowed to never let anyone get that close to your soul again. Am I describing you?"

Jason's throat tightened. Tears, the first ones in decades, began to form. Jason tried to speak, but the long-repressed emotions of deep hurt and anger tightened his chest.

"Take a deep breath, my friend. Let it out slowly."

Lew patiently sat in silence for several minutes; he knew the next spoken voice had to be from Jason.

"You are very perceptive, Lew. As I was doing my own study on the soul, I did a search on my Bible software for *soul* to see all the places it's mentioned. I kept seeing how the voices out of scripture kept crying out to God through their wounded souls. I began to wonder, what was it that so wounded their souls, and then I began to ask, what is it that has wounded my soul?"

"What did you see?"

"It felt like betrayal. It started with God. I have a deep wound in the loss of my dad. As a boy, I remember asking his pastor friends why he died in his prime—and when I needed him most. I remember one pastor saying, 'God knows. He must have needed him more than us.' Later I realized that was cliché. God does know, but God doesn't need anyone. He wants our relationship, but he doesn't *need* any of us."

"Anything else inside that pot you're carrying around?"

"You know my hotshot job at Continental Beverage? I didn't leave it to go into ministry. I was let go. The company was bought out by InterBevco, and I got caught in the downsizing. All my so-called mentors were clambering so hard to keep their own jobs, I got lost in the mad scramble. 'You're young. You're bright, Jason. Your future is all before you,' the Vice President told me. I thought these people were my friends. You know how many called to ask how I was doing after I left? Zero. Not a one. Wounded? Bitter? Yeah, I had my share of that as I sat on my pity pot. I was so humiliated, I didn't even tell Emily I was fired."

"Then came Emily's affair, our divorce and then being let go from my church staff position. Right or wrong, there comes a time when simply for survival you clench your soul into a tight, little ball and put an intelligent and smartass façade around it to make sure no one ever wounds it like that again."

"Sounds like a great way to build scar tissue."

"It is. Three things about scar tissue: it has no feelings, it makes a great barrier and it's a great container to drag around."

"Yes, it does. Ever notice how inflexible scar tissue is as well? Barrier is a great word. So, my friend, what do you think God wants to do with all this inside of you? What do you think he thinks about this scar tissue around your soul?"

"If it hurts me, it's got to hurt him. At least I understand that."

"You think he helplessly stands by with tears in his eyes, as if he's watching a terrible tragedy occurring on the internet? Do you believe he not only wants your soul healed and stripped of all that scar tissue but also that he has the power to make it happen?"

"Of course."

"So, dear friend with a wounded soul, how do you think it happens?"

"Let's see. I think you are the soul-mentor. I'm the mentor's friend. Isn't this a good place where you encourage me?"

"It is, yet self-discovery is far more valuable than instruction. I've pushed over a text that is a paraphrase of three scriptures. I hoped the conversation would get to this point. These scriptures are what started the healing for Chelsea. Take a minute to look at them, and then tell me your thoughts. I don't need your human flesh and spirit thoughts. I want you to try and dig down deep to hear the voice of your soul. Take your time; I can wait."

Are you tired? Worn out? Burned out on religion? Come to me. Pile your troubles on GOD's shoulders—he'll carry your load; he'll help you out. Get away with me, and you'll recover your life. He'll never let good people topple into ruin. Live carefree before God; he is most careful with you.

"So how do you, Lew?"

"How do I what?"

"How do you experience and live a carefree life in God. It seems so like a platitude and simplistic."

"That is your assignment for the rest of your life. And I think you have to discover that unique process for yourself. I can't give you a three-point lesson."

"I understand. So, mentor-friend, at least tell me how it happens?"

"I'm going to give you an answer that you'll, hopefully, find frustratingly incomplete."

"I'm all ears."

"Pray."

"That's it? Pray. Man, if that's not cliché or what?"

"Or what? It's either profound truth—truth that God is wanting to reveal himself to you and through you to heal you and use you even more effectively than ever before as an instrument of righteousness—or it's shallow drivel that washes off in the first rain. Here's your problem or your opportunity. You won't know until you've given it a thorough try. You've got enough pastor left in you to know I'm telling you the truth. I encourage you to spend time in the soul qualities and focus on them as a part of your prayer life. Can I pray with you before you leave?"

"Please do. I need it."

"Lord, if our souls are wounded, then you are wounded too. Still our scheming minds, quell our selfish hearts and suppress our fleshly lusts so that we can hear the still, small voice of our souls ever so desperately crying out to glorify you. Speak back so that we can know you hear. We ask that the healing balm of Jesus bind up the intentional and accidental wounds of betrayal. Help us to be willing to trust those who love us because in that process we learn again how to trust you, who loves even more. Return to us the joy of our salvation, and restore our souls as you did David's. Amen."

As Jason got up to leave, he looked at Lew and hugged him tightly. Jason began sobbing and crying like he hadn't done since the day his father died.

Dear friend, I pray that you may enjoy good health and that all may go well with you, even as your soul is getting along well.

3 John 2

REFLECTION QUESTIONS

1. *Have you ever considered the possibility that self-loathing and self-love originate from two different places in your being? Is it possible that self-loathing comes from our human spirits and genuine self-love comes from the soul? What are your thoughts? What Scriptures would seem to back up that proposition? What Scriptures would seem to argue against it?*

2. *Have you had your trust so deeply violated that it's taking a life-time to work through it? Have you been able to prepare your soul-mass to allow God to heal the violation? Has it affected your capacity to trust?*

3. *Have you been the source of deeply wounding someone else's soul-mass? How have you been able to make amends—with the victim and with yourself?*

4. *Have you ever prayed the prayer of 1 John 1:9? God is faithful and just to forgive us and to cleanse us all our unrighteousness.*

CHAPTER 14

Putting it Together

I am the true vine, and my Father is the vinedresser.
Every branch in me that does not bear fruit he takes
away, and every branch that does bear fruit he
prunes, that it may bear more fruit. Already you are
clean because of the word that I have spoken to you.
Abide in me, and I in you. As the branch cannot
bear fruit by itself, unless it abides in the vine,
neither can you, unless you abide in me. I am the
vine; you are the branches. Whoever abides in me
and I in him, he it is that bears much fruit, for apart
from me you can do nothing.

John 15:1–17

T here was over a foot of accumulated snow on yards, but the streets were clear and dry. Entering Lew's building, Jason reflected on the times with Lew, realizing this journey was coming to an end. He felt sad and hoped their time together had produced a deep friendship. It sure had for him. Lew was a few years younger than his father would have been, had he lived, yet the friendship was a combination of mentor, uncle and good friend. His stomach tightened when he thought that, like a clinical relationship, there would be some distance now that the assignment was ending.

Lew's door was open. "Good morning, friend," said Jason as he stepped in. He had hoped there would be a fire in the fireplace, and he wasn't disappointed. Jason didn't wait for a return greeting. He threw his coat and earmuffs on the chair and headed directly to the fireplace. The now-familiar aroma of rich pipe tobacco filled the air.

"Well, well, well," said Lew. "Look who came in from the cold. I've been anticipating and regretting our meeting."

Jason turned to greet Lew. The heat from the fire warmed

his back, and the radiating heat felt good. "I have too. It's great to see you too. So which one is it, anticipation or regret?"

"Both. My regret is, I know our structured time is coming to an end. I'm going to miss these conversations. My anticipation is to continue to learn what you've been working on and explore how our friendship grows from here. You've added greatly to our understanding of soul-mass. Don't underestimate the value of your contribution."

"I'm not sure what to say. Thanks for the motivation and the encouragement."

"I was just thinking, this was the longest separation between sessions. I presume this means you've been working on the soul qualities and doing some deep work."

"Yes, it's been a while, and yes, I've been working on making the list of soul qualities meaningful in my life. That was a major project you gave me and so worthwhile."

"I'm eager to hear how you're using this as a point of reference for growing your soul-mass. Grab a cup before you sit down."

As he brewed his coffee, Jason said, "Before I tell you my progress, I've got a question. Why didn't you just make the soul-qualities list from Galatians and Colossians? Seems like a good list was already started."

"If I were properly doing my work today, I'd turn the question back on you as to why you thought I thought, but that's convoluted. So let me cheat and just tell you. Those two lists are a great starting point, and you saw the qualities from those scriptures in the list. But as I searched and researched, there seemed to be so many more in other places of scripture that talked about the *be* inside of me. Actually there are 13 lists of virtues in the New Testament. The ones I gave you are a compilation of those lists."

"Okay. That makes sense."

"I'm eager to hear the results of your work."

"Here's how I've been able to apply your soul qualities list over the past number of weeks. What I did first was tape the list up in a number of locations at home and at work, so I could be reminded of those soul qualities throughout the day."

Settling in to the now-familiar and comfortable hunter green leather chair with a hot mug of coffee, Jason continued, "Then I began to get intentional."

"Sounds like having them in your face was intentional."

"Always slicing and dicing my thoughts. I love it. Okay, I then got *really* intentional. I did that by focusing on one category at a time. The first category was Caring and Loving. I started by making this an outline for prayer, and so I began by asking, 'Lord, show me today how your quality of caring and loving is expressed from my soul and through me today.' Next I wrote my own one-sentence definition of what that soul quality meant to me—my personal definition. After a day or so, I went to the next one and simply asked, for example, 'Let my caring and loving for others be through acts of being brave and being willing to give of my life as you gave up your life for me.'

"As I went through the specific qualities in the Caring and Loving list, day by day, I asked God to help me to really understand my prayer. So, for example, when I asked to be gentle, I wanted to know better what that meant and how I could express it. Next, I began to pray for and anticipate opportunities where that soul quality could show itself. Finally, I looked up some scriptures illustrating how God wants that quality to live out in me. Only when I felt I really understood what God intended me to know about each soul quality would I move on."

Jason sipped his coffee, pleased with his project but also feeling good that he didn't feel a sense of prideful justification for his work. "I pushed my chart over to you. Thanks for requesting that I create a form that would be helpful instead of providing me with a form. I had to discover it for myself. I now own it. I just sent it to your email."

"I see it just showed up on my tablet."

"Your what? Look who's come into this decade."

"Oh, stop it. I don't really need it, but my theory is, if I miss one generation of technology, I'm dead. Catching up is almost impossible. You were saying ... ?

"Here's the key for me, Lew. I only took one soul quality at a time. I wasn't on a marathon, trying to see if I came in first in a race with myself. No works. I truly was on a journey."

"My, that's impressive, Jason. Not very efficient, though."

"What do you mean?"

"This could take several months to get through the list if you really took it to heart," said Lew with a grin.

"Come on, Lew, there you go, getting sarcastic on me right in the middle of my seriousness."

"I've had a good teacher in the past several months: Jason the Sardonic."

"Just about the time we dive deep, you crack a humor nut. I'm going to miss this time."

"Don't worry, we'll find a way to continue to have fun. But after today, our relationship changes from one of mentor-to-friend to more of friend-to-friend." Lew got up to refresh his own coffee. "Getting back to serious, how's your growing exercise working out in the long run for you?"

"It's been very helpful. It's not so formulaic that I lose heart in the detail. And it's practical to the point that it's keeping my spiritual eyes open all day. It's become my 'Disciplines of the Soul.'"

"That sounds profound," Lew said, grinning over his shoulder.

"Oh, now you stop it! Here's the other thing that's been good from my focusing on this list. It's caused me to go back into scripture to find the content and the context where each of these soul qualities is mentioned. I'm regaining my hunger to consume the word. In the midst of my process, there is one discipline I'm having to work harder at than all the rest."

"Which one is that?"

"The list. As you well know, my addiction is works, and here in my list is a chronicle of my great works. I've got to be so careful I use this as a celebration list, not a task and accomplishment list testifying to my worth. I never realized how much I have to focus on devotion over duty. It's a double-edged sword."

"Have you cut yourself yet?"

"Hah, good play on words. I'm using the list to remind me of my addiction to lists. I guess you might say I'm dancing on the blade edge and trying not to get severed. But I don't know how else to form a discipline of not being focused on works. I know, it doesn't make sense on one side, but so far it is working for me."

Lew came back to his seat, set his coffee down, and picked up his new tablet.

"You know how to drive that tablet without putting it in the ditch?"

"Hey, young man, there's a lot of Lew you haven't explored yet. I'm eager to take a look at the 'Disciplines of the Soul' chart you put together. Right now take a look at the chart I sent you. There is a logical progression to explain where you are and where you're going. This is our time for you to put all the pieces together and for you to tell me how it all makes sense. Take a look at the headings. The **STATE OF MY HUMAN SPIRIT AND SOUL** determines the foundation of my **BELIEF AND BEHAVIOR VALUES**. My **FEARS AND DESIRES** strongly influence my **MOTIVES** for my **ACTIONS AND BEHAVIORS**. In the end, our actions and behaviors are what others experience.

①	②	③	④	⑤
ACTIONS AND BEHAVIORS	MOTIVES	FEARS AND DESIRES	BELIEF AND BEHAVIOR	STATE OF MY HUMAN SOUL + SPIRIT

"What we're going to do is get a final clear view of the old Jason before we bury him. Sound fair?"

"A little gruesome in the metaphor department, but I'm ready to get rid of the junk that's been slowing me down."

"I notice in your chart that the headings go in reverse order from your sentence. What's your point?"

"The way I said it is a true statement. The way we unwind is from the reverse. So we'll start at the root to get to the conclusion."

"Is there anything you do that doesn't have a strategic

purpose? Good grief!"

"I'd answer that question, but then you'd think I had a strategic motive behind my answer. Moving on, using my drilling metaphor, we're going to start at the surface. We start with a set of actions and behaviors—evidences, if you will. Then as we go deeper, we get to the core of why you—we—do what we do, ultimately reaching the soul-mass. You with me? Make sense?"

"So far, so good. You amaze me, Lew. I'm looking at this and marveling how you're able to string a succession of thoughts together into a sentence and then lay it out on a sheet of paper."

"Thanks. First of all, though, before we get to the chart, I want to lay a foundation or platform to rest our chart on that explains why we're talking. Here it is. I believe there are three fundamental temptations core to all behaviors God calls sin. I believe those temptations common to all humans are the same three Jesus experienced in the wilderness from the onslaught of Satan. You know this passage better than I, but here's my take. If Jesus experienced all temptation known to man, then these are the three categories of all sin. Permit me to give you as brief an overview as I can. Do you remember the first temptation?"

"Sure: in Matthew and Luke, Jesus' first temptation was creating bread after fasting for forty days. Satan enticed Jesus with gratifying his hunger."

"Exactly—gratification. Whether it be the lusts of the flesh or the mind, gratification is the origin of most misery on earth. Keep in mind that gratification is different than satisfaction or feeling content. What are some concrete examples that come to mind?"

"How many do you want? We want money, fame, sexual pleasure, drug highs and alcohol intoxication. We want to feel proud and take revenge. And we want a full stomach."

"It's disturbing how quickly those examples come to mind, isn't it? Gratifications: they seemingly make us feel better for the moment. I desire something, and the only way to get it is to take it for myself. What an interesting delusion. Now what was Jesus' remedy?"

"As I recall, it was consuming the bread of life, the word of God, where all the gratification you need is found."

Lew smiled. "You got it. So I eat the bread of life and drink from the streams of living water. My joy in the Lord replaces my enjoyment of the things of this world. God holds my life in his hands and is the power of all in heaven and on earth; He's promised to provide everything I need."

Lew stopped for a moment as his countenance grew serious. "Jason, as I lay the foundation, and as a follow-up to this conversation, I encourage you to periodically stop and examine yourself. See how much of what you intentionally do in life is driven by the motive to feel good. You can see in our society how much of those actions end up with us feeling bad."

"Yep," said Jason. "It's sobering, and I'm not being flip with a play on words. What you say is so true."

"You'll recall the next temptation was an offer. Satan asked Jesus to worship him in exchange for lordship over the kingdoms of earth. Ha! How ridiculous. Jesus was already Lord of all. But this was a perfect temptation for Satan to try. In Jesus' human state, the temptation He experienced was control."

Jason took a deep breath. *This one will hit home.*

"Now I'm getting personal, Jason. You've seen how much control has dictated your life. I hate to poke a needle in your balloon; you're no different than most other people. The temptation for control was no different for Jesus, either. Why are we so bent on controlling everyone and everything around us? Any ideas?"

"I'm coming to the realization I control my environment because I can't put my trust in others to watch out for me."

"You are learning well, my friend. And if we do it well— control and micro-manage our world—it feeds the temptations of gratification and preservation, the two other primal self-needs of natural man."

"Explain your thought."

"When we think we are in control, we think we possess the method and the means to gratify our sensual needs and give ourselves a sense of security. When we think we are in control, we no longer have to take the risk of trust. Jesus' remedy:

worship God—trust him, and serve him only. For us, all we need to comprehend and believe is reality: Who needs control when we worship the most powerful being in creation?"

"This is interesting, Lew. Never has that passage been so personalized before. I never saw it as a trust versus control issue; even if I had, I don't know that I could have applied it to myself."

"I'm glad you are realizing how much you've grown. Now for the last temptation: Satan taunted and challenged Jesus to prove how powerful he was. 'Throw yourself down and watch the angels catch you—maybe.' What Satan was trying to do was create doubt in Jesus that he was eternal and to focus on preserving His own life. If Jesus had attempted to prove he was immortal, it would have been because he had an inkling of doubt as to his Sonship. If Jesus had entertained that small doubt, it would have ended hope for us for all time and beyond time."

"You really know how to put drama into the gospel, Lew."

"I regard this moment in Jesus' life as the hinge point of eternity. If Jesus had blinked, it would have been over for us and eternity." He sipped his coffee, letting that idea sink in. "Well, I believe all sin can be traced back to these three temptations. They are the source of our deeply wounded souls, turning our eyes to the temporal. Jason, I don't want you to miss this point. These are your temptations too. Right now. What's your take?"

"Besides being a little blown away by the completeness of your illustration, I think this makes so much sense. I'm seeing that my behaviors of selfishness are often rooted in preservation."

"Such as?"

"Such as a lack of generosity—also known as greed. And my button-tight persona so no one can get in. Man, even my behaviors of striving and ambition are probably rooted more in preservation than ambition. Or maybe my fear of loss—which is preservation.

"Good insight. Simply you realizing and sharing that with me is loosening your grip on self-preservation.

"Let me add another 'aha' to this and see if it walks. Last time we were together, you gave me a list of soul qualities. You suggested I focus on those as a way to grow my soul. I took the list home to give it legs. What you suggest as a process is for me to do like Jesus said in rebuking Satan. Consume the word of God—containing the soul qualities—to worship him and serve him only. In addition, don't require him to prove himself every time I have doubt."

"So, your take is?"

"If I view the soul-mass qualities through the lens of the three remedies to temptation, then I can maintain a steady course. Make sense back at you, Lew?"

"You have no idea how this delights me to see these huge foundation blocks sliding into place. Ready to move on?"

"Okay. I'm with you."

"Let's look at the old Jason. I'm going to walk you through the chart I just sent you, and I'll fill in some blanks. Then you tell me if I'm hitting the targets. I'm not going to be telling you anything you haven't already said about yourself. I'm just putting it in a new frame."

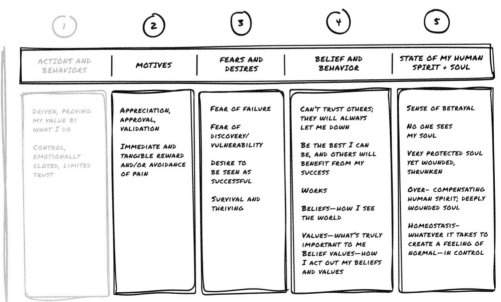

OLD JASON V1.0

1	2	3	4	5
ACTIONS AND BEHAVIORS	MOTIVES	FEARS AND DESIRES	BELIEF AND BEHAVIOR	STATE OF MY HUMAN SPIRIT + SOUL
DRIVEN, PROVING MY VALUE BY WHAT I DO CONTROL, EMOTIONALLY CLOSED, LIMITED TRUST	APPRECIATION, APPROVAL, VALIDATION IMMEDIATE AND TANGIBLE REWARD AND/OR AVOIDANCE OF PAIN	FEAR OF FAILURE FEAR OF DISCOVERY/ VULNERABILITY DESIRE TO BE SEEN AS SUCCESSFUL SURVIVAL AND THRIVING	CAN'T TRUST OTHERS; THEY WILL ALWAYS LET ME DOWN BE THE BEST I CAN BE, AND OTHERS WILL BENEFIT FROM MY SUCCESS WORKS BELIEFS—HOW I SEE THE WORLD VALUES—WHAT'S TRULY IMPORTANT TO ME BELIEF VALUES—HOW I ACT OUT MY BELIEFS AND VALUES	SENSE OF BETRAYAL NO ONE SEES MY SOUL VERY PROTECTED SOUL YET WOUNDED, SHRUNKEN OVER- COMPENSATING HUMAN SPIRIT; DEEPLY WOUNDED SOUL HOMEOSTASIS—WHATEVER IT TAKES TO CREATE A FEELING OF NORMAL—IN CONTROL

Lew pointed on Jason's tablet to **ACTIONS AND BEHAVIORS.** "Let's start at the surface, where everyone else in your life has seen you up to this point."

"Driven and proving my value by what I do? Is it that obvious? Closed, unwilling to trust and a control freak? You saw those actions and behaviors in me? You ought to be at the state fair, guessing people's soul-mass. You're too good."

"You're too obvious. In terms of your motives, I saw them revolving around your wanting to get validation from those in your circle of influence. My observation, Jason. You needed to be approved for your wholeness and your goodness, and yet you were trying to control the agenda and giving little in return. See a contradiction there?"

"Look, I know this isn't some kind of therapy session, so I'll just say yes. I longed for those I look up to, to tell me I was a talented and successful person and a man of God. I needed—and still do—external validation for the evidence of a work within me."

"That's not wrong. The 360-degree feedback perceptionaires like the *Spiritual Leader Trait Assessment* do just that. What's necessary, however, is for there to be an alignment mechanism."

"Would you explain?"

"The external views of others tell you about how they receive you. It's a perception. However, in my view, 360s are only useful when calibrated against an internal point of reference. How are you seeing yourself? Now you can compare similarities and differences."

"That's a good point. As I'm now seeing, I wanted the validation to come from my doing, not my own confidence in my being—in other words, people-pleasing to the point of dysfunction."

Lew leaned forward in his chair. "Here's a contradiction of behavior. Your difficulty in trusting others made it difficult to trust the truthfulness of their validation. See the dilemma? You discounted the very feedback you needed to validate who you are."

"Oh my gosh. I now see that lack of validation drove me to try harder to prove my worthiness. Sick cycle, huh?"

"Yes, indeed. A cycle ridden by most people I know."

"Nice double entendre."

"Nice display of your extensive vocabulary," said Lew with a fond smile, enjoying the banter with a friend. "By the way, did you notice you're describing your behaviors in the past tense. Sign of progress?"

"I hope so. I wasn't intentionally doing that."

Jason got up with his tablet and moved back to the fireplace to get warm.

"Let's drill to the next layer. As we've talked about, behind the effect of your influence was the effect that drove it, your **MOTIVES.** What might they be? Any thoughts?"

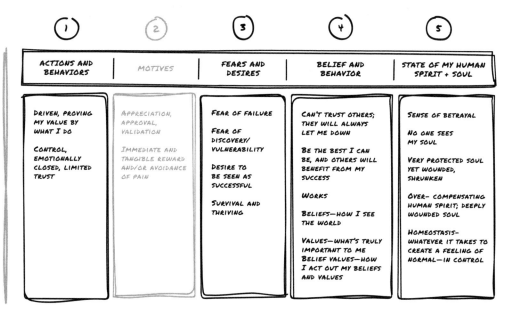

OLD JASON V1.0

① ACTIONS AND BEHAVIORS	② MOTIVES	③ FEARS AND DESIRES	④ BELIEF AND BEHAVIOR	⑤ STATE OF MY HUMAN SPIRIT + SOUL
DRIVEN, PROVING MY VALUE BY WHAT I DO CONTROL, EMOTIONALLY CLOSED, LIMITED TRUST	APPRECIATION, APPROVAL, VALIDATION IMMEDIATE AND TANGIBLE REWARD AND/OR AVOIDANCE OF PAIN	FEAR OF FAILURE FEAR OF DISCOVERY/ VULNERABILITY DESIRE TO BE SEEN AS SUCCESSFUL SURVIVAL AND THRIVING	CAN'T TRUST OTHERS; THEY WILL ALWAYS LET ME DOWN BE THE BEST I CAN BE, AND OTHERS WILL BENEFIT FROM MY SUCCESS WORKS BELIEFS—HOW I SEE THE WORLD VALUES—WHAT'S TRULY IMPORTANT TO ME BELIEF VALUES—HOW I ACT OUT MY BELIEFS AND VALUES	SENSE OF BETRAYAL NO ONE SEES MY SOUL VERY PROTECTED SOUL YET WOUNDED, SHRUNKEN OVER- COMPENSATING HUMAN SPIRIT; DEEPLY WOUNDED SOUL HOMEOSTASIS— WHATEVER IT TAKES TO CREATE A FEELING OF NORMAL—IN CONTROL

"Yes, and your chart is right on. I am realizing how much of my dysfunctional leadership behaviors were being driven by a need for approval. I needed to create an external illusion of success to counter my internal delusion of incompetence. My need for validation was sick."

"I don't know if I'd go that far, Jason. However, you certainly spread your discomfort to those around you. Don't go to self-loathing as your counter-reaction to reality. It looks unbecoming, like false humility. As you've seen, the only way to purify your motives is to ground your identity in the Word, which, as we both know, is Jesus. Of course, we do it in a comprehensible medium, the scriptures. Can we go to your **FEARS AND DESIRES?**"

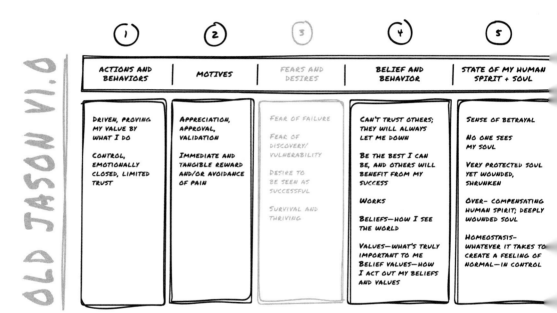

OLD JASON V1.0

① ACTIONS AND BEHAVIORS	② MOTIVES	③ FEARS AND DESIRES	④ BELIEF AND BEHAVIOR	⑤ STATE OF MY HUMAN SPIRIT + SOUL
DRIVEN, PROVING MY VALUE BY WHAT I DO CONTROL, EMOTIONALLY CLOSED, LIMITED TRUST	APPRECIATION, APPROVAL, VALIDATION IMMEDIATE AND TANGIBLE REWARD AND/OR AVOIDANCE OF PAIN	FEAR OF FAILURE FEAR OF DISCOVERY/ VULNERABILITY DESIRE TO BE SEEN AS SUCCESSFUL SURVIVAL AND THRIVING	CAN'T TRUST OTHERS; THEY WILL ALWAYS LET ME DOWN BE THE BEST I CAN BE, AND OTHERS WILL BENEFIT FROM MY SUCCESS WORKS BELIEFS—HOW I SEE THE WORLD VALUES—WHAT'S TRULY IMPORTANT TO ME BELIEF VALUES—HOW I ACT OUT MY BELIEFS AND VALUES	SENSE OF BETRAYAL NO ONE SEES MY SOUL VERY PROTECTED SOUL YET WOUNDED, SHRUNKEN OVER- COMPENSATING HUMAN SPIRIT; DEEPLY WOUNDED SOUL HOMEOSTASIS— WHATEVER IT TAKES TO CREATE A FEELING OF NORMAL—IN CONTROL

"I think that is a rhetorical question. We are going there, aren't we?"

"I know this makes you feel vulnerable, but until and unless you are willing to be courageously vulnerable, the old Jason, version 1.0, kicks back in."

"I know that. I just feel … like I'm exposed. Would you explain your term *courageously vulnerable?*"

"What I mean is, you aren't ready to have gravitational influence until you are willing, without all the explanations and excuses, for others to see you in the most authentic light. Part of that is no longer being in a state of fear over failure. The way I see it, we think other people's 'crap filters' don't work as well as ours. In truth, they're usually better. Others, just like you, see the phoniness, the hiddenness, the aloofness, and it's a put-off. We think we've mastered the art of disguise, when, in fact, we're just like Hans Christian Anderson's fable of the Emperor with no clothes."

"I remember the story. The Emperor thought he was dressed, but the reality was, everyone saw through his delusion and saw him in his naked truth. Yeah, and I'm experiencing that naked-in-public dream I have occasionally."

"So are you ready for more from the viewpoint of a friend?"

"Pour it on, Lew. For some reason I'm not as uncomfortable with this nudist colony identity as I thought I would be."

"Growth has its evidences, huh? Let's leave the naked metaphor and get back to drilling. Because you based your identity in how well you performed, I think one of your overriding fears was failure. For example, you've expressed deep and sincere regret over your first marriage. But you know what I came away hearing from you? You felt like you *failed* in your marriage. I didn't hear you talk as much about the sense of loss of relationship with Emily and Sydney. You talked as if you lost a game or a match."

"You're right, Lew. I have made most of my life about striving to be good and pounding my fist into the pillow when I failed to live up to my performance standards."

"Wrapped around that fear, what I also hear are other fears, fears of discovery and of vulnerability. It sounds like you are afraid if someone knew you like you think you know you, they would come away disappointed and certainly unimpressed. But maybe your friends and colleagues know you like you don't know you. Wrap your head around that."

Jason looked down at the chart Lew had prepared. It was hard for him to look up.

"How are you feeling at this moment, Jason?"

"I'm realizing just what you said on this chart, that at the root of my fears and desires is this overwhelming need to win at all costs. Or maybe the flip side. My overwhelming need is to *not* lose or fail at any cost."

"Interesting and insightful. What do you think would happen if you lost?"

"I would feel like a failure and that I've let a lot of people down."

"Keep in mind, Jason, we are wired for survival, and that means correcting those dangers threatening our survival. That's our selfishness. It's our God-intended flaw. Do you recall our conversation after our meeting with Bill? This ties the bow around that conversation. We were talking about change and how change was only experienced after the Fall. In Eden, everything was effortless. Food, shelter, companionship were all there. Want was not an experienced feeling. Then came banishment and the stark realization that survival meant finding and eventually growing food, building shelter, making clothing and anticipating times of want by saving the abundance in times of plenty."

"I'm seeing that my survival-oriented flesh and my control-oriented human spirit make a deadly duo. Adam and Eve and their flesh and spirit were no different than mine. Talk about feeding off of each other."

Lew pointed to the trash can; the remains of his unfinished Danish were clearly visible. "After Eden, life was hard. You could eat rotten food and die. You could drink tainted water and die. A broken limb usually meant death. Eventually some distant relative from the 'Cain' clan, who needed your land and your animals for survival, would attack you in the night."

"Referencing *Beowulf.* I'm impressed."

"Whatever. Change and survival. The story of humanity from Eden to today. Adam and Eve had no idea how difficult survival was going to be. Yet, I believe, in God's perfect plan, in order to accomplish the grand plan, humanity had to survive. Since you brought in Adam and Eve, complete the thought about our flesh and soul-mass."

"You're going to make me dig deep on this one." Jason stared at his tablet for some time. "I can see that's when the curse and the blessing kicked in. The curse for Adam was selfishness. If

Adam could exercise some degree of control over change through his toil, then survival was possible. What evolved was the sense of self, the fear-need to survive by his own effort—toil—and the greed-need to accumulate—the result of his own effort. It was also the source of the original sin."

"Which was?"

"Which was for Adam and Eve to believe they didn't need God to survive. Disobedience is easy when we see others as inessential for our living. Strangely, by contradiction, it's also the reason why the Adam clan survived more than one generation. The three same drives that drove Adam and Eve are the same three that fuel the financial markets worldwide. Power, fear and greed. And for what purpose? To exercise control over change."

"Great work, Jason. Let me tie power, fear and greed into one story. I'm thinking of Jesus' encounter with the rich young ruler. As you recall, he asked, "Good teacher, what must I do to inherit eternal life?" Now there was a man full of fear. He was in fear of not being a good enough Jew. He was in fear of being released from the dependency of things and status. In the end, his fear was rooted in vulnerability. He had never experienced living free from his possessions, his connection to princely power and his supposed knowledge. He wanted to experience God, but he wanted his power and his possessions even more. That's greed. The way I see it, Jason, the origin of all sin is rooted in our primal need to survive and control the world around us. And when the deep relationships of marriage and family fail to attach to our identity then self-reliance and self-justification become our default behaviors. The very thing we fear becomes our identity. Fear."

Jason was quiet. *What a hole I've been in. Twenty years of digging will do that.*

"But here, my friend is this amazing contradiction of such a rational and intelligent creature as we humans. The more self-reliant we become for security, the more insecure we actually are. The more we have, the more we worry about losing it. Can you identify with that?"

"Not sure I'm having a near-death experience, Lew. I'm getting all these flashing images, but they're not of my past. It's in my immediate future I see failure, unemployment, another divorce, messed-up kids, missed opportunities and more."

"That's a little dramatic, but going down the road you've been on, isn't that a real possibility? What will happen to staff if New Horizons fails? You've hinted that your—as you describe it— forever marriage, is straining under your relentless drive to make it *not fail*. Am I right?"

"Didn't think it showed."

"It does. As does most of the rest of your life. But don't be discouraged. Let's go down another layer to **BELIEF AND BEHAVIOR VALUES**. I've been debriefed by those you met with, and the consistent message I get from all of them is how impressed they are with your sharp mind, great personality, and good heart."

Jason's eyes brightened as he looked up. "They said that?"

"They did. Of course, they also mentioned what they feel is your inability to trust what you don't control."

"Really. I don't recall telling them that."

"You didn't. But just like you, they aren't where they are in life by being stupid and clueless."

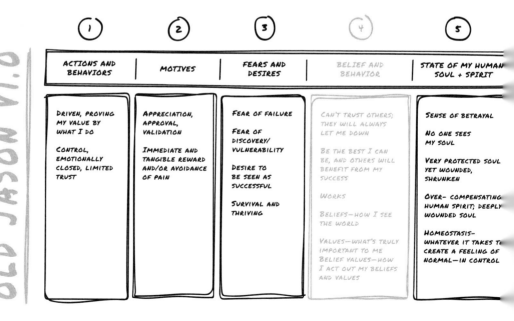

	①	②	③	④	⑤
OLD JASON V1.0	**ACTIONS AND BEHAVIORS**	**MOTIVES**	**FEARS AND DESIRES**	*BELIEF AND BEHAVIOR*	**STATE OF MY HUMAN SOUL + SPIRIT**
	DRIVEN, PROVING MY VALUE BY WHAT I DO	APPRECIATION, APPROVAL, VALIDATION	FEAR OF FAILURE	*CAN'T TRUST OTHERS; THEY WILL ALWAYS LET ME DOWN*	SENSE OF BETRAYAL
	CONTROL, EMOTIONALLY CLOSED, LIMITED TRUST	IMMEDIATE AND TANGIBLE REWARD AND/OR AVOIDANCE OF PAIN	FEAR OF DISCOVERY/ VULNERABILITY	*BE THE BEST I CAN BE, AND OTHERS WILL BENEFIT FROM MY SUCCESS*	NO ONE SEES MY SOUL
			DESIRE TO BE SEEN AS SUCCESSFUL	*WORKS*	VERY PROTECTED SOUL YET WOUNDED, SHRUNKEN
			SURVIVAL AND THRIVING	*BELIEFS—HOW I SEE THE WORLD*	OVER- COMPENSATING HUMAN SPIRIT; DEEPLY WOUNDED SOUL
				VALUES—WHAT'S TRULY IMPORTANT TO ME BELIEF VALUES—HOW I ACT OUT MY BELIEFS AND VALUES	HOMEOSTASIS— WHATEVER IT TAKES TO CREATE A FEELING OF NORMAL—IN CONTROL

"Again, didn't realize it showed. The trust issue, that is. Look, if there was a takeaway from my dad's death, it was this: you can't rely on being a good person to get you through life. You've got to work for what you get. And just like you said in that little box on this chart, 'Be the best I can be, and others will benefit from my success.' You nailed my life's motto."

"Interesting that you would use the term, nailed. Seems like someone else nailed it so you didn't have to depend on your works for justification as a worthwhile human."

"That's low, Lew. How can I come back on that one?"

"I hope you don't, Jason. If you don't, that will be a huge signal that the old Jason is ready to be put down. As I have come to know you better, I'm certain your beliefs and behavior values have a strong foundation. From the outside, though, it looks like you are in a constant state of turmoil over what you believe and how you behave."

"I think I see what you're getting at, but what exactly does 'Belief and behavior values' mean?"

"Permit me to share with you how I frame the belief values and behavior values paradigm. Values are those deep-seated senses of right and wrong, the lens through which I see my world. There are two facets to those values. One is my beliefs. These are ideas and attitudes I can articulate as foundational in defining who I think I *am*. When I can articulate them, they become my belief values. That is my ethos. The other is behavior values. These determine what I *do*. Again, when I can articulate the things I know I should do, they become my behavior values, my ethics. Now, you'd like to think they are consistent—my beliefs and my behaviors. Sadly, experience tells us, not necessarily so. For example, I believe in the value of honesty but still, on occasion, in my behavior, I will tell a lie. I believe in being peaceful until I lose my temper and destroy trust and relationships."

"Sorry to interrupt, but check if I'm tracking. In my mind, the explanation is, most of my foundational belief values come out of my soul. Most of my behavior values come out of my human spirit. Perhaps there is the source for tension and the potential for contradiction. After all, I think most people are walking contradictions, believing one way and then doing another."

"You are right on, my friend. Using my drilling metaphor, you're poking into your core. Just thought I'd better warn you: could be a gusher."

"Forewarned is forearmed."

"Okay," said Lew, finding his pipe and humidor and loading the bowl. "I'm through talking. I'm shifting the control button to you. Are you ready to talk about the **STATE OF YOUR HUMAN SPIRIT AND SOUL?**"

In the silence after the question, the crack-pop of the match being lit sounded almost like an explosion.

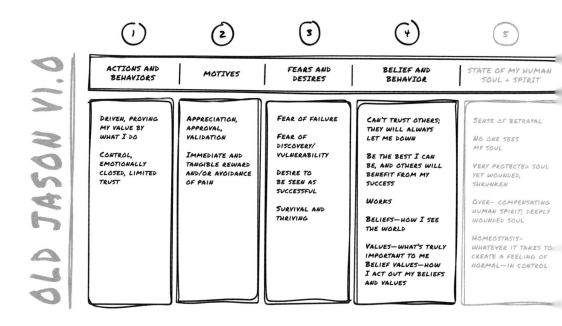

Jason saw Lew's preoccupation with lighting his pipe as Lew's intended opportunity for him to gather his swirling thoughts. Unaware that his nonverbal signals were reflecting his state of mind, Jason crossed his legs and arms and leaned back, slouching in the leather chair.

"I am, Lew. Not eager but willing. Based on our last

conversation on the soul-mass, I can't see how my life will change for the better unless I get to the core. I understand that in the next few hours or days I have the opportunity to begin to build and allow a process for the regeneration of my core, a soul-mass that will truly have gravitational attraction and influence."

"Glad you recognize the gravity of the opportunity. No pun intended."

Jason took a deep breath, puffed his cheeks and slowly let the air out. He was clearly uncomfortable with the moment. "Not sure what vulnerability feels like, since I've never allowed it before. If this is what it feels like, there is both fear and expectation. I'm afraid this is a one-way street, and yet I know it will take me to a good place. That is, as long as I'm not going the wrong way. Make any sense?"

"Been there."

"Okay, here goes. The state of my human spirit and my soul. As I've thought about our last conversation on soul-mass as well as reflecting on the conversations with these incredible people you know, what keeps coming to the surface is a feeling of anger."

"Keep in mind, Jason, I have no intention for this conversation to become a counseling session, but what you're opening up with is key. Tell me about the anger."

"Well, it's slippery and amorphous. Hard to get into a shape I can recognize, but I felt betrayed by my dad. Wasn't his fault he died. I know he'd be alive today if he had any choice about it. I also feel betrayed by Emily, my first wife. That's obvious. I feel betrayed by the pastor and church who fired me for being divorced. I know it was in their charter and theology, but it still felt like a stab in the back. I feel betrayed by Melissa, the board and my staff for the situation I'm now in. I know, I know, it doesn't make sense. No one intentionally tried to hurt me, but the anger is still there."

Lew shrugged his shoulders. "Who said it had to make sense?"

"You talk about vulnerability; here's the core piece. I've blamed everyone else, but at the center of all this stuff, I feel I betrayed myself."

"Really. Care to start pulling the thread out of the sweater?"

"Yep and nope."

"Let's take the yep first," Lew said, and he took a long gulp of his half-warm coffee.

"The more I begin to have a sense of the continuing presence of my spirit and soul, rather than just head awareness, the more this becomes real. Call it ownership, I guess. I thought getting in touch with my soul-mass would make my feelings about life better. Not really."

"What are some reasons for that?"

"For as long as I can remember, I've heard the message of how broken we are as people and how only Jesus can put the pieces together in a way that is healthy. Truth is, under the surface I thought that message was for everyone else who wasn't put together as well as I was. I'm coming to the ownership—way past realization—that I've got a lot of raw, gaping holes in the scar tissue of my soul, and like the little Dutch boy, there are way too many holes in the dike for the fingers I have.

"You want to know what the 'Old Jason V1.0' soul looks like?" Jason uncrossed his legs and arms and leaned forward. "I have so well hidden it, I'm having a hard time finding it myself. But in hiding it so no one else will see it, I've neglected it, allowed it to be beaten and wounded and starved it until it feels like a shriveled piece of dried fruit. In the absence of leading from my soul, I've allowed my human spirit to rule and even overrule the Holy Spirit. How that's possible? I have no idea. All I know is, my will is much more robust than it should be and now dominates my being."

It was clear Lew wasn't going to speak, so Jason continued. "I remember hearing a term in one of my business classes. The prof was using a medical term to describe the pressure of organizations, just like organisms, to continuously create stability. It's called *homeostasis*. That's what I've been trying to do. With a wounded soul, a spirit out of control, a mind that thinks it knows more than anyone else and a heart full of pride, this organism called Jason Cahill was simply trying to create stability when every system was spinning out of control." Jason stopped to real in his emotions. He could feel his voice cracking and his face flushing.

"Continue on. Your process of self-clarity is remarkable. Are you ready to complete the process?"

"Meaning?"

"Meaning finishing the third part of our process we started at the end of our last meeting: healing the soul. The answer, it seems to me, is found in the Apostle John's letters. You know it well, 1 John 1:9."

"You mean that if we confess our sins, Father God is faithful to forgive us of our sins and cleanse us of all unrighteousness through the saving work of Christ. Explain how that heals the soul."

"Like I've said on many occasions, you have to find your own understanding. But here's how I work that through for me. Confess means I am aware of my transgressions. Actually, the word *confess* in the Greek is *homologeous*, meaning, the same as. I confess to what God already knows. But through Christ it is no longer there. As a result, my confession is simply my ownership for what I've done and for which I've already been forgiven. A little complicated, but it works for me."

"Yeah, that is deep. Here's a huge awareness for me. There is an *if* and an *I will*. The way I tame my human spirit is by simply telling it the truth and accepting only the truth from it. I will no longer listen to stupid lies and the false fabrications of my insecurity. And the truth starts with me continually reminding myself—brain and human spirit—who God says I am. If I'm too confused to know the truth beyond that, then the truth of who God says I am is all that's necessary. That's the *if* part. The if is my responsibility."

"What about the *I will*?"

"The *I will* is God's promise. He will heal through the power of the indwelling Holy Spirit. The healing is instantaneous. The problem is the lack cooperation with the human spirit, who wants to continue to dredge up old hurts, angers and habits. Bottom line, I need to accept a healed soul in the same way I accept a fresh start, like at my point of salvation. Then I can start getting my restored soul healthy again through nourishment by concentrating on growing the soul qualities."

"That's powerful, Jason. However, if it's that simple, which I too believe it is, then why does most of humanity walk around with damaged, wounded, shrunken and bleeding souls?"

"That's the question of the ages. Could it be that the answer is so simple that we've missed the obvious looking for the mysterious?"

"Just to cement it in, restate your conclusion of how to heal the soul," asked Lew.

"As I confess my sins, I also ask the Father to make my soul new again through the saving grace of Jesus, his Son, and through the cleansing and renewing power of his Holy Spirit—the same Spirit who raised Christ from the dead. It is finished, done, complete."

"I don't mean to be flip with you, Jason, but how's that working for you?"

"Lew, I've known that scripture since I was a kid, and I've applied it as a process of obtaining God's forgiveness. But I've never thought about where and how that prayer of confession takes place. Since we've been talking over these past several months, I've come to realize the junction where God and I meet is in my soul-mass, and the healing occurs in my soul. Each time I sin, I betray my soul. Each time I sin, my soul is wounded. Yet each time I pray and ask for forgiveness, not only are my sins forgiven but my soul is healed and renewed."

"Good thought. Deep thought. You are taking care of the need for re-healing too, aren't you? As we all experience, just about the time the soul is renewed, zap, we commit a self-inflicted wound and allow the Enemy's fiery darts to penetrate once again."

"Every day, Lew, sometimes many times every day."

"The wounding or the healing?"

"Hah! Both."

"Wouldn't have expected anything other than that from you. Listen, I want you to take some time to look at the old Jason we talked about today and see what may be different in you now and going forward. Zero in on the state of your human spirit and soul. Let me know when you're ready, and we'll meet at C'est le Bon.

Besides, I have a person I want you to meet while we're there. Fascinating person. I think you already know him."

"Really? Who's that?"

"You'll recognize him when you see him."

"Can't wait."

You have searched me, LORD, and you know me. You know when I sit and when I rise; you perceive my thoughts from afar. You discern my going out and my lying down; you are familiar with all my ways. Before a word is on my tongue you, LORD, know it completely ... Search me, God, and know my heart; test me and know my anxious thoughts. See if there is any offensive way in me, and lead me in the way everlasting.

Psalm 139:1–4, 23–24

REFLECTION QUESTIONS

1. *If we name our temptations we have a better chance of overcoming them.*

Preservation*: What are your temptations of Preservation? Money, health, pride and reputation? What can you do to no longer put God to the test on these?*

Control*: What are you dysfunctionally trying to control? Your way, your version of the world, your relationships? How does worshiping God and serving Him only bring this temptation under God's realm?*

Gratification*: What are you experiencing that is giving you temporary pleasure yet taking you away from a wholly and holy relationship with God? Food, drugs, alcohol, sex, TV and entertainment, recreation? How does the Word of God provide you with the gratification your body and brain and mind demands?*

2. *Download your own Disciplines of the Soul chart at www.zzz.zzz/souldisciplines.htm.*

- *First, focus on a soul category such as, Caring/Loving or a soul-quality such as Compassionate.*
- *Next, under My Ownership, write your own one sentence definition of what that soul-quality means to you—your personal definition. Consider putting in form of a prayer.*
- *Next, begin to pray for and anticipate opportunities where that soul-quality can show itself. Record those evidences.*
- *Finally, look up Scriptures illustrating how God wants that quality to live out in you.*

CHAPTER 15

New Jason Version 2.0

*Elijah took his cloak, rolled it up, and hit the
water with it. The river divided and the two men
walked through on dry land. When they reached
the other side, Elijah said to Elisha, "What
can I do for you before I'm taken from you? Ask
anything." Elisha said, "Your life repeated in my
life. I want to be a holy man just like you." "That's
a hard one!" said Elijah. "But if you're watching
when I'm taken from you, you'll get what you've
asked for. But only if you're watching."*

2 Kings 2:8–10 (The Message)

*L*ew and Jason arrived in the C'est le Bon parking lot at the same time. As they entered the restaurant, Jason was wondering who was waiting for them. Jason scanned the restaurant. C'est le Bon's design created a feeling of privacy while maintaining a sense of community. It was a great gathering spot for casual conversation and good food. He wondered if Bill Courtland was back in town. Looking around, he took in the great smells of baked bread, simmering soups and luscious pastries.

"Any clues as to who's the mystery guest behind door number three?"

"No clues. Like I said, you've already met him."

"Really? I'm all eyes and ears? And who may that person be?"

"Jason, I'd like you to meet ... Excuse me, let's order our lunch first."

"Lew, the curiosity is killing me." Jason looked around the café, hoping to see a recognizable face.

Lew placed their order and found a table toward the

back of the café. "I got it," as he gave the server his credit card. Slipping into his seat, Lew slowly sipped his hot coffee, enjoying the suspense he was putting Jason through. Jason was smiling but still looking around in anticipation.

"You are nasty, Lew. I didn't realize you had such a devious bent. You really enjoy laying on the suspense, don't you?"

"Guilty as charged. Are you ready meet the last person who will have a significant impact in your growth as a gravitational leader?"

"Of course."

The C'est le Bon server brought their sandwiches to their table. Jason recognized the server. "Sadat, isn't it?"

"Ah, yes, it is."

"Bill introduced us when we were here several months ago. How are you doing?"

"I'm doing well, sir, and thank you for remembering me."

"Makes it easy when it was the founder who made the introduction," laughed Jason.

"Okay, Lew, enough mystery. Who's your special guest?"

"Jason, I'd like you to meet New Jason V2.0!"

"Now there's a letdown."

"Why is that? I can't think of another person I know who is more influential in shaping your life going forward than you. I think you are more than ready to start listening again to Jason Cahill. This time I think you know how to tune your speakers so you filter out the voices of the past and of self-centeredness and ignore the whispers of Satan. I think you've reconnected with your soul, and you're hearing more clearly the voice of God. However, looks like you may have a little more work to do on the celebrity part. Why are you looking for someone else to grow your living? You are the most significant and influential person in your life. Not anyone else. You believe that?"

"Yes, sort of."

"That sounded a little weak. Is there a *but* or an *and* behind it?"

"As a recovering egomaniac and control freak, it's really hard to trust myself again."

"What are some reasons for that?"

"Because I know what I did to myself and others, and I don't want it to ever happen again. I am seeing what my control fears did to shut down trust, and I don't want to go backwards."

"Jason, that's a great point of reference. Don't ever forget that fear, but don't let that fear block you from becoming the blessing God has intended your living to be. If your soul-mass is healing and you are intentionally growing it through the disciplines of the soul, your gravitational attraction and gravity are proportionally increasing. It's cause and effect. A healthy soul-mass can't help but be attractive and influential."

"I get that, but ..."

"But what? It sounds like you're stuck in neutral. Can't go backwards to being a control freak. Yet cautious about moving forward in trust, afraid you'll make it all about you. Am I right?"

"Good observation. I appreciate that you are so direct. Don't freak when I say this, but I love you as a friend and as a significant source of influence in my life. Thanks."

"Thanks. The affection and the love are mutual. Sounds like you're getting over the pushback on the love principle. So introduce me to the new Jason V2.0. Is this how you plan to move forward? I think you said you already worked on your chart. Is it on your tablet?"

"Yes, it is. You drilled down to the core with the old Jason V1.0. I'm going to start from the core and move out with the new version."

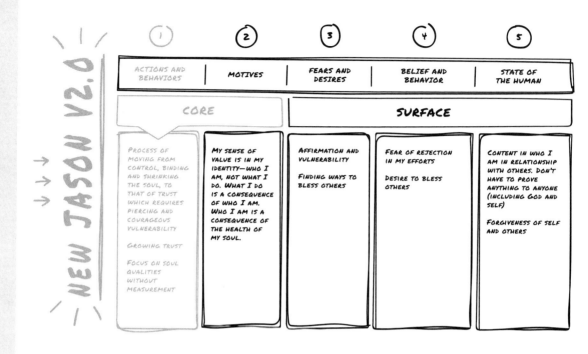

NEW JASON V2.0

① ACTIONS AND BEHAVIORS	② MOTIVES	③ FEARS AND DESIRES	④ BELIEF AND BEHAVIOR	⑤ STATE OF THE HUMAN
CORE		SURFACE		
PROCESS OF MOVING FROM CONTROL, BINDING AND SHRINKING THE SOUL, TO THAT OF TRUST WHICH REQUIRES PIERCING AND COURAGEOUS VULNERABILITY GROWING TRUST FOCUS ON SOUL QUALITIES WITHOUT MEASUREMENT	MY SENSE OF VALUE IS IN MY IDENTITY—WHO I AM, NOT WHAT I DO. WHAT I DO IS A CONSEQUENCE OF WHO I AM. WHO I AM IS A CONSEQUENCE OF THE HEALTH OF MY SOUL.	AFFIRMATION AND VULNERABILITY FINDING WAYS TO BLESS OTHERS	FEAR OF REJECTION IN MY EFFORTS DESIRE TO BLESS OTHERS	CONTENT IN WHO I AM IN RELATIONSHIP WITH OTHERS. DON'T HAVE TO PROVE ANYTHING TO ANYONE (INCLUDING GOD AND SELF) FORGIVENESS OF SELF AND OTHERS

Lew laughed. "You thought *you* were anticipating meeting someone. You have no idea how eager I am to meet this new person."

"As I've drilled into my core, I am now more aware of my spiritual entity relationships. What I mean by that is, I am binding my will to be subordinate to the Holy Spirit. It's like I've got a lifeline called desire, and if I grab ahold of it, I can begin to capture my will and begin to tame this wild thing called my human spirit."

"Sounds good. How do you do that? And take a bite of your sandwich before it goes stale."

"To start, like I mentioned the last time we met, I've got the list of soul qualities— the Disciplines of the Soul—posted on my tablet, at home in my den and at work. I try to meditate on them several times during the day until they are so much a part of me that when issues come up, I know my soul's response. I'm now tuning in to the voice of the soul."

"Impressive, Jason. What else?"

"As I meditate on the soul qualities, I'm asking the Holy Spirit hourly to reign and rule as the Spirit of Christ within me. I'm asking the Holy Spirit to make me more aware of me and thee. I guess that's what you call discernment. I'm asking the Holy Spirit to heal my soul and bind up the wounds, even as I forgetfully dig up Jason V1.0, dust him off, and start self-inflicting my soul wounds all over again. I use 1 John 1:9 as my promise for forgiveness and renewal.

"I'm in the process of moving from trying to control—thus shrinking the soul—to trusting, which requires piercing vulnerability with myself and particularly others. I haven't spent a lot of time reflecting on trust yet. That's my next project, but as long as it feels like a project, I'm not ready."

Lew's wink and nod confirmed Jason's insight. "So you're saying when you try to control, you unintentionally cause the soul to shrink. And the reverse is to trust, yet you say there is piercing vulnerability. Tell me about that. Doesn't that mean the soul becomes even more wounded instead of simply shrunk? Given the choice, seems like shrunk is a better alternative than being pierced, isn't it?"

"Lew, I know you know the answer. To me, piercing vulnerability means my soul is protected by its own health, and the piercing vulnerability is to my human spirit. That, in turn, allows my human spirit to be the protector of my soul. I know that sounds convoluted, but it makes sense to me."

"You know," said Lew with a smile of pride he couldn't hide, "that's the only person you really need to make sense to."

"Seems like before, my spirit would deflect the arrows of vulnerability, unintentionally directing them to the soul. My human spirit needs to be taken down a notch or so by deflating the bloated bladder it is through piercing vulnerability. It makes no sense to my human spirit that to be stronger, I have to be willing to be more vulnerable. What I know at this point is, trust is essential for—but nonetheless feels in opposition to—survival. In order to trust I have to be willing to become more vulnerable, and in being more vulnerable, my human spirit deflates. Does that make sense?"

"Jason, what you are saying in your self-discovery is what I prayed would be your insight. Of course it makes sense! It made sense to Paul when he talked about his weakness being strength in Christ."

"I've come to the realization that my control addiction is mostly about my exterior image management—how you perceive me. I've been externally focused and pathologically influenced by who you think I am. Like you said earlier, the opinions of people I trust do matter, but I need a healthy interior frame of reference to validate those external observations. That can only happen within a healthy soul-mass. The piercing vulnerability piece means I seek out and receive honest feedback. That requires courage on my part. I'm not going to make it any more complicated than that."

"What's the trust part all about?"

"For me, this is the biggest 'aha' of our whole process. I'm learning I can trust God, others and myself and in the process become a person worthy of trust in the lives of others. As long as I held what I thought was the control lever, there was very little trust given or received. Saw no need for it. To get to where I am is a scary, hard and slippery slope, requiring I continually dig in so I don't slip back into my old ways."

"So strengthening the core of your soul-mass is your first step. Good. Tell me a little more about focusing on soul qualities without measurement."

"When you gave that list of soul qualities to me, my first response was to try and memorize them and then break them down into a schedule."

"Kind of like the medieval book of hours?"

"How so, Lew?"

"As you may recall, it was one of the first devotionals. Copied and illustrated by monks and scribes, it became a gorgeous work of art and discipline. But it also became a book of memorization for many, and as a consequence, the life and intent of it became lost in the devotion to ritual."

"That's a good example, Lew. Memorization is good. Memorization as a task, though, is works. For the soul qualities, I just want to be able to do as the scripture says. You know, where it says, think on these things. I now realize, like you've said all along, that my gravitational influence rests in the wholeness and health of my soul and a current renovation of this old-man mind, heart and will. The hardest part for me is developing the habit of knowing I can be a blessing to others simply by my presence and not by my works. Still trying to get my head completely around that. Yet I think that's the gravitational attraction and influence we've been talking about."

"That's significant progress, Jason. In my experience, good works usually follow as a consequence of a healthy soul. What about your belief and behavior values?"

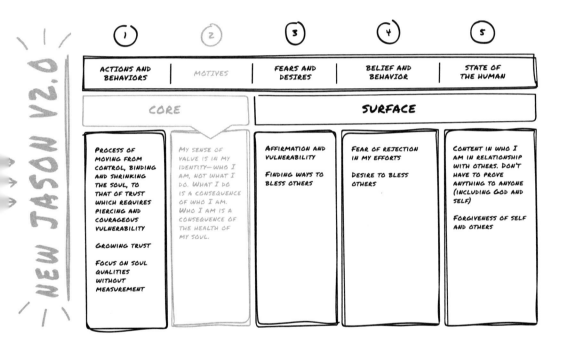

"That one is going to take a while. I know, for me, the values and beliefs I now hold came about subtly and slowly over time. Doesn't just click and change overnight. But the big one I feel shifting is the realization that my sense of value is in my identity—who I am, not in what I do. What I do is a consequence of who I am. And who I am is a consequence of the health of my soul.

"But here's a piece I'm still wrestling with: there is still this lingering feeling of unworthiness. I know compared with Christ I am unworthy. It's just that, as Paul pointed out, if I regard myself as a skin tent and it's the saving work and love of Christ empowered by the Holy Spirit that's at work within me, then, you bet I'm worthy to be loved and valued and affirmed. I think we've taken Job's lament, 'I am a worm,' to the point of being misunderstood. We played it right into the Prosecutor's hand to make us, well, at least me, feel condemned."

"That's good preaching, my friend," said Lew. "Hold tight to that: if the God of the universe loves you, you are undeniably valuable."

"Why is it so hard to believe God when he says we are so precious and loved, and yet we buy the hard lies Satan says, lock, stock and barrel?"

"Sounds like I hear a motive forming as we're starting to surface from this deep dive. How have your motives changed, Jason?"

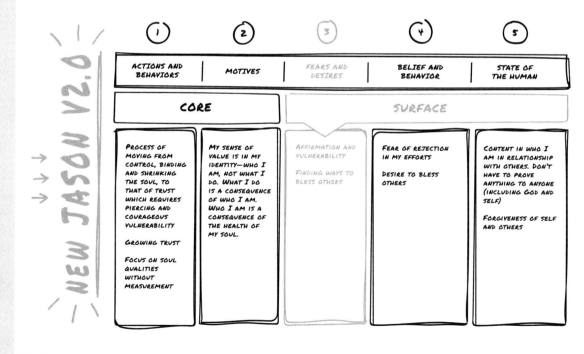

	1	2	3	4	5
	ACTIONS AND BEHAVIORS	MOTIVES	FEARS AND DESIRES	BELIEF AND BEHAVIOR	STATE OF THE HUMAN
	CORE		SURFACE		
NEW JASON V2.0	PROCESS OF MOVING FROM CONTROL, BINDING AND SHRINKING THE SOUL, TO THAT OF TRUST WHICH REQUIRES PIERCING AND COURAGEOUS VULNERABILITY GROWING TRUST FOCUS ON SOUL QUALITIES WITHOUT MEASUREMENT	MY SENSE OF VALUE IS IN MY IDENTITY—WHO I AM, NOT WHAT I DO. WHAT I DO IS A CONSEQUENCE OF WHO I AM. WHO I AM IS A CONSEQUENCE OF THE HEALTH OF MY SOUL.	AFFIRMATION AND VULNERABILITY FINDING WAYS TO BLESS OTHERS	FEAR OF REJECTION IN MY EFFORTS DESIRE TO BLESS OTHERS	CONTENT IN WHO I AM IN RELATIONSHIP WITH OTHERS. DON'T HAVE TO PROVE ANYTHING TO ANYONE (INCLUDING GOD AND SELF) FORGIVENESS OF SELF AND OTHERS

"After spending time with Joe, I am beginning to recognize my craving for approval, and I see it much like a substance abuser craves their drug of choice. And simply seeing that is helping me reframe what it is I want."

"What is it that you want, and what do you need?"

"I want to be more genuine. I'm seeing I can't have gravitational influence if I'm sending phony gravitational attraction messages. Amazing how just seeing that clarifies my hearing. The only way I can be genuine is to be vulnerable. Sounds like any oxymoron, but I understand the truth."

"Explain."

"I'm beginning to hear affirmations that were already there. It's just now I'm not relabeling them as approval statements."

"What are you hearing now, and is it perhaps related to your need?"

"I'm listening for affirmation statements from God and those around me. I need his words and his Word in my life."

"What do you see as the difference between affirmation and approval?"

"Approval statements speak to my works. Affirmation statements confirm a work within me. When I get feedback from others, I'm starting to graciously receive it without all the false humility crap attached to it. I now see my old response as nothing more than pride in my work and as a person, yet disguised as false humility."

"Deep stuff. What about your fears?"

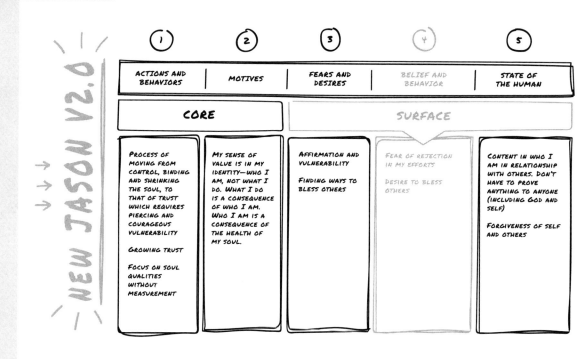

NEW JASON V2.0

①	②	③	④	⑤
ACTIONS AND BEHAVIORS	MOTIVES	FEARS AND DESIRES	BELIEF AND BEHAVIOR	STATE OF THE HUMAN
CORE		SURFACE		
PROCESS OF MOVING FROM CONTROL, BINDING AND SHRINKING THE SOUL, TO THAT OF TRUST WHICH REQUIRES PIERCING AND COURAGEOUS VULNERABILITY GROWING TRUST FOCUS ON SOUL QUALITIES WITHOUT MEASUREMENT	MY SENSE OF VALUE IS IN MY IDENTITY—WHO I AM, NOT WHAT I DO. WHAT I DO IS A CONSEQUENCE OF WHO I AM. WHO I AM IS A CONSEQUENCE OF THE HEALTH OF MY SOUL.	AFFIRMATION AND VULNERABILITY FINDING WAYS TO BLESS OTHERS	FEAR OF REJECTION IN MY EFFORTS DESIRE TO BLESS OTHERS	CONTENT IN WHO I AM IN RELATIONSHIP WITH OTHERS. DON'T HAVE TO PROVE ANYTHING TO ANYONE (INCLUDING GOD AND SELF) FORGIVENESS OF SELF AND OTHERS

"Well, one thing I'm discovering, the more I'm now able to *not* make it about me, the fewer fears I experience. I'm starting to see so many contradictions in my life. No wonder I confused people."

"For example?"

"So many of my fears had to do with my dysfunctional need for approval. So the way I thought to make sure I got the approval messages I wanted was to focus on controlling my outcomes, which made me even more hypersensitive to the need for approval. Does that make sense?"

Lew laughed. "No, in the process of life, it makes absolutely no sense. It loops. As far as an explanation as to what it was that got us to conversation, it makes perfect sense. Tell me how or if your fears are changing."

"What's replacing fear is a desire to bless others. Remember what Bill Courtland said about C'est le Bon? Their mission is to find ways to bless others. They have the privilege of using their café empire to do it. That's my inspiration as I start to build or rebuild my vision and mission."

"That's marvelous, Jason. I'm impressed with your growth. Can I warm your coffee?"

"Sure."

"What about the flip side? Are you experiencing any new desires?"

"As you would expect, I'm not looking for ways to ingratiate myself to others to feel like I'm a good person. I truly am desiring to bless others and am consciously aware to be looking for opportunities for prayer and action."

"Rich. And I'm not talking about the coffee."

Lew returned with two steaming mugs of Bon Café coffee. "Tell me about your actions. How is what you've been telling me going to translate into the New Jason V2.0? It's the old talk the talk and walk the walk. How's the talk translating into walk?"

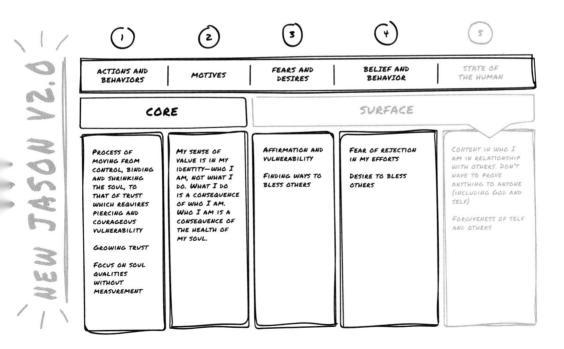

"I feel it beginning already. I feel more content in who I am in relationship with others. I'm realizing I don't have to prove anything to anyone. And because my soul is getting healthier and my spirit is being tamed to allow the Holy Spirit to rule, I'm calmer, less driven, yet full of more energy and enthusiasm than I've experienced in a long time. I really do feel like a huge burden of proof lifted off my back."

"Would you say you feel safer?"

"Yes and no. I feel more secure, and because it is becoming well with my soul, I feel I can better handle what comes my way, knowing it probably isn't just a stupid boomerang I threw out and is coming back to nail me. One other thing that is so basic and yet so fresh."

"What's that?"

"Self-forgiveness. As long as I was addicted to works as my proof of goodness—in spite of my belief in grace—I couldn't fully forgive myself for acting stupid, immature, selfish ... sinful. And because I couldn't fully forgive myself for behaving that way, my forgiveness of others was not really genuine either. It sounds so basic, but I'm just beginning to experience what I've known for a long time. My standards for myself are now the same ones I set for others. The greatest commandment is to love one another as we love ourselves. I was doing that. It's just that I didn't love myself very much unless I was performing up to expectations. I know, I know. It's so basic, but we—I—gloss over it. How could I know so much and act so ignorantly?"

"Is that a rhetorical question, Jason?"

"Yes, because I'm seeing part of the answer. When my soul-mass is in dysfunction, my theology is dysfunctional. Get the soul-mass healthy, and the rest of the skin tent follows."

"Good thinking," said Lew. "Let's return back to our continuing conversation about the 'falling in love with you' conundrum. Where are you on that?"

"As if you didn't know. I've come to the realization that if I truly love myself—meaning I have a healthy self and soul identity—then I am more than willing to accept other people's love into my soul. I'm continuing to realize and remind myself that as my soul gets healthy, love is not only the radiating essence, but it is also what causes others to be attracted to me. It's not my power, my celebrity or even my competence that causes others to follow in love with me. Maybe that's the clue I've been looking for."

"What clue?"

"To my pushback in this 'fall in love' thing you've been pushing on me."

"How so?"

"I'm not sure I want people to just fall in love with me. I now understand that's important as a result of my gravitational attraction, but what I want really want them to do is follow in love."

"If that works for you, Jason, that's fine. But keep in mind, I think your pushback to the fall in love piece is your continuing sense of unworthiness unless you feel you're competent and have earned the right for others to follow. Consider the reality that those who fall in love with you are better judges of your worthiness for trust and competency than you. Satan probably isn't talking to them about you as much as Satan is talking to you about you."

"You just won't let me off the hook will you? As you were pounding that truth into my head, here's what I think my heart was saying. Any goodness I have is found in the goodness of my soul as I gain victory over the selfishness of my human spirit. If I allow people to fall in love with the essence of goodness in me, I'm simply allowing them to fall in love with Jesus, whose virtuous love is contained in my soul."

"See. It wasn't that hard at all, was it?" Lew laughed.

"Up to this point, I've been able to figure out four big ideas or steps that are action consequences of a healthy soul-mass. Yet I've got to be careful making this list of four steps that I'm not falling back into that control trap of measuring my worth on the basis of keeping faithful to my list."

"Like you said, Jason, even the soul qualities, as helpful

as the concepts can be, can also be opportunities to strive for control—for doing rather than being."

"What a fine balance. No wonder we blow it so often. Okay, number one. When I desire God to be at work, I need to stand back and stop trying to control everything. Let God be God. Boy, is that profound, or what?"

"I take it that wasn't a real question."

"Right. The second idea is for me to become a serial killer."

"A what!" Lew was truly shocked.

Jason laughed. "I wish I could have gotten a snapshot of you. You looked truly shocked. What I mean is, every day—sometimes every hour—I have to kill the old man in me. I'm reminded of Paul's declaration in Galatians that I have been crucified with Christ. I no longer live, but Christ lives in me. Interesting how those passages I've read a hundred times all of a sudden take on new meaning. I particularly am drawn to Paul's statement in Romans that if we have died to Christ, we are free from sin. I have to die to self. That's basic, again. Well, I got news for you, Lew. My self doesn't want to die! My self hides, pleads, bargains, threatens, scares and bullies me into sparing the old man. But I know I've got to kill him. Not wound him. I've got to kill him. Sounds brutal and vicious, doesn't it? The old man is like cancer. If I don't kill every cell, it will come back and come back with a vengeance."

Lew shrugged his shoulders. "You pick the metaphors that work for you. If being a serial killer is your working metaphor, go for it."

"Okay, on a little more serious note, third is to step up and be the courageous me that God expects and who I was trying to convince myself and others that I was. All I have to do is be piercingly vulnerable, which, to me, means being authentic."

"You've explained the vulnerability before, but elaborate on authenticity, would you?"

"I need to allow people to know me as I am. I also need to know me as I truly am. None of the false humility stuff, and none of the facades of seeming success. That's the authentic part, and that requires my identity to be healthy. The courageous part is to actually do it."

"Excellent. If you want to try being piercingly vulnerable, remember, I have the *Spiritual Leader Trait Assessment* you can go through. It's a 360-degree perceptionaire of 24 leader traits. I can coach you through it if you're interested."

"Thanks, Lew, I am."

"Hey, don't worry, it's a great experience. Not much different than me asking you to stand naked in the main isle of Macy's and then ask people what they think." Lew laughed.

"On second thought ... You're quite the salesperson."

"Thank you. What's your fourth point?"

"It's to understand my will is a significant part of my conscious awareness and to begin to find ways to tame it."

"You mean to exercise spiritual disciplines?

"Exactly. Let me tell you a funny side story related to will. A dear friend of mine was the chief of a large police department. His first name was Will. So during firearms training, the typical command to start shooting at the range was, 'Ready on the left. Ready on the right. Fire at will.' Will gave an order to change the command to 'Fire when ready.'"

Lew chuckled. "I'm not sure I've heard that twist on the story before. I'd change the command too. But what's your point?"

"For me, I need to fire at my will when ready. I've got to see my undisciplined will as not necessarily being in my best interests. Somewhere between the Holy Spirit and my will is the capacity to discipline and desire the best that only God provides. To me, that is the transforming mind Paul talked about in Romans 12. I'm re-reading Dallas Willard's *Spirit of the Disciplines.* Powerful stuff. You take the soul qualities list you gave me and filter through the disciplines of the Spirit, and I'm getting re-pointed in the right direction."

"I can't adequately express how pleased I am with your realization of progress, Jason."

Lew slowly clapped his hands together. "Okay, my friend. The last thing to do today is to integrate all your learning back into the Principle of Gravitational Attraction and Influence and the seven accompanying truths. You ready?"

"Eager."

"What's the principle?"

"Sylvia says I say it in my sleep."

"Can I say, that sounds a little creepy, but let's hear it."

"Love, like gravity, influences through attraction. It causes objects to fall. To be an effective leader requires others to fall in love with you. To be an effective spiritual leader requires others to fall in love not only with you, but also to fall more in love with Jesus. Becoming a spiritual leader is a refined form of discipleship, and discipling is a refined form of love."

"Great. What about the first gravity truth?"

"LIFE if first about the kingdom of God."

"And?" Lew pushed back his lunch plate, folded his hands on his chest and slightly tilted his chin to peer through the top portion of his eyeglass lenses.

"God's given me life. My challenge or opportunity is to show my gratitude in my living. I do that as they come to mind in three frames: me as a whole person, how it affects my work and how I'm living it out in my family. Yet what I'm trying to do is to merge those three frames so I'm the same person, no matter the frame."

"How's it working for you?"

"Living is getting simpler. Trying to simply be a three-frame blessing to others, I'm beginning to experience a calmer, less intense lifestyle."

"Can you give me an example?"

"Being a recovering control freak, I lived in the future, continually planning out what's next. But now I'm reminding myself to live in the moment. It's okay to plan and anticipate, but put it in a box, Jason, for crying out loud! Don't make the future my life experience. So when I'm in a meeting or with my family, I'm focused on the moment and them, not on six steps down the road. It's hard to break old habits, but I see progress."

"Excellent. What's the next one?"

"Change enlarges the kingdom of God."

"How is your world enlarging in his enlarging world?"

"I now realize chang*es* are stylistic issues."

"For example?"

"Limiting my schedule, asking more questions, being open to feedback, focusing on our team instead of my accomplishments. Making sure Sylvia and the boys aren't the last in line for my time. Those are the kinds of *changes* things I'm focusing on. Sitting in Bill and Marge's blessing machine reminded me of the significant differences between change and changes and re-grounding vision and purpose to create a discrete culture. It is so simple. Changes is what I do. Change is who I am and who I'm becoming."

"Nice. Next?"

"This one is a longer one. I'm pulling it up so I don't get it wrong. **LOVE is the force of gravitational attraction and radiating influence.** My time with Joe Tyler was powerful. I saw how an empty soul creates this celebrity vacuum. It was scary to see what happened from his inside view. What I'm learning from that time with Joe and with you in processing it through is, this is the core element of the whole principle. As my soul heals and renews, I am more capable of unmotivated love—you know, love without expectations and conditions. How am I doing that? For me, it's just the mental and human spirit discipline of shouting, 'STOP IT!' when I find I start making it about me."

"I'm loving it, Jason. This is everything I've been praying for you. Next?"

"Thanks, Lew. You know what I now see is, the first three truths, which address life, change and love, speak to the question, Who is God?"

"Excellent. What's next?"

"The fourth gravity truth is, LEADERSHIP is the craft of a leader."

"What's happening there?"

"I am now more conscious of the roles I play. Most importantly, I keep my manager role on a tight leash, so it doesn't look to me like leading when it's not. I am now more aware that, for those I'm responsible to and for, I have a huge responsibility to serve in an intentional way. Your unpacked definition of leadership has been really helpful. For my broader relationships, I am now realizing my influence comes from my soul. That's intimidating and humbling and yet so freeing. Sure, I still try to do the best I can, but I'm no longer trying to prove my goodness and acceptability through what I do. What I do is a consequence of my sense of my soul-mass. What a great example Paul Ishii is for that gravity truth."

"Question, my friend." Lew leaned forward with a big grin. "Who's the mentor in this conversation? You are on a roll, and I am the blessed recipient. I'm taking mental notes. Seriously."

"Thanks. You've been a huge influence in my life, Lew. I'll be forever grateful. I am particularly grateful for you setting me up with Jim and Governor Barlow. We can both talk about power and influence until we're blue in the face, but to get to see living proof of it was beyond meaningful. Between the two, they brought the fifth truth to life. *LEADERS are defined by their gravitational attraction and radiating influence.*"

Lew smiled as he asked the now-familiar question, "And?"

"And the way it's working for me right now is for me to inventory my metaphorical power tools and weapons and then put them in a vault. I could be called upon to use them, but it's got to be in dire emergencies, not as a way of doing business. Kind of like having a firearms locker in your home. Always there if you need it, but locked up so no one gets accidently hurt. I'm embarrassed as I recall the times I impatiently pulled out my power chip to get my way because I didn't realize I had alternatives."

"So we're down to the core truth we talked about in our last two sessions—about soul-mass. What's happened from that conversation?"

"Lew, that conversation with you and Chelsea was really dense—in a good way, like dense gravity. Soul-mass. What a concept. I even have that gravity truth memorized. *Our capacity to influence resides within the intertwined influences of the soul and the spirit of man—our Soul-mass—and the Spirit of God.* I'm forever changed by our process and that conversation. Thanks."

Lew smiled.

"How is that gravity truth being applied in my life? Now that

I have a soul-mass awareness, it changes everything about my self-identity: how I think and how I act. Everything. The chart you gave me when we started says it all. My identity is not measured by what I do. It is evidenced in who I am. Soul-mass is the core of my being, and everything I think, say and do emanates from the condition of my soul-mass. Thank you; thank you."

"Tell me, Jason. Do those three truths answer any big questions of life?"

"Absolutely. Where the first three—life, change and love--speak to the nature of God, these three truths address the question, Who am I?"

"Deep, my friend. Deep. Well, we have one truth left to complete the principle. You remember what it is?"

"Yes, I do. I've got it here on my tablet, but I haven't committed it to memory. *The forces propelling a trajectory are the attractional gravity and radiating influence expressed through the love of a leader.*"

"Jason, we haven't gotten to that one yet because it's the simplest of all. We talk about it more than any of the other truths combined, and yet we all do such a poor job at it. I have one word for it. Discipleship—the process of each of us growing in the awareness, disciplines and behaviors of our spiritual relationship with God. In other words, falling in love with Jesus, more and more every day. The reason why it's the simplest is that it is all outcome—consequence. If we have been diligent in understanding and applying the other six gravity truths, then this one is the impact."

"I'm seeing that this truth speaks clearly to the point that if I now understand a little more who God is, and that provides a framework to better understand who I am, then the seventh truth speaks to what I do."

"Care to elaborate?"

"As I was preparing for today and thinking about this truth, I was struck by the realization that so much of what we try to do in a faith family setting is discipling, yet it seems we get such a low return for the time invested. I think Joe Tyler has a unique insight to that. You know, growing the church one soul at a time. Can I share how this is coming together for me?"

"Bring it on, Jason!"

"Okay, so a disciple is a student, a pupil of a master artisan. Here's the twist I'm coming to realize. When *ship* is put at the end of a noun, it means a craft is performed by that person, right? Leadership is the craft of leaders. Workmanship is the craft of a worker. Likewise, discipleship is the craft of a disciple, a learner. It is not the craft of the teacher, the discipler or the church. It is interesting we have made discipleship appear to be the act of helping disciples grow. In reality, discipleship is the craft of a disciple refining the process of internal spiritual formation."

"So, my young friend, you're saying that the disciples are responsible for their craft?"

"Exactly. I feel like this should have been obvious, Lew. I mean, a teacher can't force a student to learn. You know that better than anyone. It's the disciple, the learner, who is the one who perfects his or her trade. And in the process of the disciples becoming more like Jesus, the disciples form their own *trajectory*."

"Good thinking, Jason. Do you realize how radical what you said is in today's programmed environment? Radical, but good." Lew had a pleased smile on his face.

"Here's the simple truth I see missing in so many ministries. The evidence of successful discipleship is the transformation of a disciple into a discipler. That's where trajectory comes in."

"We're headed in exactly the same direction. In this truth the physics metaphor is illustrative. Gravity, as we know, is an attractional force. The larger the core mass and density of that core mass of one object, the greater the attractional pull to another object. Once the smaller object begins to move toward the larger object, there is acceleration. However, if timing is right and a pushing force of radiating love is applied, the hurling object not only turns direction but increases in acceleration due to the push of radiation."

"Got it. That's how we get satellites into deep space. We launch them around the moon and then use the slingshot power of gravity to hurl them into the far reaches of our galaxy."

"Right. And that's how we disciple one another. The reason,

I believe, why discipling efforts have been marginal in their effectiveness is low ownership. Whether it's in a church setting or one-on-one, discipleship, as long as we make it something I do to you, then you have the option as to whether you want to do it in that way and at that time."

Lew leaned forward in his seat. "The way I see it, Jason, it's a process of love. Discipleship occurs as I progressively fall more in love with Jesus. Salvation determines my destination. But my personal process of discipleship—growing in my love and understanding of Christ—defines how much the mass of my soul grows and who gets impacted on my journey. Discipleship without impact is an oxymoron. And it's intentional. I choose to learn to trust and love. I choose to grow my soul. I choose to find ways for the Holy Spirit to bind the wounds and comfort my pierced and beaten soul. I choose to increase the gravitational influence of the mass of my soul to enlarge the kingdom of God."

"You think it's really a choice, Lew?"

"I do. It happens in the process of life. This is the fragment of our will that is our lifeline to a deeper relationship with God through Christ and his Holy Spirit. There is and remains a part of our will that will never corrupt. Its name is hope. Hope begins an intentional process of taming the will. Hope grows as I progressively fall more in love with Jesus, as I become a student of the Word of Life. Hope grows as I progressively fall in love with Jesus, allowing the Holy Spirit to work through me. Then Paul ties it all up when he says we can do all this through Christ who gives us strength."

"Where's the organ music when we really need it?"

"Good grief, Jason. Don't you have a serious bone in your body, or at least one not broken with your cynicism?"

"I think you're kidding with me on that one. You're right, however, and my cynical jokes don't seem as funny anymore."

"Well, maybe I am starting to rub off on you instead of just rubbing you the wrong way." A smile from Lew signaled all was okay. "Jason, be sure and get this. While spiritual formation is the responsibility of the disciple, there can't be a disciple without a teacher. We can call them guides, mentors, teachers, disciplers or coaches. Perhaps the best word is simply *friend*."

"Yes, we do, and yes, you are," said Jason, remembering this was his last time sitting in this role and for this purpose.

"This brings us full circle. The practice of discipleship delivers the opportunity for new life through Christ. The practice of discipleship also brings the promise of a transformed and renewed mind and heart to those within the leader's sphere of influence. Discipleship, my craft as a disciple, creates an environment renewing my soul. Perhaps now we understand even better, LIFE if first about the kingdom of God—which is where we started this conversation.

"So, my young friend, from a gravitational influence point of view, trajectory is the key. A mass is being attracted to you because of your gravitational influence. If there isn't the counterbalancing radiating love, there will be a collision. If you are the large mass, your role is simply to radiate enough love to be able to help the other body find a new trajectory. It's as simple and as complex as that.

"Well, we've got just one last step—to comply with Melissa's request when you met with the board on that fateful Saturday. She said she wanted you to determine what the problems were and how you've come to correct them. Am I correct?"

"You never forget, do you?"

"Not when it comes to things as important as you, Jason. Here's my suggestion. Plan a meeting and invite your board and your leadership team at New Horizons. Then, rather than it being a *mea culpa* kind of confession about your realizations of your past behaviors, make this a time when you can talk about how things are now different in your life."

"Will you be there, Lew?"

"Wouldn't miss it for the world."

And he gave the apostles, the prophets, the
evangelists, the shepherds and teachers, to
equip the saints for the work of ministry,
for building up the body of Christ, until
we all attain to the unity of the faith and of
the knowledge of the Son of God, to mature
manhood, to the measure of the stature of the
fullness of Christ, so that we may no longer
be children, tossed to and fro by the waves and
carried about by every wind of doctrine, by
human cunning, by craftiness in deceitful
schemes. Rather, speaking the truth in love,
we are to grow up in every way into him who
is the head, into Christ.

Ephesians 4:11–15

REFLECTION QUESTIONS

1. *Lew tells Jason, "You are the most significant and influential person in your life. Not anyone else?" Do you believe that about you as well? If your answer is 'yes,' why? If your answer is 'no,' why is that?*

2. *The Principle of Gravitational Attraction and Influence starts by stating that, Love, like gravity, influences through attraction. It causes objects to fall. To be an effective leader requires others to fall in love with you. How are you doing with the falling in love with you part?*

3. *Jason had "four big ideas" as he began to put his soul-mentoring experience together.*

> 1. *Let God be God. Seems cliché but how do you relinquish control to trust?*
> 2. *Become a serial killer. A little grotesque in imagery, but how do you kill the "old man" in you?*
> 3. *Become piercingly vulnerable—be authentic. What does that look like. How is that different from being too open and too much "what you see is what you get?"*
> 4. *Tame my will through spiritual disciplines. How do discipline exercises tame the will? Are you engaged in any of them?*

4. *As you begin to put it all together, describe some strategies, thoughts and actions you now own related to each of the first six truths.*

TRUTH 1. *LIFE if first about the kingdom of God.*

TRUTH 2. *CHANGE enlarges the kingdom of God.*

TRUTH 3. *LOVE is the force of gravitational attraction and radiating influence.*

TRUTH 4. *LEADERSHIP is the craft of a leader.*

TRUTH 5. *LEADERS are defined by their gravitational attraction and radiating influence.*

TRUTH 6. *TRAJECTORY is the leader's legacy.*

CHAPTER 16

Trajectory

TRAJECTORY

is a leader's legacy

Nothing can be more cruel than the leniency
which abandons others to their sin. Nothing
can be more compassionate than the severe
reprimand which calls another Christian in
one's community back from the path of sin.

Dietrich Bonhoeffer

T he smell of early spring was in the air. A few early
    bloomers like the flowering plum were in full array, and
    the long, unusually cold winter slipped away. No one felt a
desire for it to remain or return.

Jason asked for a meeting with his board and key staff. He
told everyone not to worry, he wasn't leaving. This was a promised
update on his excursion into gravitational influence. As everyone
gathered in the conference room at New Horizons, there was a
noticeably relaxed atmosphere. No longer were staff collected
in one clan circle and board members in another. Stepping to
the front of the room, Jason announced it was time to begin the
meeting. It was hard to break into the conversations so he could
get to his agenda. Staff and guests and particularly the board
were enjoying conversation. What a difference in six short but
intense months.

Jason noticed Sylvia slipping into the room and sitting in the
furthest chair from the front. Jason had talked to Sylvia about this
meeting, but she had never made mention of wanting to attend.
Lew and Chelsea arrived as special invited guests. They greeted

and hugged Sylvia and found chairs in the back of the conference room.

"Well, let's get this party underway. Thanks for all of you taking some time away from your work to have a conversation. I have to confess, I'm uncomfortable because the conversation is about me. All of you know we have been on a rocky road for a while. We've had our challenges as an organization, and I contributed to that. I am truly sorry. I promised Melissa and the board we would have a conversation about my discovery process over the past several months. And I want to make it about all of us too. One of the things I'm learning is, if we want to be an influence force in others' lives, it's essential to be more courageous in our vulnerability. Can't get any more vulnerable than this. Right?"

The gathered guests smiled, most thinking, *Better you than me.*

"Perhaps the most fitting start to this meeting, with all due respect to Alcoholics Anonymous, is, 'Hello, my name is Jason, and I'm hopelessly addicted to self.'" There was polite laughter, knowing there was truth and a new and fresh honesty in that statement. "As you've all become aware, a number of months ago, Melissa and the board asked to speak with me, and as I clearly recall, the conversation started with, 'Jason, we've called you in because there is a problem and a crisis.' The board asked me to address my leadership challenges to assure the health and continuity of New Horizons. Melissa and Hal said they weren't going to give a laundry list of issues. Rather, I needed to discover those for myself. Well, I did, and today is my opportunity to share my discoveries with you."

Jason put his half-smile on; this was still not a completely comfortable place to be.

"If you don't already know him, I'd like to introduce the man who's been a huge part of the process of me growing in my gravitational influence. I'll explain that term in a minute, but this is Lew Merton, my soul-mentor and my good friend. Soul-mentor is what he does. Friend is who he is. And I also want to introduce his associate, Chelsea. This is one bright person and a sweet young lady. Also, I want you to meet my wife, Sylvia. I'm a little surprised but grateful to see her here. She's been a huge part of me being here today as well."

Everyone turned to look at the trio. Some already knew Lew, but Chelsea was new to the group. Sylvia looked uncomfortable having eyes on her. She was acquainted with most people in the room from Christmas parties and July 4 picnics.

"Alright, let me really get started. First, I do owe all of you an apology. I think I've already expressed this individually to each of you, but to you as a group, all deeply invested in the mission of New Horizons, I am sorry for the unnecessary tension I've inflicted on you. Hopefully, you'll be seeing less of what Lew and I now call the old Jason V1.0 and lot more of the new Jason V2.0."

"As we move forward, I want to set the record straight. I've shared my Gravity journey with many of you. We've been over a rough road in the past several months, and, at times, I haven't made it any easier for you. What I learned in the process is that the gravitational force drawing people to us is the healthy size of our soul-mass filled with love. And the counterbalancing force is radiating love. What I've come to realize even more is that what makes New Horizons so special is the abundance of radiating love flowing out and touching our communities. However, as I now realize, in the past I thought I needed your attraction to me more than any radiating capacity I may have had to bless you. That one-way sense of attraction was unhealthy. It filled some gaping holes in my soul-mass, but because of that, I allowed you to collide with me. Can't say it enough times: I apologize."

Everyone smiled, pleased Jason was demonstrating a humility not often seen in the past. Melissa nodded from the front row.

"I think I can make this fairly brief. Lew has taken me through a process of growing my gravitational influence by becoming more aware of the need for health in my soul-mass. Here's a brief physics lesson and a life lesson as well. An object under the influence of gravity continually accelerates until it impacts with the mass of a larger object. Collisions aren't good for celestial objects or for followers attracted by the gravitational pull of leaders. To avoid collision, we possess the capacity, the force, to alter a follower's course of movement. And this is a key point I missed as old Jason V1.0. Unfortunately, many of you are recalling at this moment some of the gravitational collisions we experienced."

Jason stopped for a moment and looked around the room. There were nods of agreement followed by encouraging smiles all around.

These are my friends, he thought. *I no longer feel I have to do anything to them or for them. I'm doing this with them. Wow, what a difference!*

Jason continued. "Here's what is coming clear to me. With radiating love, the process is simple. Look around the room. These are members of our tribe, all of us gathered here today. If we just stopped at gravitational attraction, we would still be experiencing collisions. But as we continue to know each other, love and grow with each other and disciple each other, we exert intentional effort to set each other on paths of influence. Consequently, our radiating love alters others' trajectory, preventing collision. What I didn't comprehend until I went through this process was that our greatest work as leaders and influencers is enabling trajectory in those who follow us as leaders. However, there is no trajectory without gravitational soul-mass.

"In my journey with Lew—" Lew feigned pain at the word *journey,* and Jason's smile grew. "—he's taken me through seven truths centered on the Principle of Gravitational Attraction and Influence. The short form of the principle says, 'To be an effective leader requires others to fall in love with you. To be an effective spiritual leader requires others to fall in love not only with you, but also to fall more in love with Jesus.'"

"The seventh truth to the principle is the one I've been talking about and around. It says, '**TRAJECTORY** *is the leader's legacy.*' I now realize as Executive Director my role isn't to make New Horizons successful. That's *our* job, team. My job is to help you become the most successful people you can be, and in the process, New Horizons will be successful. I do that by making sure I've contributed to your own trajectory. Yes, I know there are certain roles as the Executive Director I must still play that no else can, but I want the bulk of my effort to be empowering you as well as our organization's partners. I commit to you that my role is now predominantly that of creating trajectory with you. My new title, as far as this team is concerned, is Chief Trajectory Officer."

The sound of applause made Jason pause his speech. All around the room, he saw the expression of friends rooting for him. *Were those expressions always there, and I just didn't see them,* he wondered.

"That's where I feel I let you down and where I really believe there has been growth for me. I do want to influence your growth as people of God. I feel I am now better able to do that as I've come to terms with the condition of my soul. As a result, I've been freed from trying to prove to you my worth as a person and your Executive Director by continually and incessantly doing. That, in a nutshell, has been the source of my angst and your frustration."

There were the slight smiles and barely perceptible nods around the room.

"Here's the key point I want to share with you today. Becoming a spiritual leader is a refined form of discipleship for me, and discipling is a refined form of love to you. I want to be a part of your discipling process."

"Don't worry; you already have!" Chandra Boyce, New Horizons' most recent team hire, called out from her seat at the long conference table.

Jason acknowledged the comment with a smile. "You may wonder where I am going to find the time. Most of it will come from staying out of your business and letting you be the successful you. I've done way too much managing and not enough leading and influencing. From now on, I'll lead and influence by intentionally helping to shape your trajectory, assuring your success as a whole person and member of this amazing team. My role is to invest in your life. That means discerning strengths, weaknesses, potential and opportunity, as well as blind spots. It means training, testing, teaching, coaching and mentoring. It means being so transparent in life that you can see a realistic example of how a godly person of influence successfully tolerates, embraces, navigates and arbitrates surprise, tension and paradox."

Jason was feeling comfortable. He sensed his breathing had

slowed to normal, and the dryness in his mouth was no longer there. *This is different,* he thought. *I'm not having to prove anything. This is different. I am different.*

"I understand I'm setting a high expectation for myself. But now it's different. Now it's truly about my being, not about my doing. This isn't my performance goal. It's the evidence of a work within me. It's what I want to do, what I need to do and what I feel is simply the consequence of a renewing soul within me. And here's a huge discovery for me. I realize I can't radiate love *to* you unless I accept the love *from* you. That means, I want, I need and I will rejoice in receiving your love because I know it is Christ who is at work within us that is at the source of our goodness. Whatever works I produce from here on out are not the proof of my worthiness. Rather it's evidence of his work."

Jason stopped, realizing he was talking too much. But this was clearing the deck for a new start. "I ask only one commitment in return. In the end, a sign of a successful trajectory is that you, now also a renewed leader, create your own unique force of gravitational influence through your own discovery, healing and growing of your soul-mass. What a great metaphor for the gravitational influence of leaders! We contribute to the independent intentional trajectory of followers by boosting them on their own course."

Jason could hear conversation in the hall and wondered who it was. At that moment, Chelsea stood up. "Jason, if I could interrupt, we have some guests here today who want to say a few things. Since they all have busy schedules, would it be okay if they interrupted you?"

"Ah, sure," said Jason, not sure where this highjack was going but relieved to find a way to get out of the spotlight.

"First of all I want to play a clip from my dad," said Chelsea. The conference room monitor came to life, displaying the face of Bill Courtland. Jason looked at Bill on the screen and back at Chelsea, pointing his finger at the screen and back to Chelsea. She nodded with a wide grin.

"Jason, I'm sorry Marge and I couldn't be with you today. Let me say, to all your friends gathered here, how impressed we are with you as a person, a growing leader, an eager and open learner and a capable administrator. I know New Horizons has faced some recent financial challenges. And you, like most effective leaders I know, faced your own limitations. But you grew, took others with you and demonstrated you have a team able to work through those challenges.

"Because of your demonstrated capacity to grow as a leader, here's what we'd like to do. C'est le Bon is embarking on a program to bless the communities where we have the opportunity to have a footprint. Starting next month each of our stores will bake 10% more bread and make 20% more soup than is projected for that day. That's in addition to our previously planned overage. We will distribute the excess to shelters and food banks in the community to meet a need—not as leftovers at the end of the day but as fresh and intentional baking in the morning. In addition, in each store we will add one position-in-training to build skills in someone on their way out of underemployment or unemployment and poverty. We will also be donating an especially equipped delivery truck to each area where we do business to assure our goods and soup arrive at distribution centers hot and fresh. That need sparked the idea of a delivery service for our customers as well. So we don't overburden our stores, we will be funding this effort out of our family foundation. We need a coordinator for that program, and we want to contract with New Horizons to be the community linker. I've got to run, but, Jason and staff, I look forward to more great conversations with all of you."

The room broke into a cheer. What a lifeline of services and resources!

"Jason." The voice came from Alisha Bishop, who had walked to the front of the room during the video. "I come here representing the Margaret Corbin Brigade and with the good wishes of Phil Spencer of Bio-Dynetics . I've been watching you since we first met. I listened to your story and your frustration. I've also heard the stories since then of how you've humbly chosen to deepen your own sense of gravity within your soul and then reflect that to those around you. If you're not aware, you can't hide gravitational attraction and influence. So, Jason, the Margaret

Corbin Brigade wants New Horizons to work with us as we establish resource centers for first-responder women and women of the military. Phil has generously donated a $2.5 million seed grant over three years to get two centers up and running and to build a self-sustainable model for the future. We want to partner with you as the implementing agency."

Jason wasn't sure whether he was going to cry or pass out. This was incredible! Just then he noticed a big man coming in the door. He was moving like a running back with the football on his way to the goal line. It was Joe Tyler.

"Hey, Jason, can't stay for the cake and coffee, but I'm so pleased to be a part of this celebration. Just want you to know I'm in the process of finalizing the donation of a warehouse building in Leaventon. I mean we're getting it, not giving it. I think you're going to need some building space for your future projects, and we want Leaventon to be a hub. Just wanted you to know you've got the building, rent free, for as long as you have a viable ministry. I think it's important for your staff and board to know we wouldn't ask you to be a part of our ministry if we didn't believe in the reformed quality and expression of your collective soul as an enterprise."

Like groundhogs in an earthquake, the people just kept popping up. Next, it was Paul Ishii. "Jason, I've known you for some time, and the stories I'm hearing and seeing of the before-and-after are thrilling. You've clearly demonstrated the growth of a spiritual leader, and it's reflected in the growing stability of New Horizons. We're proud of you. My board has had some conversation with your board, and we would like to continue that conversation with you and your leadership team to form a strategic partnership. You've got resources and talent to develop programs. Compassion Works! has the feet on the street to make things happen. We want to work more closely together."

By this time most of the New Horizons staff were crying and cheering and hugging each other. Jason heard a group of footsteps quickly coming down the hallway. *Could it be?* thought Jason. Yes, it was Governor Wilson Barlow with Jim Oliver and two state police bodyguards. Governor Barlow stepped in and filled the room with his presence. Big personalities always do that. People weren't sure whether they were supposed to stand or just smile. Governor Barlow, sensing the hesitation, put out his hand, palm up, and spoke.

"I am so pleased to be able to be here today. I've heard a lot about New Horizons, and it hasn't just come from Jason. Folks, as a Christ-follower, I'm more convinced than ever that our role on earth for the time we have is not to create one more helping, serving or discipling program we don't even follow ourselves. What we need to do is strengthen what we already have before we create something new. As governor, I see part of my job is to try and consolidate concepts in order to communicate concrete ideas to the people we serve. In that vein, permit me to combine my version of the Great Commission, the Great Commandment and the Golden Rule into one sentence. I believe we are to love and serve others in a like manner as we have a wholesome love for ourselves. That means a healthy soul-mass. And then, we can help people know and follow Christ because they've seen an example through us in flesh and blood. That's when gravitational influence kicks in."

A big grin broke out, lighting up the governor's face and then the whole room. "Well, that's four sentences, but you get the picture. Hey, I'm a politician, what'd you expect?" laughed Governor Barlow. "Jason, here's what I'm here for. Jim and I thoroughly enjoyed your time with us. With Lew giving me some updates, I decided New Horizons is just the organization and you're just the leader people I know want to invest in. I made a few calls and I've got two long-time, well-established family foundations in this state who want to partner with your efforts and help provide the fiscal infrastructure for long-term stability." Governor Barlow winked at Jason as he nodded his head and concluded, "That's one of the ways I can use the power of my office to spread some influence around this state."

Jason truly felt lightheaded. He couldn't believe this was all happening. "I know I can speak for everyone in this room. The expressed generosity and belief in us as people and as an organization is humbling in the best sense of the word. A thank you seems so inadequate. We do regard all of your *investments* in us as stewards of your trust. We will continue to work to show ourselves faithful and worthy of your trust. I don't know what else to say." There wasn't much more Jason could say as he found himself being overtaken by emotion. He wasn't sure if the next thing from him was going to be a shout or a sob.

"Jason, my friend." It was Lew who came to the front of the room. "I am honored to call you friend. Your bright mind and sincere and good heart demonstrate a healthy soul-mass inside of you. I have been blessed to be a part of your growth and to see the evidences of your hard work—the work of introspection and intentional growth. That's not easy. I see you displaying this last truth of the principle of gravitational attraction and influence: trajectory. If we are effective leaders, we intentionally alter the trajectory of a follower to avoid collision. We help prevent collision by counterbalancing radiation in the form of love. Here's the question for all of us. What propels us forward with power, rather than keeping us coasting on the power of a leader's gravitational influence? The only sustainable energy of both followers and leaders is that of continuing to fall more and more in love with Jesus. In the process, we become more and more like Jesus, increasing our soul-mass with intentional trajectory.

"Now I know most of you haven't been studying these concepts for months. Ask Jason to explain them later." He winked at Jason. "For now, here's what I mean in a nutshell: Spiritual leaders make disciples. The disciples are followers of Christ, not merely followers of leaders."

Lew laughed. "I can't stop being the teacher. Here's the last point I want to make. There is one additional sentence that completes the seventh truth, which I expect all of you to know now. If leadership is the craft of a leader, then discipleship is the craft of a disciple. It's not what I do to someone else. It's what I do to my own soul-mass. That's discipleship."

Sylvia stood up in the back of the room and said, "Um, excuse me." She tentatively looked around, clearly uncomfortable with what she was about to say. Jason had no clue, and he too looked uncomfortable, wondering what was coming next.

"First of all, thank all of you for believing in my husband enough to help him walk through his—" Sylvia looked at Lew and smiled just a little. "—his journey. I can't tell you how often he's spoken of his love for all of you. Sometimes, in the past, it didn't show. I know that's changed now. How do I know? It's changed at home as well, although Jason's heart was and still is passionately focused on doing the right thing in the right way with the right people."

Jason's face still wasn't showing any relaxation; he was still not sure what Sylvia was going to say.

"I know things were hard at work at times. You know the reason I know that? They were hard at home too. If there's one thing Jason does not want to do, it is fail, and yet in that drive he was getting closer to the very thing he feared the most."

Jason saw an opening as Sylvia stopped to gather her thoughts. "Can I add to what you are saying, Sylvia?"

"Not yet." Several laughed, knowing that was out of character for Sylvia. "I believe anyone's identity is at risk when you're one person at work and another at home. Eventually you forget what play you're acting in, and it has *phony* written all over it. What I've seen at home is a changed man who really cares from his soul about me and our boys. I can tell you, for Jason, it's no longer just about what gets done. Now it's about who and why it's getting done as well. I know this will embarrass Jason to no end, but I'm now married to a servant leader who cares where my soul-mass and those of our boys are heading. And I know he's the same here as at home. I just wanted you to know, Jason is now, even more, the real deal."

There were a few tears in the group as everyone turned to look at Jason. He realized they were expecting him to close this love-in in some way.

"Friends, this is one of the most wonderful days of my life. Yes, Sylvia, right up there with our wedding day. I've heard the most wonderful, loving words of opportunity and affirmation that anyone could ever want—from both my wife and my friends. Thank you. Let me just say—and you've heard me say this to you individually as I've been going through this process of learning how to discover, heal and grow my soul-mass—but let me give all of you a warning: it's simply this. I'll never be the same, and because of that I intend to do everything I can to make sure you'll never be the same as well. Yes, we'll still be intensely focused on task. Good grief, think about what we just received today. We've got a lot to do! But it will now be accomplished because of who we are, not because I'm afraid of who we are if you scratched the surface a little. Our identity as a team is now defined by the size of our collective soul-mass. Our gravitational attraction and our gravitational influence will be a direct consequence of that. Okay, let's go eat some cake!"

Jesus said, "Love the Lord your God with all your passion and prayer and intelligence." This is the most important, the first on any list. But there is a second to set alongside it: "Love others as well as you love yourself." These two commands are pegs; everything in God's Law and the Prophets hangs from them: to love the world with a whole heart a whole soul and a whole mind. By this all men will know that you are My disciples, if you have love for one another.

Matt 22:37–40 (The Message); John 13:35

REFLECTION QUESTIONS

1. *The seventh truth of Gravitational Attraction and Influence says, trajectory is the leader's legacy. What are some practical examples of radiating love producing a trajectory?*

2. *What are some of the challenges you face in keeping a consistent effort of trajectory at work as well as at home?*

3. *What effort of trajectory between work and home seems to be harder? Why?*

4. *Describe the transformation that occurred in Jason. What did he go from, to what?*

5. *Do you think the path Jason was on was realistic? Why or why not?*

6. *If you were Jason, describe how you would have made the story would have turned out.*

7. *Do you know any Lew's in your life? Describe who they are.*

EPILOGUE

Cast all your anxiety on him
because he cares for you.

1 Peter 5:7

A fter Jason's divorce with Emily, Sydney and her mother moved several states away. In the past five years, Jason's relationship with Sydney has been cordial. But two weeks in the summer and a week at Christmas unfortunately had not built a bond of closeness. During her teens, Sydney became rebellious, exhibiting serious anger issues, running away, abusing substances and adopting an anarchist mindset and a 'Goth' wardrobe. Yet, like her father, she was a bright young woman.

With a combination of scholarships, student loans and financial help from Jason, Sydney graduated college with a degree in communications. Contrary to her anti-establishment teen years, she went to work for a computer hardware manufacturing company as their social media manager.

On one of her visits to see him, Jason introduced Sydney to Chelsea, hoping Chelsea's groundedness would rub off. It did, and they became fast friends.

On completion of her intern project with Lew, Chelsea began teaching at a nationally renowned seminary. But on the sudden passing of her father, Bill, she left academia to assist her mother in running C'est le Bon. Within three years, Chelsea was COO of the company. With the declining health of her mother, Chelsea took over the helm of the company as President and CEO. Three years ago, Chelsea recruited Sydney to join the company. Six months ago, she promoted Sydney to Lead Partner for Franchise Relationships.

Sydney, now 27, recently visited her mother for several days and then flew up to spend a few days with Jason and his family.

In the past 10 years Jason grew New Horizons into an international outreach nonprofit through a series of mergers with other nonprofits. With organizational health and stability well in hand, Jason felt good with his decision to leave New Horizons. Applying Lew's seven truths of influence had made a significant difference in staff development and strategic innovation.

Jason resigned his position as Executive Director of New Horizons to assume the role of Principal in the consulting company Gravity Partners, the brainchild of Lew Merton. Jason had continued to develop a deep and loving friendship with Lew through the years, and as time permitted, Jason worked as a part-time consulting associate with Lew. Lew, now in his mid-70's, wanted to cut back on his soul-mentoring clientele and speaking engagements and asked Jason to take over.

Sydney had let Jason know she wanted to see him privately when she got into town. He wasn't sure what that was all about but was delighted to have some time with her under any circumstances. It was 10:30 AM, and Sydney texted Jason she was in the building and on her way up.

As Sydney came through the door, tears were welling up in her eyes. Without saying a word, she hugged Jason and held on longer and tighter than ever before. It was clear, something was going on in Sydney, and as a father he sensed the opportunity to be available for her at a very important time. As Sydney relaxed her hug, Jason smiled at her.

"Hello, sweetheart. So good to see you."

Sydney had grown into a tall and slender woman. She wore her straight black hair stylishly bobbed and wore minimal makeup. Dressed in slacks, contrasting blouse and white cashmere sweater, she looked like the successful young woman she was.

"Your visit is a little unexpected. Do you have work in the area? You do know how proud I am of you and what you're doing."

"Thanks, Dad. That means more than you know. There's a particular reason for meeting with just you and me." Sydney hesitated and nervously played with her bracelet. "I spent last night with Mom, and we had a long conversation. She told me the reason for your divorce. She said her shame for her infidelity and your hurt couldn't bridge the gap of reconciliation. I blamed you all these years, and it was Mom who violated your trust."

"Sydney, I'm sorry you got hurt in the failure of our marriage. I'm glad the elephant in the room is now visible, but I'm still responsible. I wasn't there for your mom when she needed my affection and support. I was so wrapped up in my doing at that time that my being was only a ghost. I wasn't there for you either. I am so sorry."

"Thanks for saying that, but that's not what I want to talk with you about. Well, it is, and it isn't. Ten years ago something changed in you, and it was obvious even from my angry, long-distance view of you at the time. I know that was about the time you met Lew."

"It was. You want some coffee? I'm still brewing Bon Café."

"Sure." Sydney sat and folded her legs just like Chelsea had a decade ago. "So ... first, you know I'm not a committed believer in Jesus like you. I think I want to be, but there seems to be a barrier I just can't get over. After talking with Mom, I didn't sleep last night, as I tried, looking backwards, to put my life together. First of all, I'm sorry for all the years I was angry. I was mad at you, but I never knew why. I thought you'd abandoned me. I guess it's part of the reason I've never had a serious relationship. I was afraid my marriage would end the same as yours and Mom's. I've had some talks with Chelsea about this too, regarding my difficulties in attaching to others."

Jason brought back two mugs and sat down in a cushioned side chair. "That's a trainload to start with. Let's work backwards. What was Chelsea's advice?"

"She suggested I may have a problem in trusting others. She

even went on to say that perhaps my arm's-length relationship with God was for the same reason. She said maybe I don't trust God."

"Yes, Chelsea: The Direct. Great quality in a sweet person like her. Listen, sweetheart—"

"Hear me out, Dad, and then you'll see why I'm here. I always believed Mom was the only person I could really trust, and now I find out, not even her. Dad, please forgive me for blaming you and putting you through my anger. I'm a mess. You seem to be the only person left I can talk to, but I hardly know you. For most of my life, I regarded you as untrustworthy, and now I find out I was wrong. The only thing I know at this point is you can't trust trust. What can I do?"

At that point, Sydney started to cry, and the crying turned to sobs. Jason got out of his chair, knelt down and held her tight.

"Daddy, will you take me on as a client? I need to hear what changed your life. I need to hear if there's something in there for me too."

"Client? That might become awkward. Catch-up on father and daughter? That I can do. It will be my privilege. When would you like to start?"

ABOUT THE AUTHORS

Ron brings to *GRAVITY* diverse life experience. Trained as a pharmacist, he served 14 years in Washington State government, and formed his own consulting group, MBG Management Services, Inc. For 36 years, MBG served major employers throughout the U.S., providing a wide array of cultural and organizational development services.

Even as a young adult, Ron felt a call to bring the principles of management and leadership into a spiritual setting. He formed the Institute for Spiritual Leadership Training and developed the 360° assessment tool, the Spiritual Leader Trait Assessment (SLTA), and the accompanying resource book, Leader: Who Are You? Ron is also the author of Embracing Conflict: Finding Peace in the Midst of Tension and Growing the Soul Through Accountability, Disclosure and Feedback. Ron has authored the companion to GRAVITY– A Journey of Friends – and a conversational journal tying the books together.

Ron lives with his wife, Pat, of over 50 years in Olympia, Washington. Together they raised three children, who in turn are raising four grandchildren. Ron has served as an elder for over 30 years at Evergreen Christian Community Church.

Michael brings to *GRAVITY* a rich narrative of his own. Trained as a pastor, he has served in both pastoral and executive leadership roles for early-stage and turnaround companies, and consulted with churches for over 12 years. He met Ron several years ago, and over coffee they began to collaborate on a revolutionary leadership theory – what was to become Gravitational Leadership, LLC. Gravitational Leadership provides training and coaching services to pastors and churches throughout the U.S.

Married to his wife, Nancy, for more than 28 years, Michael has four children and has calls Bainbridge Island, Washington home. He lends his time and talent serving on boards for faith-based nonprofits like More to Life and Beyond the Blue Ministries. Michael enjoys camping, hiking, and ensuring the safe operation of his HO model train set. He reads voraciously, and listens to the blues – steaming cup of dark roast coffee in-hand.